KEY CONCEPTS IN PHONETICS AN

Palgrave Key Concepts

Palgrave Key Concepts provide an accessible and comprehensive range of subject glossaries at undergraduate level. They are ideal companions to a standard textbook, making them invaluable reading for students throughout their course of study, and especially useful as a revision aid.

Accounting and Finance
Business and Management Research Methods
Business Practice
Criminology and Criminal Justice
Cultural Studies
Drama and Performance (2nd edn)
e-Commerce
Human Resource Management
Information and Communication Technology
Innovation
International Business
Law (2nd edn)
Leisure
Management
Marketing
Operations Management
Philosophy
Politics
Psychology
Public Relations
Social Research Methods
Sociology
Strategic Management
Tourism

Palgrave Key Concepts: Literature
General Editor: Martin Coyle

Contemporary Literature
Creative Writing
Crime Fiction
Literary Terms and Criticism (3rd edn)
Medieval Literature
Modernist Literature
Postcolonial Literature
Renaissance Literature
Romantic Literature
Victorian Literature

Palgrave Key Concepts: Language and Linguistics
Bilingualism
Language and Linguistics (2nd edn)
Phonetics and Phonology
Second Language Acquisition

Further titles are in preparation
www.palgravekeyconcepts.com

Palgrave Key Concepts
Series Standing Order
ISBN 978-1-4039-3210-5
(outside North America only)

You can receive future titles in this series as they are published by placing a standing order. Please contact your bookseller or, in case of difficulty, write to us at the address below with your name and address, the title of the series and the ISBN quoted above.

Customer Services Department, Macmillan Distribution Ltd
Houndmills, Basingstoke, Hampshire RG21 6XS, England

Key Concepts in Phonetics and Phonology

Gerard O'Grady
Cardiff University, UK

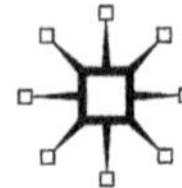

First published 2013 by
PALGRAVE MACMILLAN

Palgrave Macmillan in the UK is an imprint of Macmillan Publishers Limited, registered in England, company number 785998, of Houndmills, Basingstoke, Hampshire RG21 6XS.

Palgrave Macmillan in the US is a division of St Martin's Press LLC, 175 Fifth Avenue, New York, NY 10010.

Palgrave Macmillan is the global academic imprint of the above companies and has companies and representatives throughout the world.

Palgrave® and Macmillan® are registered trademarks in the United States, the United Kingdom, Europe and other countries.

ISBN 978–0–230–27647–5

This book is printed on paper suitable for recycling and made from fully managed and sustained forest sources. Logging, pulping and manufacturing processes are expected to conform to the environmental regulations of the country of origin.

A catalogue record for this book is available from the British Library.

A catalog record for this book is available from the Library of Congress.

10 9 8 7 6 5 4 3 2 1
22 21 20 19 18 17 16 15 14 13

Contents

Preface

This book is neither a textbook nor an encyclopaedia but something intermediate between the two. It is intended to be a resource that will enable the reader to gain entry to the related fields of phonology and phonetics. As the title of the book suggests, the book provides relatively extensive coverage of the key concepts underpinning the twin disciplines of phonetics and phonology. The book contains 136 entries presented in alphabetical order. It is not intended that a reader should read the book from cover to cover. Rather it is intended that the reader selects the entry of most immediate relevance as their entry point to the book.

Each entry starts with a brief definition of a key concept and, where appropriate, provides fuller details of the concept supported by illustrative examples. As the book has been written from a British context, many of the illustrative examples are necessarily taken from British dialects, but no specific knowledge of the varieties of English spoken in Britain and Ireland is needed in order to follow the examples. Words in bold within each entry refer to concepts that are discussed elsewhere in the book under their own entry. Many of the entries contain references to the literature, and a fairly extensive bibliography is found at the end of the book. It is my hope that the descriptions of the concepts contained in this book will enable and motivate readers to engage with the relevant literature as they further their knowledge of the twin disciplines of phonetics and phonology.

I have written the book from an atheoretical position. When describing phonological theories I have attempted to primarily describe them in their own terms. Readers who are interested in pursuing individual theories will find references in the bibliography to the seminal works underpinning those particular theories. At the start of the book I have listed alphabetically all the concepts that have been explained within their own entries. In addition, at the end of the book there is an index that lists all the concepts and terms that are mentioned in this book, and not just those which have their own entries. I very much hope that this book will prove to be an enjoyable and invaluable resource for students undertaking the study of phonetics and phonology.

Acknowledgements

I would like to thank my colleagues at the Centre for Language and Communication Research at Cardiff University for creating a space that allows books such as this one to be written. Thanks are also due to numerous Cardiff University students on the undergraduate modules *Pronunciation of English* and *Sounds of Speech* and the postgraduate module *Phonology*, whose input has shaped the final form of this work. More specific thanks are due to those who have helped me with individual queries: Tom Bartlett, Charlie Kemp, Michael Willett and Alison Wray. Paul Carley and Paul Tench have both read part of an earlier draft of this manuscript and their thoughtful questions and attention to fine detail kept me on my toes while writing this book. Thanks are also due to an anonymous reader of this manuscript whose careful reading and critical questioning proved to be invaluable. Needless to say, any infelicities or idiosyncrasies that remain are entirely my responsibility.

At Palgrave Macmillan, I am indebted to Kitty van Boxel for inviting me to write this work and to Anna Reeve and Felicity Noble for ensuring the smooth production of the book.

On a personal note, thanks are due to Georgia for putting up with disrupted holidays caused by the writing of this book. Our daughter Myrto was born during the writing of this title, and in a belated apology for not being around as much as I should have been, it is to her and her mother that I dedicate this book.

The author and publisher would like to thank the IPA for their kind permission to reproduce Figures 2 and 3. You can contact the IPA via their website http://www.langsci.ucl.ac.uk/ipa/.

List of Terms

Accent

This term has two distinct meanings. The first and more common one refers to how an individual pronounces a language; the second refers to the emphasis a speaker places on an individual word. Technically speaking, the first meaning of accent can be defined as the cumulative auditory effect of those features of pronunciation that identify where an individual is from regionally or socially, or identify the speaker's occupation or social class. As every single speaker must pronounce a word in a particular manner, which allows his/her hearer to identify either where the speaker is from or what the speaker's social class is, it is untrue to claim that accentless speech is possible (Esling 1998). The belief that one accent of British English is accentless and more prestigious will be discussed under the entry **received pronunciation**, as will discussion of social accents.

In the English speaking world there are clear differences between the English spoken between and within the main English speaking counties. Most American and most British accents differ, for instance, through the distribution of /ɹ/ within a **syllable**. In most American accents the consonant /ɹ/ is pronounced before and after vowels within syllables. In most British accents the consonant /ɹ/ can only be pronounced before a vowel within a syllable. Thus the typical American pronunciation of car is /kɑɹ/ while the typical British pronunciation is /kɑː/.

Because no two individuals speak in an identical manner, it is difficult to state how many regional accents of English exist. We can and do classify accents by country. Thus we speak of American, British, Canadian, Irish accents and so on. What is clear is that regional accents are more prevalent in the countries that have had the longest length of settlement by English speakers. In other words, there are fewer regional accents in North America and Australia, and more regional accents in Britain and Ireland. Within the United States the region with the largest number of regional accents is New England, which is also the region of earliest settlement (Kurath 1949; Nagy and Roberts 2008).

Different scholars have proposed differing typologies of accent classification, which has resulted in proposals classifying American regional accents into between three and ten types. For instance, Cassidy (1982) classifies American English as Eastern, referring to the non-rhotic accents of Boston, New England and New York City; Southern referring to the non-rhotic accents of the South, an area largely coterminous with the physical territory of the Confederate States; and General American the **rhotic** accent found in the remainder of the United States. Thomas (1958) argues that there are ten accent areas in the United States. He subdivides the Eastern accent into Eastern New England and New York City, the Southern accent into Southern and Southern Mountain; and General American into Middle Atlantic around Philadelphia, Western Pennsylvania, Central Midland centred around the middle band of states running from Ohio to Utah, Northwest, Southwest centred around California, and North-Central centred around Chicago. More recently Labov, Ash and Boberg (2006: 146) have classified North American accents of English, including Canadian English, into 17 accent regions.

In Australian English, following Mitchell and Delbridge (1965), it is useful to classify three accent categories: Cultivated, General and Broad. The overwhelming majority of the population speaks General Australian English. Cultivated Australian English is phonetically close to Received Pronunciation, with General Australian closer to the English spoken in the South East of England. Broad Australian English is noticeable for having long vowels initially in **diphthongs**. A noticeable difference between Australian and British accents is the raising of the vowel /æ/ (as in TRAP) to a vowel with the quality of a British /ɛ/ (as in DRESS). Thus, an Australian speaker's vocalization of the word *pan* may sound like a British speaker's vocalization of the word *pen*.

Within Britain and Ireland, far more accents are found within a more confined geographical area. In England alone Trudgill (2000: 66–8) identifies 16 accent regions. It must be understood that speakers are sensitized to hear significant local accent differences within the wider speech regions identified by linguists. For instance, Trudgill classifies speakers from Newcastle, Durham, Sunderland and Middlesbrough as speaking in a North East accent. Yet speakers from Newcastle have little difficulty in distinguishing their accents from those of Sunderland speakers.

The major historic split in English accents is between North and South, with Northern accents generally representing more historically conservative speech varieties. The category of historic Northern accents can be divided into modern day Northern accents and modern day Central accents, while modern Southern accents can be divided into those found in the South East and in the South West. Some key features that distinguish Southern accents from Northern and Central accents are that, in Northern and Central accents, words containing the STRUT vowel /ʌ/ are homophonous with words containing the FOOT vowel /ʊ/. Thus, for Northern and Central speakers the words *put* [pʊt] and *putt* [pʌt] are identical. This is not the case for Southern speakers. Northern and Central speakers pronounce the following set of words with a short front /æ/ vowel while Southern speakers pronounce them with a long back /ɑː/ vowel: *path*, *glass*, *raft*, *grasp*, *past*, *after*, *basket*, *laugh*, *dance*, *grant*, *branch*, *graph*, etc. (for further information see Wells 1982a: 135). There is, however, a further complication in describing accents in terms of /ɑː/ and /æ/, namely that speakers of South Western forms only use a single <a> vowel [a] which is intermediate between the fronted /æ/ vowel and the back /ɑː/ vowel.

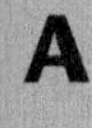

A key difference between Northern and Central accents is that Northern accents retain some long historic monophthongs whereas Central accents have undergone diphthongization. This results in the following potential pronunciation differences between Northern and Central speakers with Northern realizations first: *made* [meːd], [meɪd] *boat* [boːt], [bəʊt]. South Eastern and South Western are chiefly divided by the fact that South Western accents are unique – excluding a shrinking relic area in the Southern rural areas of Lancashire – among English accents in retaining /ɹ/ after a vowel within the same syllable. Thus, while a typical South Eastern speaker would pronounce *arm* as [ɑːm], a typical South Western speaker would pronounce it as [aɹm].

Scottish, Irish and Welsh accents are widely heard distinctive and recognizable accents found within the individual nations and more generally across the UK and Ireland. As with Northern English accents, they are essentially conservative. All three have to a greater or lesser extent been influenced by Celtic languages. Scottish accents have, in addition, been influenced by *Scots*, a distinct English dialect that was introduced into Scotland from Northumbria in the seventh century and was subsequently itself influenced by contact with Scottish Gaelic. Until the political union between Scotland and England, *Scots* was the de facto national language of Scotland. Some of the key defining features of present day Scottish accents are that it is rhotic; there is no distinction between the FOOT /ʊ/ and GOOSE /uː/ vowels that are pronounced /u/; vowel duration is dependent on the phonetic context with vowels being generally longer before /ɹ/ or a morpheme or word boundary (Stuart-Smith 2008), and the presence of the consonants /ʍ/ a voiceless labial-velar approximant, which in most other forms of English has merged with /w/ resulting in the loss of a distinction between the following pairs of words: *which/witch, whine/wine* and /x/, a velar fricative that has been retained in words such as *loch* [lɔx]. In most English accents *loch* would be homophonous with *lock* and pronounced /lɒk/. The Scottish accent also differs from most English accents in that it does not favour H dropping.

There are two main accents found in Ireland, with the accent of the North of the island Ulster English being in a sense intermediate between a Scottish and an Irish accent. However, Ulster English accents have some unique features such as the **palatization** of /k/ and /g/ before low vowels. Cat is pronounced as [kjat] (see Hickey 2008 for further details). Unlike Scottish and Southern Irish accents, Ulster English accents do not have the **phoneme** /ʍ/. All Irish accents, like Scottish accents, do not tend to favour H dropping. The chief distinguishing features of Southern Irish English accents are that it is rhotic; it retains the /ʍ/ phoneme; and, uniquely, the *th* sounds in words such as *thin* and *this* are pronounced as **dental stops** – for example, [t̪ɪn] not /θɪn/ and [d̪ɪs] not /ðɪs/ (see manner of **articulation** and place of **articulation**). Unlike most accents of English, but not Welsh accents, /l/ is traditionally pronounced in the same manner before and after vowels. However, Wells (1982b: 431) and Hickey (2008: 92) report that postvocalic /l/s are becoming dark (see **velarization** and **dark L**).

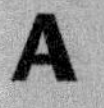

Welsh-accented English, unlike the other Celtic accents, is typically non-rhotic though there are three distinct areas of rhoticity within Wales. The first borders the rhotic English South West, the second is the site of the first historical English speaking settlement and the third is the traditional Welsh-speaking areas (Wells 1982b; Penhallurick 2008). In some Welsh accents there is a possibility of contrasts that are not found in other varieties of English, notably *blue/blew,* [bluː], [blɪu] *pain/pane,* [peːn] [peɪn] *no/know* [noː], [nou]. Somewhat surprisingly, a widely commented-upon feature of Welsh accented English – its lilting or singsong intonation – has not yet been systematically investigated. In a study aimed at producing a phonetic description of Welsh-accented English in the South Wales valleys, Walters (2003) points out that the most notable feature that contributes to the melody of the Rhondda valley is **intonation**. Unlike other varieties of English the most common pitch movement prior to the tonic syllable was downwards, while after the tonic syllable the most common initial tone movement was rising.

Accent 2

An accented syllable refers to a syllable that is realized by auditory prominence within a word. This auditory prominence enables the word to stand out in a stream of speech. Accenting results from a combination of **pitch**, **loudness** and **duration**. The accent within a word is normally placed on the primary stressed syllable within the word. But if the speaker wishes to highlight a contrast he/she may move the accent on to another syllable, for instance Bolinger (1962: 83) reports a speaker saying: *This whiskey wasn't **EX**ported from Ireland it was **DE**ported.* The speaker, in order to signal the contrast, has moved the accent from the primary stressed syllable *por*. The communicative value produced by accented syllables is discussed under **intonation**.

Acoustic phonetics

Acoustic phonetics is the subfield of **phonetics**, which studies the physical properties of speech. It complements **articulatory** and **auditory** phonetics. Advanced study of acoustic phonetics requires some mathematical knowledge and familiarization with the relevant equipment such as spectrographs or relevant software, such as Praat. Acoustic analyses reveal the physical facts of a sound wave, which can be used to corroborate articulatory analyses and provide a firm phonetic underpinning for phonological analyses. However, acoustic analyses of **intonation** contours may conflict with our perception of intonation contours; what we perceive as a rising tone movement may be measured instrumentally as neither an increase nor decrease in **fundamental frequency**. In cases where acoustic analyses conflict with human perception it is by no means clear which analysis a phonetician should prefer, nor how a phonetician should reconcile the difference (see Wichmann 2000: 2).

Acoustic phonetics describes the physical effect of speech on the air molecules surrounding the speaker. When people speak they disturb the air molecules near their mouths, which in turn bump into other molecules and displace them. This results in a chain reaction, which continues until the energy imparted by the **vocal organs** dissipates and the sound dies out some distance from the speaker. When an air molecule is displaced it rebounds back to its starting point and continues to oscillate to and fro until it runs out of energy, at which point it eventually stands still again. The sounds we hear are related to the characteristic vibrations of molecules around their places of rest. It is these cycles that acoustic phoneticians plot in order to measure the frequency of a sound. There are two ways in which the oscillation of an air molecule can vary. The first is if the molecule is given a harder initial bump: it will travel further from its place of rest. We perceive the increased **amplitude** as an increase in loudness. The second way to vary the oscillation is to increase or decrease the speed in which the cycle can be completed. A faster cycle with amplitude kept constant is perceived as a higher **pitch**, and a slower cycle as a lower pitch.

Sounds whose periods remain almost the same for cycle after cycle, such as a note on a piano, are known as periodic sounds. Other sounds are known as aperiodic sounds. Only periodic sounds give rise to a clear sensation of pitch. The sound waves of some speech sounds, chiefly **vowels**, can be decomposed into a combination of more than two periodic sounds, known as harmonic components. The waveform of an aperiodic sound, such as a consonant, does not repeat itself and cannot consequently be broken down into harmonic components. However, aperiodic sounds can be identified instrumentally in terms of the overall shape of their spectra. This is because the amplitude of any individual aperiodic sound is greater in some frequency regions than others. It is these differences in the overall amplitude profile of the sound over the frequency range that enable us to distinguish one aperiodic sound from another (see also **formant**). Phoneticians can identify all individual speech sounds either through the combination of fundamental frequency and harmonic structure or the overall spectra shape, and can produce spectrographic illustrations of each individual speech sound. For accessible accounts of acoustic phonetics see Ball and Rahilly (1999: ch. 9); Clark, Yallop and Fletcher (2006: ch. 7); Ladefoged (2001: ch. 8); Harrington (2010); and Lodge (2009: ch. 9).

Acute

This term has three distinct meanings all of which contrast with **grave**. The first is slightly old-fashioned and is used in descriptions of **tone** languages to refer to a rising lexical tone. The second meaning is used in some accounts of **intonation** to describe a rising tone. The third meaning refers to one of the features of a sound in **distinctive feature** theory (see Jakobson and Halle 1956), where it defines sounds involving the combination of a medial articulation in the mouth and a concentration of acoustic energy in the higher frequencies. Sounds that contain the feature acute are front **vowels**, and **dental**, **alveolar** and **palatal consonants**.

Advanced tongue root

In most languages differences in **vowel** quality can be described in terms of variations in height, backness and lip-rounding. However, in some African languages, such as Akan and Igbo, there are sets of vowels that cannot be distinguished solely by variations in these three dimensions. In one set of vowels, the root of the tongue is drawn forward and the larynx is lowered. These vowels are described as advanced tongue root (ATR) vowels. In the other set, the root of the tongue is not drawn forward and the larynx is not lowered. This set of vowels is described as retracted tongue root (RTR) vowels. However, Ladefoged (2001: 211) notes that not all speakers of Akan make the difference between ATR vowels and RTR vowels by bunching-up their tongues. Instead, what seems to signal the distinction is either tongue root movement or larynx lowering, which results in an enlargement of the middle and lower pharynx. In English, while no sets of vowels are distinguished solely by this articulatory gesture, the vowels in FLEECE and GOOSE have a more advanced tongue root than do the vowels in KIT and FOOT. See **tense** and **lax**.

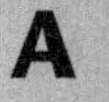

Affricate

An affricate is a term used to refer to the classification of a **consonant** on the basis of its manner of **articulation**. An affricate results from the sequential articulation of a **stop** that is released slowly into a **fricative** within the same syllable in the same place in the mouth. Affricates, like all consonants, may be **voiced** or **voiceless**. Voiceless affricates may be **aspirated** or **unaspirated**. Phonetically, affricates differ from a sequence of a stop followed by a fricative in that the duration of the fricative component is shorter than the duration of an independent fricative. There are two affricates found in English, namely the first sounds in *chip* /tʃ/ and in *judge* /dʒ/. The **voiceless palato-alveolar** affricate /tʃ/ is a very common speech sound. It is present in 45 per cent of the world's languages. Other well-known affricates are the voiceless labiodental affricate /pf/ found in German and the **alveolar** affricate /ts/ found in numerous languages such as Chinese and German (see Ladefoged and Maddieson 1996). In theory, an affricate can be articulated anywhere in the mouth. The International Phonetic Association (IPA) provides symbols for voiced and voiceless **velar** and **uvular** affricates but, in practice, languages tend to favour affricates produced between the **alveolar** ridge and the hard palate.

In many languages, including some accents of English, stops are often affricated. This means that the speaker releases the stop very slowly, which causes a short but audible phase of frication. In effect, by not lowering the tongue cleanly and swiftly, the speaker releases the stop into a fricative. Affrication is a noted feature of Liverpool speech, where some speakers often realize the following stop phonemes: /p/, /t/, /d/ and /k/ as [p$^{\Phi}$], [t^{s}], [d^{z}] and [k^{x}].

Phonologically, affricates realize one **phoneme**. Sounds that may be pronounced phonetically as affricates may be classified on **phonological** grounds as either affricated **allophones** of stops, or as a sequence of two consonant phonemes. In many accents of English the initial consonant cluster in the words *train* and *drain* are pronounced as affricates with the onset of the [ɹ] producing audible friction. Despite this phonetic reality, the initial consonant cluster is not classified as an affricate. Three justifications may be advanced for not analysing [tɹ] and [dɹ] in strict accordance with the phonetic facts. The first is that native English speakers feel that words such as *train* and *drain* begin with two consonant sounds, whereas words such as *church* and *judge* are felt to begin with only one consonant. The second reason is that the affricate /tʃ/ can be found in all phonetic environments, for example, word initially in words such as *chip*, word medially in words such as *richer* and word finally in words such as *match*. The sequence [tɹ] can only be found word initially in words such as *train* and word medially in words such as *metrical*, it is never found word finally. However, this second argument is not as convincing as it initially seems. Some English consonant phonemes are restricted in their distribution, for example, /ŋ/ is only allowed medially and finally but not initially, and /h/ and /w/ are only allowed word initially and medially.

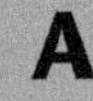

The final reason is that the initial sound in the consonant sequences [tɹ] and [dɹ], and in some rare cases the second consonant may be substituted by another consonant, and this substitution leads to the formation of a new lexical unit (see **phoneme**), for example:

/tɹeɪn/ *train*: /t/ replaced by /b/ becomes /bɹeɪn/ *brain*.
/tɹeɪn/ *train*: /ɹ/ replaced by /w/ becomes /tweɪn/ *twain*.
/dɹein/ *drain*: /d/ replaced by /g/ becomes /gɹeɪn/ *grain*.
/dɹein/ *drain*: /ɹ/ replaced by /w/ becomes /dweɪn/ *Dwayne*.

In affricates such as /tʃ/ it is not possible to substitute either the stop or the fricative component alone. The entire phonological unit contrasts with other English consonant phonemes; for example, if the initial affricate /tʃ/ in *chip* is replaced by the following consonants /p/, /t/, /d/, /n/, /l/, /ɹ/, /s/, /ʃ/, /k/ and /h/, the following set of words results: /pɪp/, /tɪp/, /dɪp/, /nɪp/, /lɪp/, /ɹɪp/, /sɪp/ /ʃɪp/, /kɪp/, /hɪp/.

Airstream mechanism

Speakers need a source of energy to power their speech. The airstream mechanism is the physiological process, which provides the energy used in speech production. The air used to power speech may be produced by an outward flow of air known as an **egressive** airstream or, in less usual circumstances, by an inward flow of air known as an **ingressive** airstream. Most speech is powered by an outwards flow of air initiated by the lungs. This is known as a **pulmonic** egressive airstream. However, as readers who have talked while simultaneously engaging in strenuous physical activity will realize, it is perfectly possible to articulate a speech sound or a sequence of speech sounds when inhaling. Technically this airstream mechanism is known as a pulmonic ingressive airstream.

The movement of air used to power a speech sound may be initiated other than by the lungs. An airstream mechanism can be initiated by the movement of the **glottis**. As with a pulmonic airstream the flow of air known as **glottalic** may be egressive or ingressive. A further power source for speech sounds found in language is an airstream known as **velaric**, which is initiated by the pressing of the back of the tongue against the **velum**. The airstream initiated by the velum is ingressive and produces a sound similar to the 'tut tut' paralinguistic sound produced by English speakers to signal displeasure.

In principle, speech can be powered by any airstream mechanism initiated at any point in the **vocal tract**. Patients who have undergone a laryngectomy have been taught to power their speech by swallowing air into their stomachs and then pushing the air out from their stomachs as a substitute for an egressive pulmonic airstream. Chapter 6 of Laver (1994) and Ladefoged and Maddieson (1996: 77–89) provide a comprehensive and reader-friendly description of airstream mechanisms.

Allophone

An allophone is a phonological term for an audibly distinct variant of a **phoneme** within a language which does not affect the phoneme's functional unity. Allophones within a language system are found in *complementary distribution*. They do not exist in the same phonetic environment. For instance, in most dialects of English there are two variants of /l/ clear <L> [l] and dark <L> [ɫ]. Clear <L> is normally produced by contact between the tip of the tongue and the upper teeth, which allows the air to escape over the sides of the tongue. Simultaneously, the front of the tongue is raised in the direction of the **hard palate**. In contrast for dark or **velarized** <L> the front of the tongue is somewhat depressed, while the back of the tongue is raised towards the **soft palate**. Dark <Ls> consequently have an auditorily perceptible back vowel resonance which clear <Ls> lack. Yet despite the clear phonetic dissimilarity between clear and dark <Ls> in English they are considered to be allophones and not separate phonemes. This is because, in English, clear and dark <Ls> are in complementary distribution with clear <Ls> preceding vowels and /j/, while dark <Ls> follow vowels. In other words, substitution of a clear <L> by a dark <L> does not lead to the formation of a new lexical item. For instance, regardless of whether a Southern English speaker pronounces a word as [lɪɫt], a Southern Irish speaker as [lɪlt] or a Northern English speaker as [ɫɪɫt], all three speakers have articulated the lexical item *lilt*.

In English the **nasal** /n/ is normally realized in **alveolar** position (e.g. /pæn/) but in the word *panther* – see **assimilation** – it is realized as a **dental** nasal (e.g. [ˈp^{h}æ̃n̪θə]). In English the realization of a nasal as dental before /θ/ is predictable. Both variants of the nasal are in complementary distribution and can be classified as allophones. However, it is worth noting that complementary distribution alone is not sufficient to identify allophones. The phones /h/ and /ŋ/ occur in complementary distribution in English with /h/ present only in **syllable onset** position and /ŋ/ restricted to **syllable coda** position. If we relied solely on complementary distribution to identify allophones we would have to argue that the two phones were allophones of the same phoneme. However, this is clearly not a satisfactory solution as English speakers intuitively feel that the two phonemes are not allophonic realizations of a single phoneme. Indeed I cannot even imagine what kind of phoneme they could be allophones of!

In deciding whether a particular phone is a phoneme or an allophone we must also consider the notion of phonetic similarity. Phonetic similarity is a vague concept that differs across languages. For instance, in Irish Gaelic, dental nasals are not in complementary distribution with alveolar nasals. Instead their distributions overlap and the choice of a dental or an alveolar nasal realizes lexical meaning. Irish contrasts nasals with six different places of articulation, or, in other words, has six nasal phonemes (Ní Chasaide 1999: 112); English has only three nasal phonemes, one of which /ŋ/ is restricted to coda position. Hence what is phonemic in Irish will be allophonic in English.

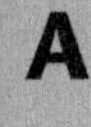

To an English speaker it is intuitive that the first, second and third phones in the following words are all realizations of the /p/ phoneme *pot* [p^{h}ɒt], spot [sp̬ɒt] and top [t^{h}ɒp], yet speakers of some other languages do not have the same intuition. Hindi, Korean, Mandarin and Cantonese contrast /p/ and /p^{h}/ phonemically (for an enlightening discussion see Silverman 2006: 69–80). The following illustrative examples are from Ladefoged and Maddieson (1996: 58) and Bok Lee (1999: 121).

	Hindi		Korean
/pal/	*take care of*	/pal/	*sucking*
/p^{h}al/	*knife blade*	/p^{h}al/	*arm*
/bal/	*hair*	/bal/	*foot*

For speakers of Hindi and Korean the presence or absence of **aspiration** is as phonetically dissimilar as is the presence or absence of **voicing**. English speakers by contrast barely recognize the phonetic dissimilarity between an aspirated and unaspirated stop. Conversely for English speakers the initial phones in the words *they* /θeɪ/ and *day* /deɪ/ sound phonetically dissimilar enough for them to be able to distinguish between the phones and to contrast them phonemically. However, cross-linguistically dental **fricatives** /θ/ and /ð/ are rare – see Table 9 – and for most languages [θ] and [ð] are allophonic realizations of /s/ and /z/.

Yet even establishing that phones are in complementary distribution and that they seem to be phonetically similar is not always conclusive evidence in establishing whether or not two phones are allophones of the same phoneme. Clark, Fletcher and Yallop (2007: 97–8) report that in Italian there are three nasal phonemes: the bilabial /m/, the alveolar /n/ and the palatal /ɲ/. The nasal phoneme, before the velar consonants /k/ and /g/, assimilates predictably to [ŋ] as in [baŋka] *bank*. However, it is by no means clear what phoneme [ŋ] is an allophone of. The closest sounding phoneme is /ɲ/ but Italian orthography suggests that it is an allophone of /n/. There does not seem to be any principled reason why it could not be an allophone of /m/. Indeterminacies such as this have led some scholars to abandon phonemic analysis and propose alternate analyses based on **underlying representations**.

Alveolar

The term alveolar refers to the classification of a **consonant** sound on the basis of the place of **articulation** of the sound. Alveolar consonants are produced by contact or close proximity between the alveolar ridge, which is the bony structure behind the front teeth, and the tip or blade of the tongue. Assuming a normal **pulmonic egressive airstream mechanism** the following classes of consonants are classified by the IPA as alveolar: **plosives** [t, d], **nasals** [n], **trills** [r], **taps** [ɾ], **fricatives** [s, z], **lateral fricatives** [ɬ, ɮ], **approximants** [ɹ] and **lateral appoximants** [l].

The **voiceless** alveolar plosive consonant [t] is one of the most favoured consonants across languages. It is estimated (Ladefoged 2005: 156) that around 98 per cent of the world's languages contain a variant of [t], though in some languages, such as French, the [t] has a **dental** place of **articulation**. Languages including French, Hungarian, Persian and Russian do not contain any alveolar phonemes; instead they have dental phonemes.

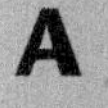

Table 1 summarizes the presence or absence of alveolar consonant **phonemes** across a number of major languages. Table 1 and all other tables that list phonemes in the 25 languages are based on data mostly found in the 1999 IPA handbook. It can be seen that there are eight possible alveolar manner of **articulations** with plosive, fricative and lateral approximants being the most favoured across the languages surveyed. The most marked manner of **articulation** is the lateral fricative which is found in Welsh and represented orthographically as *ll* as in place names such as *Llanelli* [ɬan'ɛɬi] and *Llangollen* [ɬan'goɬɛn]

In English, in addition to the alveolar phonemes listed above, in some accents alveolar **allophonic** variations may be heard. In some forms of **received pronunciation** an <r> pronounced between two vowels may be realized as a tap, as in [vɛɾi] Scottish English is commonly said to favour taps [ɾ], though this is a matter of some dispute. For further information see Wells (1982b: 411)

Table 1 List of alveolar phonemes found in 25 languages

Language	Plosive	Nasal	Trill	Tap	Fricatives	Lateral Fricatives	Approximants	Lateral Approximants
Amharic	t d	n	r		s z			l
Arabic			r		s z			
Bulgarian	t d	n	r		s z			l
Cantonese	t	n						
Czech	t d	n	r					l
Dutch	t d	n		ɾ	s z			l
English	t d	n			s z		ɹ	l
French								
German	t d	n			s z			l
Greek		n	r		s z			l
Hausa	t d	n	r		s z			l
Hebrew	t d	n	r		s z			l
Hindi		n		ɾ	s z			l
Hungarian								
Igbo		n			s z			
Italian			r		s z			l
Japanese					s z			
Korean	t t^h d	n			s z			l
Mandarin	t	n			s			l
Persian								
Portuguese				ɾ	s z			
Russian								
Spanish		n	r	ɾ	s			l
Swedish							ɹ	
Thai	t t^h d	n	r		s			l
Welsh	t d	n	r		s	ɬ		l

Here and in the other tables the cells that are shaded in grey indicate that the particular language does not contain any phonemes articulated at the relevant place of **articulation**.

and Stuart-Smith (2008: 64–5). A noticeable feature of American English and an apparently increasing feature in working-class New Zealand speech is what sociolinguists refer to as *t-voicing*. The speaker substitutes a tap for an alveolar stop. Thus, Ladefoged (2001: 151) claims that a General American pronunciation of *petal* will resemble a Scottish pronunciation of *pearl*. In both cases the speaker will say something like [p^{h}ɛɾɬ].

Amplitude

Amplitude is an **acoustic** phonetic term that refers to the extent to which an air molecule moves to and fro around its place of rest. The greater the amplitude, or the distance between the points of rest, the greater the **intensity**. The greater the intensity the louder the sound will be perceived as.

Aperture

Aperture is a phonological term that is used to refer to contrasts involving the degree of openness of an **articulation** in models of phonology such as

autosegmental, **metrical** and **firthian**. For consonants, a tertiary classification of aperture is recognized. Complete closure of the oral tract results in **stops** and **nasals**. An aperture sufficient to generate a turbulent **airstream** results in **fricatives**. A more open aperture that is insufficient to generate a turbulent airstream mechanism results in **approximants** and **semi vowels**. For **vowels** the degree of aperture correlates with tongue height, with **close** vowels having a less open aperture than do **open** vowels.

Approximant

An approximant is a term used to refer to the classification of a **consonant** on the basis of its manner of **articulation**. Approximants are produced by a narrowing of the opening through which the airstream occurs. The narrowing is not close enough to produce friction. As a result these sounds are also known as **frictionless continuants**. The IPA recognizes two types of approximants: one where the airstream escapes over the tongue; the other known as a **lateral**, where the airstream escapes around the sides of the tongue. Approximants can be articulated at the following places of **articulation**: **bilabial**, **labiodental**, **alveolar**, **dental**, **palato-alveolar**, **retroflex**, **palatal** and **velar**.

In English there are four **voiced** approximant phonemes /ɹ/, /w/, /j/ and /l/. Voiceless approximants are possible in language though there are none in English. Approximants can be subdivided into two further classifications: **liquids** – in English /ɹ/ and /l/; and **semi vowels** – in English /j/ and /w/.

Archiphoneme

An archiphoneme is a phonological solution to the problem of **phonemic** neutralization. Phonemic neutralization refers to cases where the contrast between phonemes within a word is lost. For instance, in **coda** position in English there is no contrast between **nasal** phonemes, which are immediately followed by a **plosive**. The nasal before /p/ must be **bilabial** (e.g. *limp* /lɪmp/); the nasal before /t/ must be **alveolar** (e.g. *lint* /lɪnt/); and the nasal before /k/ must be **velar** (e.g. *link* /lɪŋk/). By choosing to transcribe the nasals in *limp, lint* and *link* as /m/, /n/ and /ŋ/, respectively, an analyst attributes a contrast that is not there! The contrast between the coda final plosive determines the place of **articulation** of the preceding nasal phoneme.

After /s/ in **onset** position the voicing contrast between plosives is lost. Yet *speech* is transcribed as /spiːtʃ/ and not /sbiːtʃ/, *stitch* is transcribed as /stɪtʃ/ and not /sdɪtʃ/ and skate is transcribed as /skeɪt/ and not /sgeit/. The plosive, though, cannot be voiced because the voicelessness of the initial fricative perseveres and devoices the following segment (e.g. *snow* [sn̥əʊ] and *slow* [sl̥əʊ]). The transcription of /p/, /t/ and /k/ after /s/ incorrectly implies the existence of an available voicing contrast. The solution to this problem proposed by the Prague School linguist Nikolai Trubetzkoy was to explicitly signal the phonemic neutralization by notating an archiphoneme, indicated by a capital letter, which is not identified with a particular phoneme but rather with the suspension of contrasts between the relevant phonemes. Thus, *limp, lint* and *link* are transcribed as

/lɪNp/, /lɪNt/ and /lɪNk/, respectively. The N symbol transcribes a nasal that is underspecified for place of **articulation**. Similarly *speech* is transcribed as /sPiːtʃ/ with the P symbol notating a bilabial stop that is unspecified for voicing.

Articulation

Articulation is a phonetic term that refers to any physiological movement which modifies an **airstream mechanism** in the production of the sound. There are two distinct sets of articulators: the active articulators that move to create the stricture, and the passive articulators that the active articulators move towards. The active articulator is usually the tongue. However, in **bilabial** and **labiodentals** the active articulator is the lower lip and, in the articulation of /h/, the **vocal folds**.

The tongue itself is usually segmented into five distinct regions. The tip or apex, which is the front-most extremity of the tongue, is especially flexible and can touch the roof of the mouth as far back as the hard palate. It is the active articulator in **retroflex** sounds and in **trills**. Sounds that are articulated with the tip of the tongue are classified as apical. The blade is the upper surface of the tongue immediately behind the tip. When the tongue is at rest it is opposite the alveolar ridge. It is the active articulator in the production of **dental**, **alveolar** and **palato-alveolar** sounds. Sounds that are articulated with the blade of the tongue are classified as laminal. The front is the region of the tongue below the hard palate when the tongue is at rest. It is the active articulator in the production of **palatal** sounds. It may be used to articulate fronted **velar** stops in words such as *key* and *geese*. The back is the region of the tongue below the soft palate when the tongue is at rest. It is the active articulator in the production of velar sounds. Sounds that are articulated with the back of the tongue are classified as dorsal. The root of the tongue is the region opposite the pharynx and it is not used as an active articulator in languages other than Semitic ones. However, the root of the tongue is involved in the production of sounds that are classified as being made with an **advanced tongue root**. It may be involved in the production of **tense** sounds.

Sounds are classified in terms of their manner of **articulation**. This refers to the degree of closure caused by the movement of the active articulator and the passive articulator. If the airstream mechanism is able to flow out of the mouth unimpeded the sound is a vowel or a semi-vowel. Sounds produced with a closure that impedes the airflow are consonants. Those produced with a complete closure of the mouth are known as stop consonants. If the soft palate is raised and the airstream is unable to flow out the nasal passage the sound is a **plosive**, as in /p/, /b/, /t/, /d/, /k/ and /g/. Conversely, if the soft palate is lowered and the airstream is free to flow out through the nose the sound is a **nasal** stop, as in /m/, /n/ and /ŋ/. Sounds where the active articulator approaches the passive articulator so closely that it results in audible friction are **fricative** consonants (e.g. /f/, /v/, /θ/, /ð/, /s/, /z/, /ʃ/, /ʒ/ and /h/). Sounds where the organs do not approach closely together are known as **approximants**, for example, g /l/ and /ɹ/.

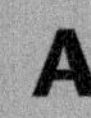

The passive articulators define the place of **articulation**. If the upper lip is the passive articulator the sound is **bilabial**. /p/ and /b/ are bilabial plosives, /m/ is a bilabial nasal stop. Sounds produced at the teeth have a **labiodental** or **dental**

place of **articulation**. /f/ and /v/ are labiodental fricatives, and /θ/ and /ð/ are dental fricatives. Those produced at the **alveolar** ridge, the bony prominence behind the upper teeth, have an **alveolar** place of **articulation**. /t/ and /d/ are alveolar plosive consonants, /n/ is an alveolar nasal, /s/ and /z/ are alveolar fricatives and /l/ and /ɹ/ are alveolar approximants. Sounds produced at the part of the mouth between the alveolar ridge and the beginning of the hard palate have a **palato-alveolar** place of **articulation**. /ʃ/ and /ʒ/ are palato-alveolar fricatives. Sounds produced at the hard palate, the arched bony structure behind the front teeth, have a **palatal** place of **articulation**. /j/ is a palatal approximant.

Sounds produced at the soft palate or velum, the mobile fleshy area contiguous to the back of the hard palate, have a **velar** place of **articulation**. /k/ and /g/ are velar plosives and /ŋ/ is a velar nasal. Sounds that are made at the uvula, the small appendage that dangles from the back of the soft palate, have an **uvular** place of **articulation**. There are no English uvular phonemes. The remaining passive articulators, with the exception of the **glottis**, are not used in the English sound system. These are the pharynx, the tubular cavity immediately above the larynx and the epiglottis, the anatomical structure that closes over the larynx. The larynx itself is made up of cartilage and muscle and contains the **vocal folds**. The space between the vocal folds is the glottis and sounds that are made by the narrowing of the space between the vocal folds have a **glottal** place of **articulation**, for example /h/, which is a glottal fricative. The remaining place of **articulation** is **retroflex**. This refers to a sound produced by the touching of the tip of the tongue against the front of the soft palate.

Articulatory phonetics

Articulatory phonetics is the subfield of **phonetics**, which studies how speech sounds are articulated by the vocal organs. It complements **acoustic** and **auditory** phonetics.

Articulatory setting

An articulatory setting is the medium to long term setting of all the articulators in relation to one another. It varies both between languages and **accents**, and between individual speakers of the same dialect. Differences in articulatory settings between languages/accents account for many of the stereotypical differences between accents. For instance, Laver (1994: 411) explains how differences in the setting of the tongue body result in a 'velarized voice' typical of Liverpool and Birmingham accents. Differences in articulatory settings between speakers result in some speakers producing more nasalized or pharyngealized speech compared to others in their speech community.

Aspiration

Aspiration is a phonetic term for the audible breath that accompanies a sound's, usually a **plosive's**, **articulation**. Aspiration is notated by a superscript [h] placed immediately after the consonant symbol. In almost all English accents **voiceless** plosives are aspirated when initial in stressed syllables, as in *pin, tin* and *kin* are pronounced as [pʰɪn], [tʰɪn] and [kʰɪn]. Celtic-influenced accents tend to have more strongly aspirated syllable initial plosives than RP does. If [l, ɹ, w, j] immediately follow an aspirated phoneme they are devoiced and articulated as [l̥, ɹ̥, w̥, j̊]. Readers may note the difference in voicing by slowly and carefully articulating the following pairs of words:

Lay [leɪ]	*Play* [pʰl̥eɪ]
Ray [ɹeɪ]	*Pray* [pʰɹ̥eɪ]
Ween [wiːn]	*Queen* [kʰw̥iːn]
You [juː]	*Pew* [pʰj̊uː]

There are a number of exceptions to the 'rule' that initial voiceless plosives are aspirated. Wells (1982b: 370) reports that speakers from the Pennine Valleys north of Manchester may have little or no aspiration before a stressed vowel. Clark (2008: 169) reports that aspiration of syllable final plosives may be a feature of West-Midland accents. South African speakers, presumably because of interference from Afrikaans, tend not to aspirate voiceless plosives that precede stressed vowels (Wells 1982c: 618). Wells further reports (ibid.: 625) that it is a well-known feature of Anglo-Indian accents that voiceless plosives are unaspirated in all positions.

A simple test that readers can do to check if, and how strongly, they aspirate voiceless plosives is to slowly and carefully pronounce words with initial and final voiceless plosives such as *pan, nap, tan, gnat, can, knack* with their hand held a few inches in front of their mouth. If a plosive is aspirated readers will perceive a burst of air striking their hand. When I read the above words my pronunciation – and no doubt that of the majority of the readers – is [pʰæn], [næp], [tʰæn], [næt], [kʰæn] and [næk]. Readers are likely to notice that the burst of air following [p] is the strongest, and that following [k] the weakest. This is because the closure for [p] is at the lips, thus there is a far larger amount of compressed air waiting to be released once the lips are opened than there is when the stop closure is made by the back of the tongue against the velum.

Many languages have voiceless aspirated plosives either as **phonemes** or **allophones**, but a few languages such as Hindi and Igbo are reported to have voiced aspirated plosives. Ladefoged and Maddieson (1996: 69–70) note, however, that voiced aspirated plosives do not contain a period of voicelessness or audible breath. Consequently they argue that if these sounds are truly aspirated, aspiration must be redefined in terms of **voice onset time** 'as period after the release of a stricture and before the start of regular voicing in which the vocal folds are markedly further apart than they are in modally voiced sounds'.

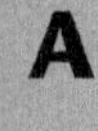

Assimilation

Assimilation is a process that can lead, in historical terms, to a sound change. Sounds assimilate when a feature of one sound changes to match those of another feature, which either precedes it or follows it. In connected speech where words are pronounced without audible gaps between them the pronunciation of one **phoneme** may alter how a nearby phoneme is pronounced. In English, assimilation is more likely to occur in rapid casual speech rather than in slow careful

Table 2 Assimilation in Greek from nominative to accusative

Nominative	Accusative	
[i porta]	[tim borta]	*the door*
[i trapeza]	[tin drapeza]	*the bank*
[i kori]	[tiŋ gori]	*the girl*

speech. This, however, is not the case in other languages where assimilation is not optional but rather obligatory. Table 2 (adapted from Lodge 2009: 149–50) provides examples of assimilation from Greek when a nominal feminine element switches from the nominative to the accusative case. In Greek the clitic /i/ signals a feminine singular noun in the nominative case while /tin/ signals a feminine singular noun in the accusative case.

The Greek examples illustrate that there is more than one kind of assimilation. In the /porta/ example, the place of **articulation** of the final **nasal** in /tin/ is influenced by the **bilabial** place of **articulation** of the initial consonant /p/ in *porta*, and that nasal assimilates to the bilabial place of **articulation**. Thus /n/ is realized as [m]. Simultaneously, the voicing produced during the articulation of the nasal /n/ is maintained and the word initial voiceless phoneme /p/ is realized as a voiced sound [b]. In the *trapeza* example, the final nasal of /tin/ and the initial consonant in /trapeza/ are both **alveolar** but, as in the previous examples, the voicing of the nasal is maintained. The initial phoneme of the nominal element /t/ is realized as [d]. In the final example *kori*, as in the earlier /porta/ example, the place of **articulation** of the nasal assimilates to that of the initial consonant and /n/ is realized as [ŋ]. As in the other two examples, the voicing of the nasal is maintained and /k/ is realized as [g].

The examples set out in Table 2 indicate that there are two main types of assimilation: *regressive* (also known as *anticipatory*) and *progressive* (also known as *perseverative*). In the Greek examples, above, the place assimilation is regressive while the voicing assimilation is progressive. Regressive assimilation means that a phoneme that comes later in time influences a phoneme which comes earlier in time. For instance, if an English speaker wishes to say the phrase *ten guns* in fast casual speech, it is likely that the /n/ in *ten* will assimilate to [ŋ] in anticipation of the following **velar** stop /g/.

Progressive assimilation, which is not as common as regressive assimilation, is the opposite case and refers to a situation where the phoneme that is earlier in time influences the pronunciation of a phoneme that is later in time. English examples of progressive assimilation may occur in fast and casual pronunciations of words such as *happen* and *quicken*. Assuming that the nasal is syllabic the words may be realized as ['hæpm̩] and ['kwɪkŋ̩]. The place of **articulation** of the plosive is preserved and continues during the articulation of the nasal. In fast and casual articulations, the sequence of words *in the* is often realized as [ɪn̪ n̪ə]. The influence of the alveolar nasal perseveres and changes the dental fricative /ð/ into a dental nasal [n̪]. At the same time, the dental articulation of the fricative influences the place of **articulation** of the nasal and both are articulated as dentals, which is an example of regressive assimilation.

A further type of assimilation is coalescent assimilation, where each of the adjacent sounds reciprocally influence one another's pronunciation. In English the sequence /t/, /d/, /s/ and /z/ plus /j/ may coalesce to /tʃ/, /dʒ/, /ʃ/ and /ʒ/. Within word boundaries this coalescence has led historically to the presence of /tʃ/, /dʒ/, /ʃ/ and /ʒ/ medially in words such as *nurture, grandeur, mission* and *pleasure*. Some examples of possible coalescences across word boundaries are:

They hit you	/ðeɪ hɪt juː/	becomes	[ðeɪˈhɪtʃu]
I need you	/aɪ niːd juː/	becomes	[aɪˈniːdʒu]
I miss you	/aɪ mɪs juː/	becomes	[aɪˈmɪʃu]
I lose you	/aɪ luːz juː/	becomes	[aɪˈluːʒu]

In connected speech, assimilation may change a phoneme's place of **articulation**, voicing or (more rarely) manner of **articulation**. A typical example of regressive assimilation leading to a change in voicing is where a voiced obstruent is followed by a voiceless consonant, for instance the /b/ in [ˈæb̥səluːtli] is devoiced. Voiceless fricatives found in a fully voiced environment tend to be voiced. This happens in three phonetic environments: first between two vowels in words such as *Asia* realized as [ˈeɪʒə]; second where the fricative is immediately preceded by a voiced consonant and immediately followed by a vowel, as with transit realized as [ˈtɹænzɪt]; third where the voiceless fricative immediately follows a vowel and is itself immediately followed by a voiced consonant, as with *Muslim* realized as [mʊzlɪm].[1]

In this section, the assimilation described is continuous or contact assimilation but the influence of a phoneme may extend beyond the immediately adjacent sound. For instance, Crystal (2003: 38) reports that a possible articulation of the expression *turn up trumps* is [tɜːməptɹʌmps] where the nasal phoneme in *turn* has assimilated to the place of **articulation** of later consonants. While non-continuous or distance assimilation is rare in English it is common in many other languages where it is known as **harmony**.

Auditory phonetics

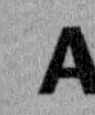

Auditory phonetics is the subfield of **phonetics** that studies how people perceive speech sounds and how they interpret their meaning. It complements **acoustic** and **auditory phonetics**. Traditionally auditory phonetics has been ignored in many treatments of phonetics, which have gone no further than (1) describing how a speech sound is made and (2) detailing the physical properties of the speech sound. A solid and approachable introduction to auditory phonetics is Ball and Rahilly (1999: chs 10 and 11). Today, as a result of numerous psychoacoustic studies, much is known about how people perceive sound, including speech, but far less is known about how people interpret meaning from the speech signal. Accordingly, the following paragraphs describe how people hear sound, including speech, prior to sketching some of the little that is known about how people listen to speech.

Air set in motion by the **vocal organs** oscillates. As speech is directed at hearers the vibrating air reaches the hearer's outer ear, the visible part of the ear, the pinna or auricle. The pinna itself is largely irrelevant to the ability to hear. It serves merely to channel the vibrating body of air into the ear canal. The ear canal is a tube that connects the pinna with the middle ear. It is approximately 25 mm long with a diameter of around 7 mm, although the shape and size vary between individuals. The ear canal functions as a resonator. It amplifies the sound waves that travel through it. It is particularly responsive to sounds between 3,000 Hz and 4,000 Hz, although it can amplify sounds between 500 Hz and 12,000 Hz.

After passing through the ear canal the sound wave enters the middle ear and strikes the air-filled eardrum, or tympanic membrane, which acts as a seal between the outer and middle ear. The eardrum contains three connected bones collectively known as the ossicles. The bones individually are the malleus (hammer), the incus (anvil) and the stapes (stirrup). Sound entering the middle ear pressurizes the bones and causes them to vibrate. The vibration of the bones of the middle ear converts the lower-pressure eardrum vibrations into higher pressure sounds that can be transmitted to the inner ear. The eardrum, as well as amplifying sounds, regulates the volume and protects the inner ear from damage.

Sound is transmitted to the inner ear through the oval window that is connected to the stapes. By the time the sound exits the middle ear it has been amplified by a factor of between 20 and 30 times. The inner ear contains the cochlea, which is the organ that converts sound waves into neural impulses. The cochlea is a coiled structure rather like a snail's shell. It is filled with a watery liquid and divided by two membranes, the vestibular membrane and the basilar membrane which divide the cochlea into two chambers, the scala vestibule and the scala tympani. It contains the organ of Corti, which is a structure deep inside the inner ear consisting of hair cells resting on the basilar membrane.

Sound pressure variations at the oval window cause the fluid in the upper chamber, the scala vestibule, to vibrate. This in turn triggers vibration in the fluid inside the scala tympani, the organ of Corti and the basilar membrane. The nature and location of the vibration along the basilar membrane is dependent on the frequency of the sound waves, with higher frequencies causing vibrations near the oval window and lower frequencies causing vibrations near the organ of Corti. The vibration of the basilar membrane results in movement in the hair cells in the organ of Corti. It is this movement that converts the vibration into the electrical impulses which are transmitted to the auditory centre of the brain as neural impulses.

The organ of Corti contains thousands of hair cells. As people age they experience a loss in the number of hair cells. This results in them being unable to hear higher frequency sounds. However, it is worth remembering that humans, unlike some other animals, can only hear sounds up to around 20,000 Hz and that speech sounds are relatively low frequency sounds.

Little is as yet known about how the brain categorizes sounds, though it is believed that that there is a feedback loop from the brain to the organ of Corti, which helps hearers monitor their hearing. Experiments have demonstrated that humans categorize speech digitally. For instance, rather than hearing multiple potential vowels between **cardinal vowels** 1 and 2, hearers tend to perceive two categorical vowels and experimenters have succeeded in identifying the point at which one vowel switches into the other.

Some of the acoustic cues that allow listeners to decode the speech signal are known. Speakers of English distinguish word initial voiced and voiceless **stops** in syllables such as [pɑː] and [bɑː] by the amount of time it takes voicing to commence on the vowel – see **voice onset time**. They use perceived vowel length to distinguish whether a final stop consonant is voiced or voiceless (e.g. /æt/ and /æd/) – see **fortis** and **lenis**. It is believed that speakers use **formant2** (F2) transitions to perceive the place of **articulation** of a consonant. An F2 value that is lower than would be expected had the vowel been produced in isolation signals a **bilabial** consonant, while an F2 value that is higher than had the vowel been produced in isolation signals a **velar** consonant.

However, far less is known about how hearers become listeners and decode meaning from the speech signal. Two models of listening, active and passive, are proposed in the literature (see Crystal 1997: 148). Both of the proposed models are problematic in one way or another. So it may well be that both models of listening are available to listeners to utilize when appropriate. Active models of listening claim that listeners use their pre-existing knowledge of the language to decode novel strings of speech. There are two main types of active models. The first, 'the motor theory' of speech perception (see Liberman 1996) proposes that listeners identify sounds by internally shadowing the articulatory movements of the speaker. This model is able to explain the rather puzzling McGurk effect, which suggests that speech perception is multimodal. The effect can be produced by video recording a speaker repeatedly producing an open syllable such as [gagagaga], removing the original soundtrack and dubbing the speaker's production of a different string of open syllables, such as [dadadada]. Hearers who watch the video recording will perceive the string of sound as [gagagaga], though if they close their eyes they will hear it as [dadadada]. However, it singularly fails to explain how individuals with pathological speaking disorders are able to successfully listen to speech.

The second influential active listening approach is 'analysis by synthesis' (e.g. Stevens and Halle 1967), which proposes that humans perceive speech by implicitly synthesizing speech by using their internal **distinctive feature** matrix to match the auditory input. Perception begins when the listener analyses the speech signal into a series of auditory patterns, which are then represented in terms of distinctive features. The resulting distinctive feature matrix, assuming that there has been no significant contextual interference, is assigned to a phoneme. In cases where there has been significant contextual interference, the listener hypothesizes a representation of the distinctive feature matrix and compares it with various representations generated by the listener's own internal phonology. All proposed models of active listening – readers interested in an accessible description of various active listening models are advised to read Yeni-Komshian (1998) – are able to account for attested experimental effects such as the listener's ability to fill in missing phonemes or words in a contextualized speech signal. However, they are unable to explain misidentifications such as /dɒn/ being perceived as /dʒɒn/ – see below.

Passive models of listening propose that listeners hear a message and match the incoming signals to a set of templates stored in the brain. If a match is located the sound is recognized, but if (as in the case of a foreign language) no internal template is available the listener is unable to decode the sound signal. Ball and Rahilly (1999: 187) note that it is by no means clear what type of internal templates listeners would need to enable them to decode the speech signal. Passive models are, however, able to account for data which active models struggle to explain. Listeners in response to the question, *Was it John or Mike?*, who hear the answer string it was /dɒn/ are almost certain to interpret /dɒn/ as /dʒɒn/. To account for these facts, Crystal (1997: 148) proposes that a combination of active and passive theories is required to explain the process of speech perception.

Autosegmental phonology

Autosegmental phonology is an influential **generative** model of phonology that was developed by John Goldsmith in his 1976 PhD dissertation. The most accessible theoretical introduction to the model is Goldsmith (1999); Goldsmith (1990) is a comprehensive textbook on the model. While Goldsmith overtly situates autosegmental phonology within the generative tradition some scholars, notably Lass (1984: 269fn.10.2.3), have noted the strong resemblance between autosegmental phonology and earlier models, especially **firthian prosodic phonology**. Despite this resemblance, autosegmental phonologists share many assumptions with generative phonologists, notably the existence of an underlying lexical representational level, which generates forms that represent the input to a series of linearly ordered rules, the operation of which generates surface forms.

The model was developed through the study of African **tone** languages and designed to provide a more phonetically grounded and less abstract phonological representation of language. The main insight of the model is that the phonological representation of a language comprises several autonomous *tiers* or levels with each tier consisting of a linear arrangement of elements. Tiers are linked by *association lines*, which formally represent the relation between the elements notated on the different tiers.

To illustrate using an English example based on Goldsmith (1999: 137–8), the phonological representation of /tɛn/ is:

/t/	/ɛ/	/n/
+ Coronal	+ Vocalic	+ Coronal
− Nasal	+ Dorsal	+ Nasal
+ Consonantal	− High	+ Consonantal
− Voice	− Low	+ Voice
− Continuant	− Back	− Continuant
+ Anterior		+ Anterior

Yet a speaker is likely to pronounce *ten* as an utterance that can be notated as following: [t^{h}ɛ̃n]. This utterance is produced by the following articulatory sequence, or in Goldsmith's terminology *orchestration* (see Table 3).

The aspiration that in segmental models is linked to [t] where it is classified as [+heightened subglottal pressure] continues into the articulation of the vowel. Nasality that is classified as belonging to the [+Nasal] /n/ in fact commences during the articulation of the vowel. To account for these facts, autosegmental

Table 3 A score for the orchestration of *ten* assuming a falling tone

Lips:	Spread		
Tongue:	Touch the palate	High and Front	Touch the palate..............
Velum:	Raise	Lower	
Vocal folds:	Apart	Vibrate faster	Vibrate slower ....
Segments:	/t/	/ɛ/	/n/

phonology proposes a representation where certain features are autonomous and linked simultaneously with more than one feature, for example:.

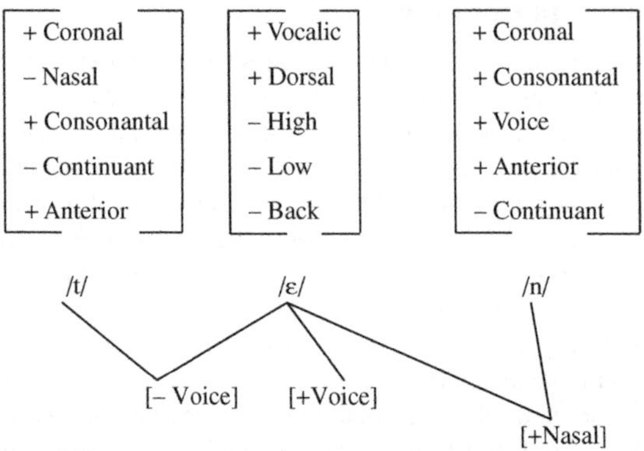

In the autosegmental representation of *ten* the nasality and voicing features are represented on their own autonomous tiers where they are free to associate with more than one segment.

The model was initially developed to account for five problems found in the study of African tone languages. The first of which *contour tones* is where a falling, rising or compound tone movement is attached to a word final vowel. Convincing phonetic evidence exists – see **tone** – demonstrating that lexical tones in African tone languages can be usefully analysed as a series of High or Low pitch targets. Thus, where the lexical tone on a word final vowel falls or rises, a segmental description runs into trouble, as with the word *àkálâ* (from Goldsmith 1999: 143):

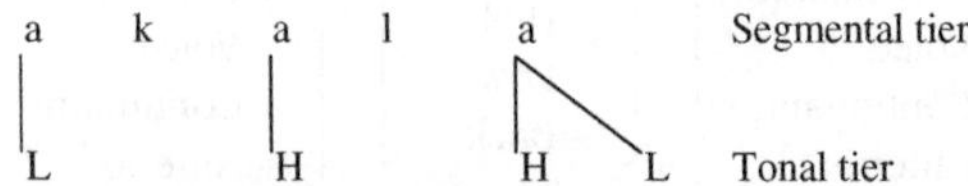

It is impossible to ascribe the feature [+high pitch –low pitch] and [–low pitch +high pitch] to the final vowel but the contour tone on the final vowel is easily explainable if tone is represented on an autonomous tier. A similar argument would be made by intonation scholars whose work is grounded in autosegmental phonology, for instance B's utterance with a rising tone in the following example:

A: Who wants this?
B: ↗ ME

In autosegmental notation *me* would be represented as:

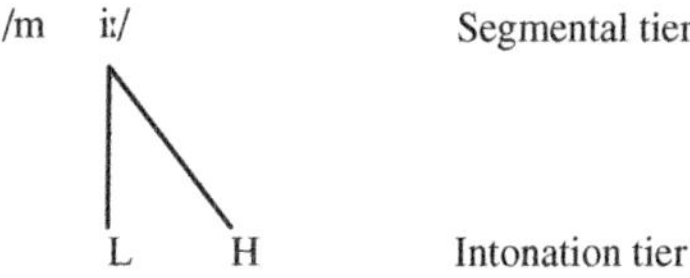

Goldsmith labelled his second reason *stability*. This refers to the situation where a vowel is elided but the accompanying tone is not deleted. If the tone were a feature of the vowel there would be no reason why it and not some other feature of the vowel segment should be preserved. His third argument, *melody levels*, is similar to Firth's notion of prosodies. Goldsmith notes that different types of features attach to different segments in different lexical contexts. For instance, English voiceless stops in stressed syllable onset initial position are aspirated while voiceless stops in coda position are normally not aspirated. If the feature [+Delayed Release] is part of the phonological matrix which forms [p] it would be equally likely to occur in final or middle position as in initial position. Yet, this is demonstrably not the case. A description that places aspiration on an autonomous tier, where it is free to associate with the relevant feature, is more theoretically accurate.

The fourth justification for the model refers to *floating tones*. These are tones that are not known to be attached to any underlying vowel. While easy to explain in an autosegmental model, these are theoretically suspect in segmental models. According to segmental models the underlying vowel that the floating tone is posited to be attached to must surface in the pronunciation. As the vowel fails to surface, floating tones are an awkward anomaly for generative segmental descriptions. The final reason is **harmony**. Segmental models can notate phonological features such as vowel harmony. However, unlike autosegmental models they are unable to offer descriptions, which can generalize all instances of harmony in an economical manner.

Bilabial

The term bilabial refers to the classification of a **consonant** sound on the basis of the place of **articulation** of the sound. Bilabial consonants are produced (or in the case of the approximant partly produced) by contact or close proximity between the upper and the lower lips. Assuming a normal **pulmonic egressive airstream mechanism**, the following classes of consonants are classified by the IPA as bilabial: **plosives** [p, b], **nasals** [m], **fricatives** [ɸ, β] and **approximants** [w]. Bilabial plosives are extremely common across languages. Maddieson (2008a) in a survey of 567 languages reports that only 5 marginal Amerindian languages lack bilabial phonemes.[1] The voiceless bilabial plosive /p/ is perhaps the most common sound found across languages although, as Table 4 indicates, it is possible to find languages such as Arabic that only contain the voiced variant. French is unusual in that it contains two labial approximants, one **palatal** and the other **velar**. As can be seen from Table 4, bilabial fricatives are quite rare across languages.

In English, fricatives may be heard as **allophones** of plosives in syllable final position, for example, a Liverpool pronunciation of *stop* might be [stɒɸ], *sit* might be [sɪs] and *cake* might be [keɪx].

The phonemic system of English, unlike languages such as Hindi and Mandarin, contrasts bilabial stops only in terms of **voicing**. However, the phonetic picture is more complicated. In most accents of English a word initial stop is aspirated while a word final stop is unaspirated. For instance, in the word *pop* [p^{h}ɒp] the two <p>s realize different **allophones** of the same **phoneme** with the initial <p> aspirated. A noticeable feature of some Lancashire dialects is that voiceless bilabial stops are unaspirated or weakly aspirated. Conversely, some Celtic influenced accents are more aspirated. Gimson (2008: 168) notes that in fast casual speech between vowels speakers may not fully close their stops. The bilabial plosives /p/ and /b/ are in effect replaced by their fricative counterparts /ɸ/ and /β/. This results in the following pronunciations: *pepper* ['pɛɸə] *rubber* ['ɹʌβə].

Table 4 List of bilabial phonemes found in 25 languages

Language	Plosive	Nasal	Fricatives	Approximants[1]
Amharic	(p)[2] b	m		w
Arabic	b	m		w
Bulgarian	p b	m		
Cantonese	p p^h	m		
Czech	p b	m		
Dutch	p b	m		
English	p b	m		w
French	p b	m		w ɥ
German	p b	m		
Greek	p b	m		
Hausa	b	m	ɸ	w
Hebrew	p b	m		
Hindi	p b p^h $b^{ɦ}$[3]	m		
Hungarian	p b	m		
Igbo	p b	m		w
Italian	p b	m		w
Japanese	p b	m		
Korean	p p^h b	m		
Mandarin	p p^h	m		
Persian	p b	m		
Portuguese	p b	m		
Russian	p b	m		
Spanish	p b	m		
Swedish	p b	m		
Thai	p b	m		w
Welsh	p b	m		w

[1] /w/ is a labial-velar approximant and as such has been included in this table as a bilabial consonant and simultaneously in Table 39 as a velar consonant.

[2] /p/ is extremely rare and confined to words of foreign origin (Hayward and Hayward 1999: 45).

[3] /$b^{ɦ}$/ is a voiced bilabial stop that is accompanied by a voiced glottal fricative, but see **aspiration**.

Breathy voice

Breathy voice, also known as murmur, is a term used in the **phonetic** classification of **voice quality**. It refers to a vocal effect produced by allowing a great deal of air to pass through a partially open **glottis**. Breathy voiced sounds are produced when the **vocal folds** are kept apart, though not as far apart as for **voiceless** sounds. The rate of airflow coming from the lungs is significantly higher than the airflow required to produce either a voiced or voiceless sound. Catford (1977: 99) reports that an airflow in the range of 900 to 1,000 cc per second is sufficient to set the vocal folds 'flapping in the breeze'. Laver (1994: 418) labels breathy voice 'a very inefficient use of air'. It is therefore not surprising that breathy voice does not have **phonemic** status in many languages. Instead it is used by individual speakers as a paralinguistic device to signal intimacy. In English, some speakers produce breathy voice on an intervocalic /h/ in words such as *ahead* and *aha.*

There are a number of Indian languages that assign phonemic status to breathy voiced phonemes, for example Hindi, which has breathy voiced **stops** that contrast with voiceless and voiced stops, and Gujarati, which contrasts breathy voiced and normal vowels. Breathy voiced phonemes are notated by [..] beneath the symbol for the voiced consonant or vowel.

Cardinal vowels

The system of cardinal vowels was devised by the illustrious twentieth-century phonetician Daniel Jones (see Jones 1956). They are reference points aimed at establishing grid references by which we can map all the vowel sounds of all the languages in the world. The cardinal vowel chart, also known as the cardinal vowel quadrilateral, is a set of standard reference points based on a combination of articulatory and auditory judgements. The front centre and the back of the tongue are distinguished, as are four levels of tongue height: close, close-mid, open-mid and open (Figure 1).

The corners of the vowel quadrilateral represent the highest and lowest positions that the tongue can achieve without producing audible friction. Thus, cardinal vowel (CV)1 [i] is pronounced with the tongue raised as close to the palate as possible without producing audible friction. If a speaker moved their tongue any closer to the palate they would produce a [ʝ] instead of a vowel. When producing CV5 a speaker opens their mouth as wide as possible and lowers their tongue as much as possible, as if a doctor wished to inspect their tonsils. The two intermediate areas are supposed to divide the intervening space into auditorily equidistant areas. In other words, when producing the cardinal vowels speakers should have the sensation that their tongue is stepping up or down an equal distance between them. I certainly do when producing CVs 1 to 4. Gimson (2008: 34) notes that X-ray positions of tongue height show that the steps down from CV1 to CV2, from CV2 to CV3 and from CV3 to CV4 are 'fairly equidistant'. Jones labelled the vowels with numbers from 1 to 8 the primary cardinals, with the secondary cardinal vowels numbered 9 to 16. The distinction between the primary and secondary vowels is based solely on lip position. Primary CVs 1 to 5 are unrounded, with 6 to 8 rounded. The reverse is true for the secondary cardinal vowels, where 9 to 13 are rounded and 14 to 16 are unrounded.

The cardinal vowels provide an easy reference point for plotting vowels from different languages. For instance, the English FLEECE vowel and the initial French vowel in *livre* /ˈliːvʁ/ are both notated by [iː] though they are not phonetically identical. The French vowel is closer and more fronted than the English vowel. It approaches CV1 position, while the English vowel is noticeably backed and realized in a position which, when mapped on a vowel chart, is about one-third of a way towards CV2. Despite the clarity that the cardinal vowel system brings to cross-linguistic and cross-dialectal comparison of vowel qualities there are a number of problems with the system, both practical and theoretical. Learning the cardinal vowel system, as Jones himself noted, requires intense practise and oral instruction from a trained teacher. However, a self-critical learner with access to

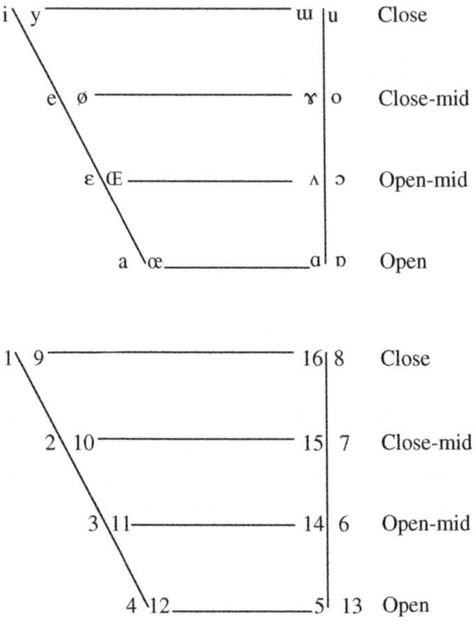

Figure 1 The cardinal vowel chart: primary and secondary cardinal vowels

the recordings should be able, with practise, to produce close approximations of the cardinal vowels. A copy of Jones's original recordings is on an internet tutorial available at http://www.youtube.com/watch?v=6UIAe4p2I74.

A more serious problem with the system of cardinal vowels is that it is not clear how acoustic analysis of Jones's own renditions of the cardinal vowels can be reconciled with his notion of equidistance between the vowels. His back vowels are closer together than his front vowels. X-rays of trained speakers producing cardinal vowels, which have been validated as accurate renderings of the cardinal vowels, illustrate that the position of the highest points of the tongue for the back vowels are not reliable indicators of vowel quality (Ladefoged 2001: 203). CVs 6 and 7 appear to be produced with similar degrees of tongue height. Yet despite these problems, cardinal vowels have enabled phoneticians to plot vowels with far greater accuracy than earlier impressionistic accounts. Acoustic plots of the first two **formants** of the primary cardinal vowels result in charts similar to the original cardinal vowel charts.[1] If cardinal vowels are reinterpreted in terms of their formants, and not as articulations, Jones's system proves to be an accurate map of the edges of the vowel space.

The cardinal vowels as originally set out are not particularly helpful for describing central vowels. So the IPA introduced the following symbols [ɨ] and [ʉ], which are known as CVs 17 and 18 in close central position. There is also a pair of close-mid central vowels [ɘ] and [ɵ] and a corresponding pair of open-mid CVs [ɜ] and [ɞ]. Two other central vowels have been introduced schwa [ə] between close-mid and open-mid and [ɐ] between open-mid and open. Finally, the IPA note three other vowels [ɪ ʏ ʊ] that are centralized versions of [i y ʊ], respectively. Figure 2 shows the full set of vowel symbols recognized by the IPA plotted on a vowel quadrilateral.

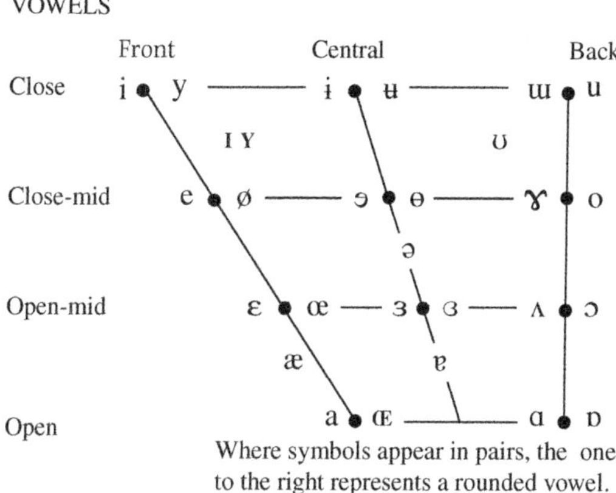

Figure 2 Vowels according to the IPA. Reprinted with permission from the International Phonetic Association. Copyright 2005 by International Phonetic Association

Click

A click is a term used to classify **consonants** on the basis of their manner of **articulation**. Clicks are the only speech sounds that are produced on a **velaric ingressive airstream mechanism**. They are an important part of the consonant systems of some languages, especially those found in Southern Africa. Clicks result from the combination of two closures in the mouth; the back one made by the back of the tongue against the **velum**. The front closure can be made at any location forward of the velum.

While clicks are not part of the consonant systems of any European languages, English speakers are very familiar with the paralinguistic use of three types of clicks. The first is made with a closure formed by the **tip** or **blade** of the tongue being held in contact with the upper teeth. It is often written as *tut-tut* or *tsk-tsk* and is used to signal displeasure. The second is made with a closure of the lips and is used to simulate kissing. The third is made with a closure formed by the tip or blade of the tongue being held in contact with the **alveolar ridge**. It is used to gee-up horses.

Ladefoged and Maddieson (1996: ch. 8) report that clicks play a very important part in the sound system of Khoisan languages, for example, !Xóõ, !Xû and Nama, spoken in the Western parts of Southern Africa. They cite data showing that 70 per cent of all lexical entries found in a !Xóõ dictionary begin with a click. Khoisan languages are presently spoken by an estimated 330,000 speakers. Clicks are also relatively common in some languages, such as Zulu and Xhosa, which are spoken in regions historically contiguous to lands occupied by Khoisan speakers.

There is some controversy in the literature as to how to classify **clicks** (for further details, see Ladefoged and Maddieson 1996) in terms of their place of **articulation**. But the International Phonetic Association currently recognizes five clicks that differ in their manner of **articulation**. Table 5 taken from the IPA

Table 5 Click phonemes in IPA

Symbol	Place of articulation
ʘ	bilabial
|	dental
!	(post) alveolar
ǂ	palatoalveolar
||	alveolar lateral

Table 6 Click phonemes in Xhosa

Dental	Alveolar	Lateral	
Voiceless	|	!	||
Aspirated	|ʰ	!ʰ	||ʰ
Breathy voiced	..|	..!	..||
Voiced nasal	n|	n!	n||
Breathy voiced nasal	n̤|	n̤!	n̤||

handbook (1999) sets out the current symbols that were adopted by the Kiel Convention of the IPA in 1989.

The only language known to exploit contrasts between all five possible places of articulation is !Xóõ. All click languages exploit **phonation**, **voicing** and manner articulation contrasts in order to substantially increase the number of language-specific click phonemes. For instance, Xhosa, which contrasts Dental, Alveolar and Alveolar Lateral places of articulation, has 15 click phonemes. Table 6, adapted from Ladefoged and Maddieson (ibid.: 260), illustrates contrasting click phonemes in Xhosa.

A recent study, Wright (2011), argues that clicks function in English not only to signal paralinguistic meaning by conveying the emotional state or attitudinal stance of the speaker but also may demarcate sequence boundaries. Clicks are, it is claimed, a resource that speakers may employ in managing their contributions to interactive discourse.

Coalescence

Coalescence, also known as fusion, is a phonetic term that is used in historical linguistics to refer to the fusion of linguistic units that were originally distinguishable. For instance, many cases of modern English /ʒ/ were originally pronounced as a series of /z/ + /j/, which in time coalesced into /ʒ/. The word *treasure*, which was formerly pronounced as /ˈtɹɛzjə/, is now pronounced as /ˈtɹɛʒə/. Coalescence occurs in everyday speech when words that phonemically contain two syllables are articulated as monosyllables with a fused long vowel, such as *drier* /ˈdɹaɪə/ → [dɹɑː], *tower* /ˈtaʊə/ → [tɑː], *mower* /ˈməʊə/ → [mɜː] and *slower* /ˈsləʊə/→ [ʃlɜː]. There is a view that coalescence is more likely to happen inside morpheme boundaries, as in for some speakers *hire and higher* are not homophonous. But as the above examples indicate, fusion may take place across morpheme boundaries.

Coarticulation

Coarticulation is a phonetic term that refers to the successive or overlapping articulation of two successive phones at more than one point in the vocal tract. In the usual articulation of *swim* the lip-rounding of /w/ usually overlaps with the articulation of the /s/ and the word is pronounced as [sʷwɪm]. Coarticulation differs from **double articulation** in that it involves the pronunciation of two successive phonological units and not the pronunciation of a single phonological unit. See **assimilation**.

Compensatory lengthening

Compensatory lengthening is a phonological term used in historical linguistics to describe an effect in which the deletion of one segment, usually a consonant, is accompanied by an increase in the length of a vowel. In English, the effect can be seen in the lengthening of vowels in non-rhotic varieties after the deletion of /ɹ/ in words such as *bird* /bɪɹd/ → /bɜːd/, *bard* /bɑɹd/ → /bɑːd/ and *horse* /hɔrs/ → /hɔːs/ (for further details see McMahon 2000a: 174). The effect of compensatory lengthening can be seen in fused pronunciations – see **coalescence** – of words such as *tower*.

Consonant

In phonetic terms, a consonant is a sound that is made either by a closure of the **vocal tract** or by a narrowing of the vocal tract sufficient to generate a turbulent **airstream** resulting in audible friction. This, however, is not an entirely satisfactory means of identifying consonants. Some consonants, notably the **semi vowels**, are made without a narrowing of the vocal tract sufficient to generate audible friction. Yet consonants alone are found outside the nucleus of the **syllable**. Thus /j/ and /w/ are clearly consonants as they are found only outside the syllable nucleus, for example, *yet* /jɛt/ and *wet* /wɛt/. Some sounds that are made either by a complete closure of the vocal tract, /n/ and /m/, or by a narrowing of the vocal tract /l/, may occur in the syllable nucleus, for example, *little* [lɪtl̩], *button* [bʌtn̩] and *bottom* [bɒtm̩]. In these examples, the final syllable consists solely of a syllabic consonant in the nucleus. Syllabic consonants are notated by the IPA diacritic ̩ placed under the consonant symbol. The American linguist Kenneth Pike coined the terms contoid and vocoid (Pike 1943) and proposed that they should be used for the phonetic description of speech. This reserved the terms vowel and consonant for phonological descriptions: the semi vowels would be classified as vocoids and consonants, while syllabic consonants would be classified as contoids and vowels. Table 7 illustrates the set of **pulmonic** consonants recognized by the IPA.

Constraint

A constraint is a phonological term that in **generative phonology** restricts the application of a rule and, by so doing, ensures that the phonetic output is well formed. In phonology there are two types of constraints: simultaneous ones that

Table 7 The pulmonic consonant system. Reprinted with permission from the International Phonetic Association. Copyright 2005 by International Phonetic Association

CONSONANTS (PULMONIC)											
	Bilabial	**Labiodental**	**Dental**	**Alveolar**	**Postalveolar**	**Retroflex**	**Palatal**	**Velar**	**Uvular**	**Pharyngeal**	**Glottal**
Plosive	p b			t d		ʈ ɖ	c ɟ	k g	q ɢ		ʔ
Nasal	m	ɱ		n		ɳ	ɲ	ŋ	ɴ		
Trill	ʙ			r					ʀ		
Tap or Flap				ɾ		ɽ					
Fricative	ɸ β	f v	θ ð	s z	ʃ ʒ	ʂ ʐ	ç ʝ	x ɣ	χ ʁ	ħ ʕ	h ɦ
Lateral fricative				ɬ ɮ							
Approximant		ʋ		ɹ		ɻ	j	ɰ			
Lateral approximant				l		ɭ	ʎ	ʟ			

Where symbols appear in pairs, the one to the right represents a voiced consonant. Shaded areas denote articulations judged impossible.

apply to individual segments, and sequential ones that apply to sequences of segments. An example of a simultaneous constraint is that a vowel cannot be [+Front, +Back]. An example of a sequential constraint is the **obligatory contour principle** which, however, is not an absolute constraint but rather more of a tendency. In recent years, because of the recognition that not all constraints are inviolable in all contexts, the concept of constraint has been recast as an explanatory method of explaining language universals – see **optimality theory**.

A short-lived school of research, but one that shares much in common with optimality theory, was *natural phonology*. Natural phonology was grounded in Stampe (1979), whose work primarily focused on how children developed their native phonology. Stampe argued that, rather than acquiring a series of rules, learners learnt not to produce sounds based on the innate constraints of their articulatory mechanisms. In learning their native phonology, children suppress their innate physiological constraints, and this enables them to produce utterances that match the phonological system of their native language.

Constriction

Constriction is a term in **articulatory** phonetics that refers to the narrowing of the **vocal tract**. **vowels** are articulated with a more open constriction than are **consonants**.

Creaky voice

Creaky voice, also known as glottal or vocal fry, is a term used in the **phonetic** classification of **voice quality**. It refers to a vocal effect produced when the arytenoid cartilages are held tightly together so that the **vocal folds** can only vibrate at the anterior end (Catford 1977). The vibration of the vocal folds is at a very low rate, thus ensuring that creaky voiced sounds are produced on a low **pitch**. Creaky voiced sounds are notated by [̰] under the respective voiced sound, as in [b̰] or [ḛ].

Some individual speakers may, because of their individual voice quality, speak with a creaky voice. Creaky voice can be widely heard across languages in the speech of people suffering from a cold. A creaky voice may also be heard in the low-pitched **intonation** of speakers immediately prior to the finishing of their speaking turn (Crystal 1969). Wells and Peppé (1996: 122), however, report that while creaky voice is a phonetic cue for turn delimitation in the speech of London Jamaicans, it does not correlate with turn-taking in Ulster or Tyneside speech. Local (1996) reports that what he labels 'free-standing oh tokens' – which may be produced as acknowledgement by a speaker that their interlocutor has informed them of something newsworthy – are often articulated with creaky voice.

Creaky voice is not phonemically contrastive in European languages. But Ladefoged and Maddieson (1996: 53–5) report that languages which exploit creaky voice in the production of **stops** are 'areally diverse'. They are found in Africa, the Americas and Asia. Hausa, a language spoken by around 39 million people in West Africa, distinguishes between voiced stops with regular voicing [b, d] and ones with a creaky voice [b̰, d̰] (Ladefoged 2001: 125).

Dark <L>

Dark <L> is a phonetic term used to describe a **lateral** sound that is pronounced with a **secondary articulation**. The speaker simultaneously raises the back of the tongue towards the **soft palate** while producing the lateral consonant. A dark <L> is transcribed as [ɫ]. It is the usual pronunciation for [l] in RP, except where the [l] is immediately followed by either a vowel or /j/. An [l] that is followed by a vowel or [j] is not pronounced with any secondary articulation and is known as a clear <L>. The difference between a clear and dark <L> can be heard in the word *little* [lɪtəɫ]. Some predictable examples of dark and clear Ls are:

bottle	*Loot*	*Liverpool*	*kiln*	*please*
['bɒtɫ̩]	[luːt]	['lɪvəpuːɫ]	[kɪɫn]	[pliːz]

There are, however, a number of differences in the realization of /l/ across English accents. In basilectal London speech the tongue tip contact required to produce [ɫ] is omitted and some speakers may produce a short vowel, most likely either a short [o] or [ʊ]. Thus, Wells (1982b: 313) reports *fill* and *people* being pronounced as [fɪo] and ['piːpo]. There are other accents of English where the RP distribution of clear and dark <L> does not occur. For instance, Penhallurick (2008: 118) reports that in North Wales (and particularly in Gwynedd) dark <L> dominates in all positions, while in South Wales, possibly because of contact from Welsh, clear <L> dominates in all positions. In Southern Irish varieties, Hickey (2008: 97) reports that the <L> in words such as *feel* may be clear for some speakers but dark for others. In Northern Irish varieties it is either dark or pronounced as a vocoid. In Scotland, with the sole exception of Highland speakers, dark <L> is realized in all positions within the word (Stuart-Smith 2008: 65). Wells (1982b: 411) notes that in Glasgow dark Ls may be realized as [ɒ] type vocoids.

In Lancashire accents, dark <L> is used in all contexts whereas in other Northern forms, such as Tyneside and Northumbria, clear <L> is used in all word positions. Mathisen (1999: 173) illustrates the complexity of the issue by noting that in the West Midlands male speakers typically produce dark <L> in all contexts, whereas female speakers typically produce clear <L> in all contexts. Among younger speakers, there appears to be an increased tendency to vocalize Ls found after vowels or /j/.

Wells (1982c: 490) reports that speakers of General American tend to favour dark <L>; though preconsonantally it appears to be far less velarized than it is after vowels. Kretzschmar (2008: 48) reports a sociolinguistic variation in the production of post-vocalic /l/ by speakers of General American. The more educated the speaker, the more likely it is that post-vocalic /l/ will be vocalized, unless the /l/ is in word final position. Kretzschmar reports *milk* as being pronounced [mɪʊk], a pronunciation identical to basilectal London speech. Thomas (2008: 107) reports that speakers of Southern (American) English produce dark <L>s before vowels and tend to vocalize their <L>s after vowels. Speakers of Australian and New Zealand English produce dark <Ls> in all contexts and may vocalize <L> after vowels (Wells 1982c).

Dental

The term dental refers to the classification of a **consonant** sound on the basis of the place of **articulation** of the sound. Dental consonants are produced by contact or close proximity between the teeth and the tip or blade of the tongue – see also **labiodental**. Assuming a normal **pulmonic egressive airstream mechanism**, the following classes of consonants are classified by the IPA as dental: **fricatives** [θ, ð]. Table 8 illustrates that for many languages consonants such as [t] are produced not by contact or close proximity between the tongue tip or blade and the **alveolar ridge** but rather by contact or close proximity between the tongue tip or blade and the upper teeth. In Southern Irish English, /θ/ and /ð/ are often produced as **allophonic** dental stops. *Three* and *they* are pronounced as [t̪ʰɹɪː] and [d̪eɪ], respectively. For an Irish speaker, though not for a speaker of another variety of English, the **phonemic** contrast between the following pairs of words will be maintained: *tree/three* [tʰɹiː]/[t̪ʰɹiː] and *day/they* [deɪ]/[d̪eɪ]. Other speakers are likely to hear the Irish pronunciations of the words as homophonous.

There appears to be an **articulatory** though not **acoustic** difference in the realization of /θ/ and /ð/ between the standard British and American accents. Gimson, a British author (2008: 195), states that in order to articulate /θ/ or /ð/ speakers make a light contact with the tip or rims of the tongue and the edge or inner surface of the upper incisors, and a firmer contact with the upper teeth. Ladefoged and Maddieson (2006: 143) report the findings of a small experiment which found that 90 per cent of American speakers pronounce /θ/ or /ð/ with the tip of the tongue protruding between the teeth, but only 10 per cent of British speakers produced /θ/ or /ð/ with a protruding tongue – see **interdental**.

In basilectal London speech, and in some popular Southern American accents, dental fricatives are replaced by labiodental articulations. Thus words such as *throw* and *brother* are pronounced as [fɹəʊ] and [ˈbɹʌvə] – see Kerswill (2003: 229–36) for a historical account of dental fricatives being replaced by their labiodental counterparts in England.

Table 8 List of dental phonemes found in 25 languages

Language	Plosive	Nasal	Trill	Fricatives	Approximants
Amharic					
Arabic	t d	n		θ ð	
Bulgarian					
Cantonese					l
Czech					
Dutch					

Table 8 (Continued)

Language	Plosive	Nasal	Trill	Fricatives	Approximants
English				θ ð	
French	t d	n		s z	l
German					
Greek	t d			θ ð	
Hausa					
Hebrew					
Hindi	t̪ d̪ t̪ʰ d̪ʱ				
Hungarian	t d	n	r	s ʒ	l
Igbo	t d				
Italian	t d	n			
Japanese	t d	n			
Korean					
Mandarin					
Persian	t d	n	r	s z	l
Portuguese	t d	n			l
Russian	t d	n	r	s z	l
Spanish	t d				
Swedish	t d	n		s	l
Thai					
Welsh				θ ð	

The use of the symbols /t/, /d/, /n/, /s/ and /z/ in the languages Arabic, French, Hungarian, Igbo, Italian, Japanese, Persian, Portuguese and Swedish indicates that the phonemes in these languages are to some extent intermediate between dental and alveolar sounds.

Diphthong

Diphthongs are vowels whose quality changes perceptively in one direction within a syllable. To put it another way, they are vowels that have two targets. Phonologically, diphthongs represent one vowel in **syllable** nucleus position. They are relatively frequent and occur in around one-third of the languages surveyed by Maddieson (1984). Of the languages in which diphthongs are present, diphthongs of the [aɪ] type were present in 75 per cent of languages, while diphthongs of the [au] type were found in 65 per cent of the surveyed languages. Major languages such as English, Chinese, Arabic and Hausa contained both types of diphthongs (see Lindau, Norlin and Svantesson 1985: 40). Non-rhotic varieties of English contain a third type of diphthongs that end in /ə/. In rhotic forms of English, these diphthongs are replaced by a sequence of vowels followed by an <r> consonant.

As Figure 3 indicates, there are two types of closing diphthongs, those that end in the front of the mouth and those that end at the back of the mouth. The FACE /eɪ/ vowel in RP begins slightly below **cardinal vowel** (CV)2 position and moves

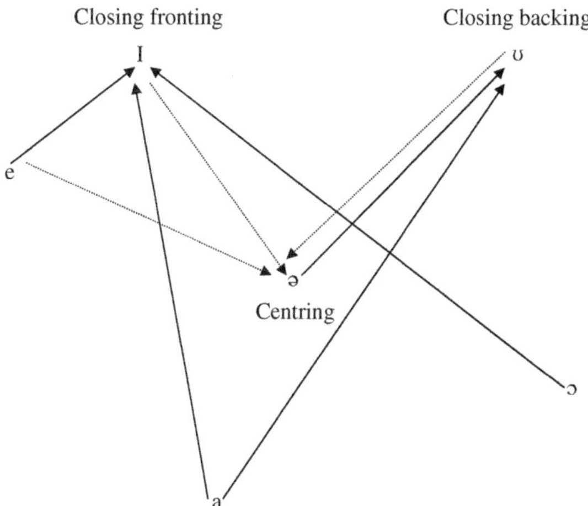

Figure 3 The diphthongs of English

in the direction of the RP KIT vowel. There is considerable variation in the actual articulation of this vowel, with speakers of more traditional or upper RP having a starting point of CV2. Australian English, New Zealand English and Cockney have much more open starting points, with the glide commencing from the position of the TRAP vowel. Many English accents realize the face vowel as a monophthong: see Vowel.

The PRICE vowel is realized as a diphthong in most varieties of English but again its actual realization is quite different in different accents. In RP, the glide begins at a point slightly behind and a little raised from CV4. The glide moves in the direction of the position associated with the KIT vowel, although the tongue is not usually raised to a level closer than CV2. One notable feature of this vowel is that for many people the closing movement of the lower jaw is obvious. During the course of the glide, the lips change from a neutral to a loosely spread position. On Tyneside the starting and the end point of the glide are fronted. The glide is roughly from CV3 to a position slightly closer than CV2. In the broad West Midlands accent, the starting point of the glide is slightly more open than that of CV6. The glide reaches a mid-central position. In Australian English, New Zealand English and Cockney, the glide commences from a back open position and never reaches a position above CV3. Gimson (2008: 134–5) notes that such a change in the articulation of the FACE and PART vowels is part of a more general sound change known as the *Southern Diphthong Shift* found south of Birmingham in England. This has resulted in the FLEECE vowel being realized as [əɪ], the FACE vowel being realized as [aɪ], the PRICE vowel being realized as [ɑɪ] and the CHOICE vowel being realized as [oɪ].

The CHOICE vowel is typically realized as a diphthong. In RP the glide begins slightly above CV6 and moves in the direction of the KIT vowel. There is less regional variation in the realization of this vowel, though in Southern Ireland the starting point of the glide is in a centralized open position and the glide doesn't reach higher than a point midway between close-mid and open-mid. In Cockney the position of the starting and end points of the glide are slightly closer than in RP.

On Tyneside there is a more extended glide, which starts from a backed position below open-mid, and which approaches to CV1 position.

The two closing backing diphthongs are the MOUTH and GOAT vowels. In RP the glide in the MOUTH vowel begins at an open central position that is slightly further back than the beginning point of the PRICE vowel. The diphthong glides in the direction of the tongue position of the FOOT vowel but does not reach a position closer than close-mid. All the main regional variants of the MOUTH vowel are realized as diphthongs. There is, however, considerable variation in how the vowel is actually pronounced. Cockney has the broadest glide with the starting position being between CV3 and CV4, and the end position aiming at the tongue position of the FOOT vowel but falling short and reaching a point midway between open-mid and close-mid. In South Welsh accents, the starting point of the diphthong is a central vowel and the end point of the glide approaches to CV8. In Northern Ireland the starting point of the glide is close to CV5 and the glide reaches a position approaching CV11. In the West of England the glide has a starting point backed slightly from CV3 and an end point approaching CV9. In other words, phonetically, in Northern Ireland and the West of England the vowel is realized as a fronting diphthong, though one that ends with a rounded lip position.

The GOAT vowel is realized as a diphthong in most accents, though in GA, Scottish English and on Tyneside it is realized as a long monophthong similar to CV7. In RP the glide starts at the position of the RP NURSE vowel and moves towards the position of the FOOT vowel. During the glide there is, for many speakers, a slight closing movement of the jaw. While the lips are neutral at the start of the glide they may become rounded on the second element of the glide. Both O'Connor (1973: 167) and Gimson (2008: 140) suggest that the goat vowel has undergone a slight sound change in recent years, with younger speakers producing a shorter glide owing to a closer beginning point and the fronting of the end point. Gimson proposes that in general RP the GOAT vowel be notated as [əʉ], a transcription identical to that used to in recent transcriptions of Australian English (Cox and Palethorpe 2007).

There is some dispute as to how many centring diphthongs are found in non-rhotic English accents. Figure 3 listed three /ɪə/, /ʊə/ and /eə/. Collins and Mees (2008: 100) do not list /eə/ in their description of the English vowel system. They argue that modern day Southern English speakers produce the SQUARE vowel as a long monophthong /ɛː/. The diphthong /eə/ represents, for them, an earlier pronunciation that may still be heard as a variant.[1] However, Gimson (2008: 151) and Wells (2000) still transcribe the SQUARE vowel with the diphthong. O'Connor (1973: 171) alone argues that in RP a fourth centring diphthong /ɔə/ is used to distinguish *pour* from *paw* but acknowledges that this diphthong is quite rare. More recent authorities (such as Wells 2000: 597) consider *pour* and *paw* to be homophonous. This book considers /ɔə/ to represent an outdated historical pronunciation and only describes three centring diphthongs.

The first centring diphthong to be discussed is the NEAR vowel. In RP the glide begins with a tongue position approximately equal to that used for the KIT vowel and moves in the direction of the commA vowel. If the NEAR vowel is lexically non-final, the glide is not so extensive and the ending point is closer. The only major variant among non-rhotic accents is Tyneside English, where the glide starts from a position near CV1 and reaches an open position approaching but backed from CV4. In recent years, however, this vowel is increasingly being realized as a monophthong for Southern English speakers.

The SQUARE vowel starts slightly below CV3 and glides into a more central and more open position. Traditionally, in both Tyneside and Liverpool English, the square vowel has been realized as a long monophthong between CV2 and CV3, with the Tyneside variant being considerably more fronted than the Liverpool one, which is produced in the centre of the mouth. The final diphthong is the CURE vowel, which is articulated starting with a tongue position similar to that used for the FOOT vowel and moves in the direction of the COMMA vowel. There are a couple of significant regional variants, with the CURE vowel in Tyneside English starting from a position very near CV8 and finishing in a central position between open-mid and open. Among younger speakers, there is a tendency to pronounce words such as *poor* with the THOUGHT vowel. Wells (2000: 592) in a poll panel of 275 adults found that 57 per cent of British speakers considered *poor* and *paw* to be homophonous. But if only speakers born since 1973 were considered, then 82 per cent considered the words to be homophonous and pronounced as /pɔː/. However, the diphthong is still retained in the pronunciation of *cure*.[2]

Distinctive feature

A distinctive feature is a phonological term referring to the minimal contrastive unit of sound. For some scholars (e.g. Jakobson and Waugh 1987), the **phoneme** is made up of bundles of distinctive features, but other scholars such as Chomsky and Halle (1968) argue that the phonemic level is redundant. They employ distinctive features alone to describe a language's sound system.

In the original work on distinctive features, Jakobson (1952) reprinted in Jakobson (1990: chs 15 and 16), all meaningful oppositions or contrasts between sounds were binary. Thus, individual sounds differ in what value of the feature they possess, for instance /p/ is [+voice] while /b/ is [–voice]. More recently, linguists have begun to pursue unary analyses, for instance Hayes (2009: 95ff.). This brief sketch of distinctive features starts with a historical discussion of binary analyses in order to underpin the rationale behind the approach, then discusses unary feature approaches before describing some criticisms of distinctive feature theory. The entry concludes by illustrating the power and economy of a phonological description couched in features.

Distinctive feature theory, in its original binary form at least, attempted to produce an inventory of all the phonemes within an individual language. The inventory was not based on how the phonemes functioned in the sound system of the language but rather it took account of the articulatory and acoustic differences between the phonemes in a language. It was hoped that by focusing on the phonetic reality of the phonemes that distinctive feature analysis would succeed in sorting the sounds into natural classes.

Jakobson proposed ten binary features that allowed him to distinguish the English phonemic inventory[3] (see Jakobson and Waugh 1987, ch. 2; Waugh and Monville-Burston 1990: 259–60) for further details. Jakobson's distinctive features are summarized in Table 9.

Table 9 Feature description of English Phonemes based on Jakobson

Feature	**Acoustic description**	**Articulatory description**
[±Consonantal]	Low total energy	Obstruction in vocal tract
Example: all English consonants are [+Consonantal]		
[±Vocalic]	Clearly defined formant structure[1]	No obstruction in vocal tract
Example all English consonants are [−Vocalic] except /l/ /ɹ/ /w/ and /j/		
[±Compact]	Strong concentration of energy in central area of the spectrum	Stricture in front of mouth is relatively larger
Example: /ʃ/ /ʒ/ /tʃ/ /dʒ/ /k/ /g/ /ŋ/ and /ɑ/ are [+Compact]		
[±Nasal]	Additional anti-formants which reduce formant intensity	Soft palate raised
Example: /m/ /n/ and /ŋ/ are [+Nasal]		
[±Tense]	Higher energy with greater spread across the spectrum	More strain and duration or a stronger airflow
Example: /p/ /t/ /k/ /f/ /θ/ /s/ /ʃ/ /tʃ/ /iː/ /uː/ /ɑː/ /ɔː/ and /ɜː/ are [+Tense]		
[±Voice]	Periodic low frequency excitation	Vocal fold vibration
Example: all vowels plus /b/ /d/ g/ v/ /ð/ /z/ /ʒ/ /dʒ/ /m/ /n/ and /ŋ/ are [+Voice]		
[±Continuant]	Interrupted sound	Rapid opening and closing of Oral tract
Example: all vowels plus /f/ /v/ /θ/ /ð/ /s/ /z/ /ʃ/ /ʒ/ /l/ /ɹ/ /j/ and /w/ are [+Continuant]		
[±Strident]	High intensity noise	Relatively complex stricture
Example: /s/ /z/ /ʃ/ /ʒ/ /tʃ/ dʒ/ are [+Strident]		
[±Grave]	Energy concentrated in lower frequencies	Articulated at peripheries of mouth

D

Example: /uː/ /ʊ/ /ɔː/ /p/ /b/ /m/ /f/ /v/ /k/ and /g/ are [+Grave]		
[±**Flat**}	Weakening of upper frequencies	Lip-rounding or other forms of narrowed aperture
Example: /uː/ /ʊ/ / /p/ /b/ and /w/ are [+Flat]		

[1]This does not seem to be a totally reliable acoustic description as nasal sounds have clear formant structures.

Table 10 employs Jakobson's distinctive feature classification to contrast the nine English plosive consonants. Features that are not applicable have been indicated with the symbol 0. Redundant features have not been included in the Table.

Table 10 Distinctive features of the nine English plosives according to Jakobson

Distinctive Feature	**/p/**	**/b/**	**/t/**	**/d/**	**/k/**	/g/	**/m/**	**/n/**	/ŋ/
Compact	–	–	–	–	+	+	–	–	+
Nasal	–	–	–	–	–	–	+	+	+
Tense	+	–	+	–	+	–	0	0	0
Voice	–	+	–	+	–	+	+	+	+
Grave	+	+	–	–	+	+	+	–	+

Chomsky and Halle (1968) noted that while Jakobson's system of distinctive features was a contribution that went beyond the IPA description of sounds, it was itself in need of some revision. The features [compact ~ diffuse] they noted were used to characterize the distinction not only between high and non-high vowels but also between consonants produced with an obstruction before the **palato-alveolar** region of the mouth with consonants produced behind the palato-alveolar region. This resulted in high vowels such as /iː/ and consonants such as /t/ being classified together as [–Compact] or [+diffuse]. This they noted was both 'complex and rather implausible' (ibid.: 307).

In Chomsky and Halle's revised distinct feature theory the features were mainly described in articulatory terms, though they referred on occasions to acoustic features. The following paragraphs list the features that are relevant to English only. Chomsky and Halle (1968: 301ff.) grouped their classification into four types of features: (1) Major class features, (2) Cavity features, (3) Manner of **articulation** features and (4) Source features.[4]

The term *Major class* features, a grouping of three binary features, refers articulatorily to the alternation of openings and closings within the vocal tract. Each of the binary features describes the positive or negative value of a different aspect of the open versus close phase. The first feature [±Sonorant] refers to whether or not sounds are produced with a vocal tract configuration in which voicing is possible. In English, all vowels, nasals, /l/, /ɹ/, /w/, /j/ and /h/[5] are described as [+Sonorant]. The other English phonemes are classified as [–Sonorant]. The second major class feature is [±Vocalic] or [Syllabic], which refers to whether or not the sound is produced with a vocal tract configuration not exceeding that found in the production of the high vowels. The vocal folds must be positioned to allow for spontaneous voicing. Hence all sounds that are [+Vocalic] must be [+Sonorant]. Not all sounds that are [+Sonorant], however, are [+Vocalic]. Sounds in rhotic varieties of English that are [+Vocalic] are the vowels and /l/ and /ɹ/. The remaining sounds are [–Vocalic]. The final major class binary feature is [±Consonantal], which refers to whether or not a sound is produced with a radical obstruction in the mid-sagittal (the line that divides the body into left and right halves of equal proportion) region of the vocal tract. The constriction must be as least as narrow as that found for **fricatives**. It is important to note that [+Consonantal] sounds are not necessarily [–Vocalic]. /l/ is produced with the tip of the tongue touching the roof of the mouth. Thus, it blocks the mid-sagittal region. Yet the airstream is able to flow unimpeded out on one or both sides of the tongue ensuring that spontaneous voicing is not suppressed. /l/ is [+Sonorant], [+Vocalic] and [+Consonantal]. English sounds that are [+Consonantal] are, not surprisingly, the consonants minus the semi vowels /w/ and /j/!

Chomsky and Halle's system of cavity features covers very much the same ground as Jakobson's compact, diffuse and grave features. It combines what has traditionally been described in terms of place of **articulation** for consonants, and in terms of tongue position for vowels. There are eleven binary features contained under the heading of cavity features. The features [±Glottal] and [±Covered] are not relevant to the English phonemic sound system and are not discussed below. Readers interested in further information should see Chomsky and Halle (1968: 314–16). The first binary cavity feature is [±Coronal], which refers to whether or not a sound is articulated by the blade of the tongue raised from its neutral position in the mouth. Sounds in English that are [+Coronal] are /θ/, /ð/, /t/, /d/, /n/, /s/, /z/, /l/, /ʃ/, /ʒ/, tʃ/, /dʒ/ and /ɹ/. [+Coronal sounds] are in Jakobson's terminology [–Grave]. Sounds that are produced with an obstruction of the tongue located before the palato-alveolar region of the mouth are [+Anterior] and in English are /θ/, /ð/, /t/, /d/, /n/, /s/, /z/ and /l/. These sounds in Jakobson's terminology are [–Compact].

The next three binary cavity features are connected with the body of the tongue. The first of them is [±High], which refers to whether or not the body of the tongue is raised above the level it occupies when at rest. In English /iː/, /ɪ/, /uː/, /ʊ/, /ʌ/, /k/, /g/, /ŋ/, /j/ and /w/ are [+High]. The next feature is [±Low], which refers to whether or not the body or the tongue is lowered below neutral position in producing the sound. English sounds that are [+Low] are /æ/ and /ɑː/. The features [±High] and [±Low] are mutually exclusive in the sense that a sound cannot be either [+High +Low] or [+High +Low] as it is physically impossible for the body of the tongue to be simultaneously above and below neutral position. It is, however, perfectly possible for the tongue to be in a position that is neither above nor below the neutral position and for a sound such as /ɛ/ to be [–High –Low]. The third binary feature is [±Back], which refers to whether or not the body of the tongue is retracted from the neutral position in the production of the sound. English sounds that are [+Back] are /uː/, /ʊ/, /ʌ/, /ɔː/, /ɒ/, /ɑː/, /k/, /g/ and /ŋ/.

The next distinctive cavity feature is [±Rounded], which refers to whether or not sounds are produced by the narrowing of the lip orifice. In English, the sounds that are [+Rounded] are /uː/, /ʊ/, /ɔː/, /ɒ/ and /w/. [±Distributed] is a feature that refers to sounds produced by a constriction that extends for a considerable distance along the direction of airflow. The feature is designed to distinguish between sounds articulated with the tip of the tongue and sounds that are articulated by the blade of the tongue. Sounds that are [+Distributed] in English are likely to be [+Coronal]. However, on page 313 Chomsky and Halle state that [±Distributed] 'does not correspond precisely to the distinction between laminal and apical'. They argue that the relevant distinction is between sounds with long constrictions and those with short ones. This allows them to claim that **bilabials** are [+Distributed][6]. In English, the sounds /p/, /b/, /m/, /θ/, /ð/, /ʃ/, /ʒ/, /tʃ/ and /dʒ/ are [+Distributed]. The cavity feature [±Nasal] refers to whether or not the soft palate is raised. Sounds in English that are [+Nasal] are /n/, /m/ and /ŋ/. The final cavity distinctive feature is [±Lateral], which refers to whether or not the sound was produced by lowering one or both sides of the tongue. [+Lateral] sounds must be [+Coronal] as no other articulation allows for the possibility of air escaping over the sides of the tongue. In English /l/ alone is [+Lateral].

Chomsky and Halle group seven sets of binary features under the set of manner of **articulation** features. Only three of these sets of features are relevant to English and will be discussed below. The other features [±Velar suction], [±Implosion] and [±Ejection] refer to the production of **clicks**, **implosives** and **ejectives**, respectively. The remaining feature [±Velar pressure] is not evidenced in any known language. The first of the three sets of binary features relevant to English is [±Continuant], which refers to whether or not the airflow in the mouth is unblocked. Sounds that are [+Continuant] are made without a complete closure in the mouth, and in English are the vowels plus, /f/, /v/, /|θ/, /ð/, /s/, /z/, /ʃ/, /ʒ/, /h/, /ɹ/, /w/, /j/ and /l/.[7]

The next relevant manner of **articulation** feature is [±Instantaneous Release], which refers to whether or not a closure in the oral tract is released instantaneously or with a delay. This feature is used to distinguish **stops** and **affricates** with /p/, /b/, /m/, /t/, /d/, /n/, /k/, /g/ and /ŋ/ being [+Instantaneous Release] and /tʃ/ and /dʒ/ being [– Instantaneous Release]. [±Tense] is supposed to refer to sounds that are produced 'with a deliberate, accurate, maximally distinct gesture which involves considerable muscular effort' (ibid.: 324). In English, /iː/, /uː/, /ɔː/, /ɜː/, /ɑː/, /p/, /t/ and /k/ are [+Tense] – but see **tense**.

The final class of features set out in Chomsky and Halle are source features that refer to the airstream mechanism. They are three sets of source features, one of which [±Heightened subglottal pressure] may correlate with **aspiration**. [±Voiced] refers to whether or not the sound is produced with an airflow of a sufficient magnitude to produce vibration of the **vocal folds**. In English, all vowels and the consonants /b/, /m/, /d/, /n/, /g/, /ŋ/, /v/, /ð/, /z/, /ʒ/, /l/, /ɹ/, /w/ and /j/ are [+Voiced]. The final feature is [±Strident], which refers to whether or not the sound is produced with a noisy and turbulent airflow caused by the nature of the surface over which the airstream flows. The feature is restricted to **fricatives** and **affricates**. In English, the sounds /s/, /z/, /ʃ/, /ʒ/, tʃ/ and /dʒ/ are [+Strident].

Table 11 details the distinctive features of the English consonant phonemes using the relevant features in Chomsky and Halle (1968).

While it is clear that the feature system set out in Chomsky and Halle (1968) is able to satisfactorily map out the English sound system, not all the features it describes are necessarily binary. Some are better described in terms of unary features – which are either present or not in the vocal tract. Current research indicates that the roof of the mouth contains three or four primary regions that can be represented by unary features. Within each set of unary features there are sets of binary features (Nathan 2008: 63). The first unary feature is [Labial], which refers to whether or not sounds are made at the lips. This feature includes **bilabials**, **labiodentals** and **labial-velars**. The second major unary feature is [Coronal], which includes the subcategory features [±Distributed], [±Anterior] and [±Strident]. The next unary feature is [Dorsal], which denotes sounds produced by the back of the tongue. The final unary feature [Guttural] refers to glottals and pharyngeals, which phonologists studying Semitic languages (see Hoberman 1995: 839) argue form a natural class of sounds. The remaining features are largely left unrevised. Table 12 details the distinctive features of the English consonant phonemes with unary features notated by a √ symbol.

The adoption of a unary features approach reflects the fact that since the seminal work of Chomsky and Halle (1968) phonologists have recognized that phonolological processes typically affect some related combinations of features rather than others – see **autosegmental phonology**. This has led to current models where the structure of segments are no longer treated as simply a random list of features but rather as a hierarchical configuration of features that can be represented either as a series of submatrices or more commonly through a feature tree. There are a number of superordinating nodes, printed below in small capitals, which dominate the features and segment them into natural classes. Figure 4 illustrates a feature tree for /n/.

D

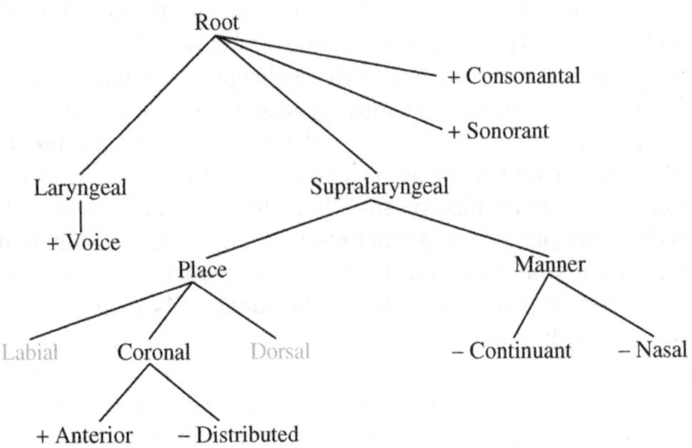

Figure 4 A tree for /n/

Table 11 The English consonant phonemes based on Chomsky and Halle (1968)

Feature	**p**	**b**	**m**	**f**	**v**	**θ**	**ð**	**t**	**d**	**n**	**s**	**z**	**l**	**tʃ**	**dʒ**	**ʃ**	**ʒ**	**ɹ**	**k**	**g**	**ŋ**	**w**	**j**	**h**
Sonorant	−	−	+	−	−	−	−	−	−	+	−	−	+	−	−	−	−	+	−	−	+	+	+	+
Vocalic	−	−	−	−	−	−	−	−	−	−	−	−	+	−	−	−	−	+	−	−	−	+	+	−
Consonantal	+	+	+	+	+	+	+	+	+	+	+	+	+	+	+	+	+	+	+	+	+	−	−	+
Coronal	−	−	−	−	−	+	+	+	+	+	+	+	+	+	+	+	+	+	−	−	−	−	−	−
Anterior	−	−	−	−	−	+	+	+	+	+	+	+	+	−	−	−	−	−	−	−	−	−	−	−
High	−	−	−	−	−	−	−	−	−	−	−	−	−	−	−	−	−	−	+	+	+	+	+	−
Low	0	0	0	0	0	0	0	0	0	0	0	0	0	0	0	0	0	0	0	0	0	0	0	0
Back	−	−	−	−	−	−	−	−	−	−	−	−	−	−	−	−	−	−	+	+	+	−	−	−
Rounded	−	−	−	−	−	−	−	−	−	−	−	−	−	−	−	−	−	−	−	−	−	+	−	−
Distributed	+	+	+	0	0	+	+	−	−	−	−	−	−	+	+	+	+	−	0	0	0	0	0	0
Nasal	−	−	+	−	−	−	−	−	−	+	−	−	−	−	−	−	−	−	−	−	+	−	−	−
Lateral	0	0	0	0	0	−	−	−	−	−	−	−	+	−	−	−	−	−	0	0	0	0	0	0
Continuant	−	−	−	+	+	+	+	−	−	−	+	+	+	−	−	+	+	+	−	−	−	+	+	+
Instantaneous Release	+	+	+	−	−	−	−	+	+	+	−	−	−	−	−	−	−	−	+	+	+	−	−	−
Tense	+	−	0	0	0	0	0	+	−	0	0	0	0	0	0	0	0	0	+	−	0	0	0	0
Voiced	−	+	+	−	+	−	+	−	+	+	−	+	+	−	+	−	+	+	−	+	+	+	+	−
Strident	0	0	0	−	−	−	−	0	0	0	+	+	0	+	+	+	+	0	0	0	0	0	0	0

Table 12 The consonant phonemes of English unary analysis

FEATURE	p	b	m	f	v	θ	ð	t	d	n	s	z	l	tʃ	dʒ	ʃ	ʒ	ɹ	k	g	ŋ	w	j	h
Sonorant	−	−	+	−	−	−	−	−	−	+	−	−	+	−	−	−	−	+	−	−	+	+	+	−
Consonantal	+	+	+	+	+	+	+	+	+	+	+	+	+	+	+	+	+	+	+	+	+	−	−	+
Nasal	−	−	+	−	−	−	−	−	−	+	−	−	−	−	−	−	−	−	−	−	+	−	−	−
Continuant	−	−	−	+	+	+	+	−	−	−	+	+	+	−	−	+	+	−	−	−	−	+	+	+
Instantaneous Release	+	+	+	−	−	−	−	+	+	+	−	−	−	−	−	−	−	−	+	+	+	−	−	−
Voiced	−	+	+	−	+	−	+	−	+	+	−	+	+	−	+	−	+	+		+	+	+	+	−
LABIAL	✓	✓	✓	✓	✓																	✓		
Rounded	−	−	−	−	−																	+		
CORONAL						✓	✓	✓	✓	✓	✓	✓	✓	✓	✓	✓	✓	✓						
Anterior						+	+	+	+	+	+	+	+	+	−	−	−	−						
Distributed						+	+	−	−	−	−	−	−	−	−	−	−	−						
Strident						−	−	0	0	0	+	+	0	+	+	+	+	0						
Lateral						−	−	−	−	−	−	−	+	−	−	−	−	−						
DORSAL																			✓	✓	✓	✓	✓	
High																			+	+	+	+	+	
Low																			−	−	−	−	−	
Back																			+	+	+	−	−	

Table 13 The Monophthongs of RP based on Halle (1995)

Feature	iː	ɪ	uː	ʊ	ɛ	æ	ʌ	ɔː	ɒ	ɜː	ɑː	ə
Labial			√	√				√	√			
Rounded			+	+				+	+			
Dorsal	√	√	√	√	√	√	√	√	√	√	√	√
High	+	+	+	+	–	–	–	–	–	–	–	–
Low	–	–	–	–	–	+	–	–	+	–	+	–
Back	–	–	+	+	–	–	+	+	+	–	+	–
Radical	√		√					√		√	√	
Tense	+		+					+		+	+	

There are two important things to note from this tree representation. The first is that it is not the individual features that are subject to the application of phonological rules but rather the natural class of features that are subject to their application. The second is that tree representations such as Figure 4 are referred to as underspecified because only the relevant features are specified in the tree. The remaining features are filled in by default rules. To indicate the underspecification, I have included (but grey shaded) the place features Labial and Dorsal. Underspecified representations allow phonologists not only to write more economical and insightful rules, but more importantly imply that predictable information is absent from the underlying representation (see **generative grammar**). Useful introductions to feature geometry are found in Davenport and Hannahs (2010: Sections 10.1 and 10.2), and Gussenhoven and Jacobs (2005: chs 11 and 12).

Vowels can be similarly described in terms of features, though it is worth remembering that traditional articulatory descriptions of vowels appear to be less accurate than acoustic descriptions in terms of their **formants**. All English vowels by definition are [+Vocalic], [–Consonantal], [–Nasal], [+Continuant], [+Voiced] and [0 Instantaneous Release], [0 Distributed], [0 Strident] and [0 Lateral]. As with consonants, vowel features are classified into a number of unary features which themselves contain sets of binary features. The three relevant unary vowel features are [Labial], [Dorsal] and [Radical]. Radical features refer to the articulations produced by the tongue root and are notoriously difficult to define – see **tense** and **advanced tongue root**. The features detailed in Table 13 simplify Halle (1995) by including only the feature [±Tense] under the radical category.

In current phonology, distinctive features are primarily grounded in articulations with a secondary grounding in perception. In other words, they are supposed to represent the physical reflexes and the acoustic correlates of actual stored mental entities. Yet, originally, features were considered solely in terms of 12 perceptual features, which did not, however, always succeed in characterizing sound patterns in a manner that corresponded to native speaker intuition. Chomsky and Halle, as detailed above, recast distinctive features in articulatory terms and, by so doing, largely solved the problem of aligning features with native speaker intuition. Yet, articulatory-based feature systems do not completely capture every attested feature of speech, for instance the tendency for dark <L>s to vocalize in some varieties of English, for example, words such as *shelf* and *milk* may be articulated as [ʃɛɤf] and [mɪɤk] by London speakers. A feature chart based on articulatory measures does not fully capture the perceptual similarity between the dark <L> and the [ɤ] vowel: though this would be less of a problem for a feature system grounded in perception.

MacNeilage (2008: 227) after reviewing such facts concludes that, 'some aspects of the sound patterns of languages are articulatory motivated while others are perceptually motivated'. He notes that this implies that sound systems emerge from and are maintained by a trade-off between the ease of articulation and perceptual distinctiveness. Such an observation is problematic for views of language that maintain an absolute division between language competence – the innate mental level of language – and language performance. Features that are posited as actual mental entitles are identified by their performed realization in speech!

A further problem with distinctive features is that they are intended to represent a small finite set of features that are applicable to the description of the sound system of any natural language. Yet, even in the case of English, certain features, notably [Tense] and to a lesser extent [Distributed], are themselves based on opaque and disputable phonetic underpinnings. They may represent nothing more tangible than ad hoc descriptive convenience. In other words, they may not represent universal features. Ladefoged and Maddieson (1996: 369ff.) when reviewing the findings of their survey of over 500 languages conceded that their initial hopes that their findings might provide a phonetic underpinning for further developments in phonological feature theory proved to be in vain. In their own words, 'The great variety of data that we have presented shows that the construction of an adequate theory [especially for vowels] is much more complex than hitherto thought.' Indeed, distinctive features provide a less rigorous description of the vowel system than the one of **cardinal vowel**, for instance CV2 and CV3 would both be classified as [– High] and [– Low] rather than opposed as mid-close versus mid-open.[8]

Since the work of Jakobson in the 1950s there has been an assumption that distinctive features are innate cognitive entities specified in Universal Grammar. Permissible phonological patterns are built directly out of features – see for instance Clements and Hume (1995). In recent times, an alternative view has emerged – see for instance Pierrehumbert (2003) and Mieke (2008) – namely that features are learnt by speakers in response to phonological patterns and that features can be described as properties of sounds within phonologically active classes. A phonologically active class is a group of sounds that to the exclusion of all other sounds does one of the following: (1) undergo a phonological process; (2) trigger a phonological process; or (3) exemplify a static distributional restriction.

In an extensive survey of patterning into phonologically active classes in more than 6,000 languages, Mieke (2008) found that an innate feature description was incapable of describing around 25 per cent of the attested phonologically active classes. This evidence, coupled with the lack of strong experimental and psycholinguistic evidence in favour of innateness, led him to conclude that features are emergent and arise out of phonetic similarity and phonetically driven sound change. Hence there is no reason to expect that all languages will pattern in similar ways. However, he also noted that a description of features as emergent should not be considered as a rejection of the work of scholars such as Jakobson, Chomsky and Clements but rather as a continuation of it (ibid.: 113).

Regardless of whether or not features are innate or emergent, it is clear that phonological rules typically affect natural classes of phonemes, and that phonological rules couched in distinctive feature theory are accurate and economical. Analysts can usefully employ feature theory to describe sound patterning within a language or a cluster of related languages without worrying about whether or not they are investigating part of Universal Grammar. The following paragraphs illustrate three examples of the power and economy of a phonological description couched in features.

It is well known that **nasals** assimilate to the place of **articulation** of a following consonant. An economical way of stating this rule for the English Nasal phonemes, assuming that /n/ is the unmarked segment is:

$$\begin{bmatrix} +\text{Nasal} \\ +\text{Alveolar} \end{bmatrix} \rightarrow [+\text{Labial}]/ \underline{\qquad} [+\text{Labial}]$$

This rule accounts for examples such as [ɪmp] and [bʌmp] etc. The pronunciation of the nasal in words such as /iŋk/ and /mʌŋk/ follows:

$$\begin{bmatrix} +\text{Nasal} \\ +\text{Alveolar} \end{bmatrix} \rightarrow [+\text{Velar}]/ \underline{\qquad} [+\text{Vela}]$$

In words such as *panther* the nasal assimilates to a dental place of assimilation as [ˈpæn̪θə] and the rule is:

$$\begin{bmatrix} +\text{Nasal} \\ +\text{Alveolar} \end{bmatrix} \rightarrow [+\text{Dental}]/ \underline{\qquad} [+\text{Dental}]$$

Rather than writing three rules, however, the rule can be written more economically as:

$$\begin{bmatrix} +\text{Nasal} \\ +\text{Alveolar} \end{bmatrix} \rightarrow [\alpha\ \text{Place}]/ \underline{\qquad} [\alpha\ \text{Place}]$$

The rule states that the place of **articulation** of the nasal consonant comes to match the place of **articulation** of the following consonant. The Greek letter α stipulates that the two places of articulation are identical.

Voiced obstruents in numerous languages other than English – such as German, Dutch and Russian – tend to be devoiced word finally. The rule or formal description is as follows:

$$\begin{bmatrix} +\text{Consonantal} \\ +\text{Sonorant} \end{bmatrix} \rightarrow [-\text{Voice}]/ \underline{\qquad} \#]$$ [9]

When pronouncing words, speakers often insert segments to help ease the burden of articulation – see **epenthesis**. Well-known examples are *hamster* → [ˈhæmpstə], *monster* → [ˈmɒntstə] and *youngster* → [ˈjʌŋkstə]. In each case, a voiceless stop has been inserted after a homorganic nasal and before [s].

The insertion is noted as follow:

$$\varnothing \rightarrow \begin{bmatrix} \alpha \text{ place} \\ + \text{Consonantal} \\ - \text{Voice} \\ - \text{Nasal} \\ + \text{Instantaneous} \\ \text{release} \end{bmatrix} / \begin{bmatrix} \alpha \text{ place} \\ + \text{nasal} \end{bmatrix} \_\_\_ \begin{bmatrix} - \text{Sonorant} \\ + \text{Consonantal} \\ + \text{Continuant} \\ - \text{Voice} \end{bmatrix}$$

The rule describes how a segment is inserted between a nasal and [s]. The inserted segment is a voiceless stop that has a homorganic articulation with the preceding nasal.

Distribution

Distribution is a phonological term that refers to the set of contexts within a word in which a sound can appear in a language. Sounds that have overlapping distributions contrast with one another and are **phonemic**. Sounds whose distributions do not overlap are in complementary distribution and are **allophonic**. In English, /l/ before vowels and /j/ is clear while after vowels it is dark. As the distributions of the two types of <L> do not overlap clear and dark <L> are in an allophonic relationship.

Double articulation

Double articulation, also known as co-ordinate articulation, is the production of a sound that has two simultaneous primary articulations of the same **manner**, for example, *stop +stop*, *fricative +fricative*, *nasal +nasal* or *approximant +approximant*. The IPA symbolizes double articulation through the use of a tie bar, which can be placed above or under the phonemic symbols, as in [p͡k] or [p͜k]. Double articulation is not a feature of the sound system of English if one assumes that the **labialization** of /w/ is a **secondary articulation**. However, double articulations can be heard in some fast articulations of words such as *apt, act, ragtime*, etc. Similarly, some French pronunciations of words such as *Louis* [lwi] and *lui* [lɥi] *(him)* involve an approximant +approximant double articulation (Catford 2001).

Double articulations, however, are present in the sound systems of numerous non-European languages. For instance, West African languages such as Yoruba and Idoma contain voiced and voiceless bilabial-velar and nasal-nasal articulations. The following Idoma data from Ladefoged and Maddieson (1996: 333) illustrates:

Voiceless stop	[àk͡pà]	'bridge'
Voiced stop	[àg͡bà]	'jaw'
Voiced nasal	[aŋ͡màa]	'body painting'

Duration

Duration is a phonetic term for the physical length of a sound or syllable as measured on a time scale usually in milliseconds. Duration is perceived by hearers as length. For instance, the FLEECE vowel is perceived as longer than the KIT vowel in most varieties of English. In other words, the articulation of the FLEECE vowel for most speakers involves a longer duration than that of the KIT vowel. However, because speech tempo varies both across and within speakers, the duration of a sound or syllable must be examined relative to the rest of an individual speaker's talk. In conversation, hearers use duration as a clue to identify tonic syllables, which allows them to identify the parts of their interlocutor's message that is signalled as being informationally in focus – see **intonation**.

Egressive

Egressive is a phonetic term that is used to classify speech sounds produced using an outwards moving airstream mechanism. Egressive contrasts with **ingressive**. As an egressive airstream mechanism is by far the most efficient means of powering speech it is the most common power source for speech. All English **phonemes** are produced with an egressive airstream mechanism initiated by the lungs. An egressive airstream may, however, be initiated by the **glottis**. Consonants known as **ejectives**, which are produced by a **glottalic** airstream, are found in numerous languages.

Ejective

An ejective is a consonant that is produced by a flow of air initiated by an **egressive glottalic airstream mechanism**. Ejectives are produced when the vocal tract is blocked by a closure of the **glottis** and by the raising of the **velum**, which seals off the **nasal passage**. In addition, the mouth is blocked either by the tongue or the lips. As the glottis is closed, ejectives are **voiceless**. The most common type of ejective found cross-linguistically are **stops**, though ejective **fricatives** and ejective **affricates** are reported in the literature. Ejectives are transcribed by placing an apostrophe after the phonemic symbol for the corresponding **pulmonic** egressive consonant, for instance [k'] symbolizes an ejective **velar** stop.

In order to articulate [k'] a speaker first closes her glottis in order to produce a **glottal** stop while simultaneously making a **velar** stop by putting the back of her tongue into contact with the **soft palate**. The speaker must ensure that the velum is raised and that the nasal passage is sealed to ensure that air cannot enter from the nasal passage into or out of the **pharynx**. Next, the speaker must raise her closed glottis, which compresses the air in the pharynx. The speaker then releases the velar stop by lowering the back of the tongue while almost simultaneously releasing the glottal stop. This results in a very different quality of sound than [k].

Ladefoged (2005) reports that ejectives occur in around 20 per cent of the world's languages. He argues that the relative paucity of ejectives in comparison with oral stops is because ejectives are more physically demanding to make **uvular** and especially **velar** ejectives are more common cross-linguistically than **bilabial** or **alveolar** ejectives. This is because ejectives made at the back of the mouth are more auditorily distinct from their pulmonic egressive counterparts than those made towards the front of the mouth. To illustrate, the articulation of [k'] results in the formation of a small body of air trapped between the glottis and the back of the tongue. A small upward movement of the glottis causes a significant compression of the trapped air, which when released results in an audible pop. During the articulation of [p'] there is a much larger body of air trapped between the glottis and the mouth. The upward movement of the glottis results in a far less significant compression of the trapped air, which when released results in a much less audible pop. The resulting [p'] is thus not easily distinguishable from a [p].

Ejectives are characteristic of Caucasian languages such as Georgian (also known as Kartvelian), which has bilabial, alveolar, velar and uvular ejective stops in addition to bilabial, alveolar, velar and uvular oral stops. Ejectives are also found in many African and Amerindian languages where they contrast with oral consonants. Quecha – a language spoken in the Andean regions of Bolivia and Peru – contrasts ejective stops with **unaspirated** and **aspirated** stops, for example:

[kujui]	[kʰujui]	[k'ujui]
to move	to whistle	to twist

(Ladefoged 2005: 149)

While ejectives are not part of the sound system of English, Gimson (2008: 30) notes that some speakers of English, for instance speakers from South-East Lancashire, may produce ejective stops as **allophonic** variants of oral stops in word final position. Thus the word *bike* might be pronounced as [baɪk'].

Elision

Elision is a phonetic term that refers to the omission of sound segments especially in connected speech. **consonants**, **vowels** and **syllables** may all be deleted. The sound segments are deleted in order to aid the ease of pronunciation by smoothening the transition between two sounds. Traditionally, some people when they notice elisions may castigate them as examples of slovenly language use. However, such a view fails to take account of the fact that today's elisions may be tomorrow's innovations. Modern French has partly emerged through the elision of numerous Latin case endings, for instance the classical Latin word for *peach* was *persica malcus*, which underwent a series of elisions: first, the word *malcus* was elided leaving *persica*, next the middle vowel [i] was elided resulting in *persca*, which over time lost the post-vocalic [r] and became *pesca* before ending up as the modern French *pêche,* (Deutscher 2005: 89).

In English, consideration of the orthographic spelling system provides copious examples of historic elisions that have reified into language changes, for example *knot,* /nɒt/ with a historically elided /k/, *often* /ˈɒfən/ with a historically elided /t/,[1] *Christmas* /ˈkɹɪsməs/ with a historically elided /t/, *palm* /pɑːm/ with a historically elided /l/, *wren* [ɹɛn] with a historically elided /w/ and *light* /laɪt/ with a historically elided orthographic <gh>, which was pronounced as /x/.

Words in connected speech have to retain a certain phonetic shape in order to ensure that they are comprehensible, therefore instances of elision are largely predictable and include:

- /h/ is regularly elided in the **weak form** of pronouns, for example, *him* [ɪm] and *he* [iː] or [i].

E

- If an **alveolar plosive** is in **syllable coda** position and preceded by a consonant that agrees in voicing is found medially between consonants it is regularly elided, for example, *last dance* [læsdɑːns], *next place* [nɛkspleɪs], *west coast,* [wɛskəʊst], *old man* [əʊlmæn] and *hold firm* [həulfɜːm].
- If a word final cluster containing either a **voiceless** plosive or **affricate** and followed by /t/, or a **voiced** plosive or affricate followed by /d/, the alveolar plosive is regularly elided, for instance /t/ in *stopped playing* [stɒppleɪŋ], *looked like* [lʊkleɪk], watched them [wɒtʃðəm] and /d/ in *urged them* [ɜːdʒðəm], *changed shape* [tʃeɪndʒʃeɪp] and *rubbed them* [ɹʌbðəm]. It will be noted that the elision of the alveolar plosive results in the loss of any explicit marker of past tense. Speakers must use the context and especially the previous co-text to aid their comprehension.
- If /t/ is found in the clitic negative marker <n't> it is regularly elided especially before a consonant, for example, *mustn't go* [mʌsn̩gəʊ], *wouldn't win* [wʊdn̩wɪn] and *couldn't lose* [kʊdn̩luːz]. It may also be elided before a vowel in fast casual speech, as in *wouldn't eat* [wʊdn̩iːt].
- /t/ and /d/ may be elided if they are part of a word final and word initial cluster formed from the phonemes /t/ and /d/, for example, *I've got to*... [aɪvgɒtə] and *what do you*... [wɒdəjuː] or [wɒdʒuː].
- The elision of a member of a boundary cluster of two consonants may occur in casual speech, though it is usually stigmatized as slovenly pronunciation. This is more likely to happen across a word boundary, for instance /v/ in *Give me (gimme) the ball* [ˈgɪmɪðəˈbɔːl], /t/ in *I want to (wanna) dance*, [aɪˈwɒnəˈdɑːns].
- In fast casual speech a **fricative** in a sequence of fricatives may be elided, for example, *fifths,* /f/ in [fɪθs] and *twelfth* [twɛlθ], and /θ/ in *asthma* [ˈæsmə].

Epenthesis

Epenthesis is a phonetic term that refers to the insertion of additional sound segments. The sound segments are inserted for a number of reasons such as to aid the ease of pronunciation by smoothing the transition between two sounds, ensuring that a syllable is well formed and ensuring that the word is long enough for it to be prosodically parsable. Sounds that are inserted epenthetically may, over generations of speakers, become accepted as part of the standard pronunciation of a word and result in a sound change. McMahon (2000b: 61) notes that the Latin word *schola* has mutated into *école* in French and *escuela* in Spanish partly as a result of the insertion of the initial /ɛ/ vowel. Second-language speakers of English with native languages that contain only open syllables frequently insert epenthetic vowels into their English. For instance, a Japanese learner beginning English is likely to produce the following English monosyllables as:

Book	/bʊk/ → [bɯkɯ]
Milk	/mɪlk/ → [mɪɽɯ]
Spin	/spɪn/ → [sɯpɪnɯ]

In compliance with the **phonotactic** rules of the speaker's native Japanese, the speaker inserts a back vowel between consonants in consonant clusters.

Epenthesis is a noted feature of many broad Irish accents. Wells (1982b: 434–5) identifies two types of epenthesis prevalent in Ireland, which are an areal hangover from Gaelic, involving [ə] and [d]. [ə] may be inserted between a **plosive** and **liquid** or **nasal**, for instance *petrol* → [p^{h}ɛt̪əɹəl], or between two consonants one of which is a liquid and the other a nasal, as in *film* → [fɪləm]. A [d] can be inserted between two consonants if the preceding consonant is either /l/ or /n/ and the following one /z/, or if the preceding consonant is /ɹ/ and the following one is either /n/ or /l/, such as *tons* → [tundz] and *girl* → [gɪɹdl].

In most British accents, epenthesis may be found in the following cases:

- [t] may be inserted into consonant clusters containing two **alveolar** consonants, for example, *tense* → [t^{h}ɛnts] and *prince* → [p^{h}ɹ̥ɪnts]. It will be noted that this leads to a phonetic neutralization between the following words: *tents/tense* and *prints/prince*.
- [t] may be inserted between a preceding /n/ and a following /θ/ or /ʃ/, for instance, *anthrax* → [ˈæntθɹæks] *tension* → [ˈtɛntʃən], *anthem* → [ˈæntθəm] and *tenth* → [tɛntθ].
- [p] may be inserted between a preceding /m/ and a following fricative, as in *hamster* → [ˈhæmpstə], *warmth* → [wɔːmpθ].[2]
- [k] may be inserted between a preceding /ŋ/ and a following fricative, as in *tungsten* → [ˈtʌŋkstən].

The above may be summed up by the phonetic rule presented earlier on page 48.

Estuary English

The term Estuary English (EE) was coined by Rosewarne (1984) in a rather impressionistic and brief article, and adopted by the media to describe an alleged supraregional prestige accent. Rosewarne proposed that EE was a novel variety of English, originating in the counties adjacent to the Thames estuary. He claimed that it is gaining in prestige and that it may be replacing **received pronunciation** as the favoured supraregional pronunciation of younger middle-class speakers throughout the UK. Rosewarne argued that EE consisted of a mixture of RP and basilectal London speech features. He proposed that the identifying phonemic features are the substitution of a short back vowel for a **dark** <L>; the replacement of a word medial **alveolar stop** by a **glottal** stop; the replacement of a syllable final alveolar stop by a glottal stop, J dropping after /l/, /t/, /s/ and /n/; a distinctive realization of <r>; and the diphthongization of the FLEECE and HAPPY vowels.

However, while there is little doubt that (1) features from basilectal London speech have spread into the speech of the higher social classes in the South East; (2) there has been an increased retention of South-Eastern regional features by speakers who might have been anticipated to adopt RP; (3) that speakers of RP use some features of basilectal London speech in some less formal registers of speech; (4) that there has been extensive dialect-levelling in recent decades in the Home Counties – it is doubtful that these four developments amount to the creation of a new supraregional variety (Altendorf and Watt 2008). Przedlacka (2002) failed to find homogeneity in the speech of 16 teenage informants in the Home Counties and concluded that claims for the emergence for a new accent that is on the cusp of replacing RP have been overstated. However, at the same time she recognized that there are considerable sound changes in progress that have led to regional influences on RP and that these can be described by the cover term EE.

E

Firthian prosodic phonology

Firthian prosodic phonology, also known as the 'London School' of linguistics, is a school of phonology associated with John Rupert Firth and his followers. As a theory, it shares much in common with the later theory of **autosegmental** phonology; though unlike autosegmental phonology, Firthian prosodic phonology does not posit language universals. It argues that each language must be described on its own terms.

Firth's starting point was his objection to what he felt was the mistaken preoccupation with the **phoneme** and the resulting description of speech as a series of paradigmatic oppositions between segments. Firth (1957) argues that an adequate description of speech needs to focus equally on the syntagmatic structure of the utterance while at the same time not neglecting paradigmatic oppositions. The cornerstone of Firth's approach was his belief that the speech signal does not easily lend itself to analyses in terms of discrete segments. Rather, he postulated that some features had the potential to spread across segments. To account for these facts, Firth created the theoretical notion of *prosodies*, which are any features that may extend across the utterance such as **secondary articulations**, **junctural features** and **intonation**, etc.

A further key innovation in Firth's theory was his polysystemic principle that recognized that different paradigmatic contrasts are allowable in different places of phonological structure. The permissible contrasts in word initial and final position for voiceless stops differs. Before the vowel the stops are **aspirated**, after the vowel they are not. Firth's notation (ibid.: 123) of *i* for initial position and *f* for final position, plus the abstract symbols C and V, can be used to illustrate the different prosodic paradigms, for instance:

> [pʰɑː], [tʰɑː] and [kʰɑː] are represented as *i*Cʰ V while
> [ɑːp], [ɑːt] and [ɑːk] are represented by as VC*f*.

In English, the consonant cluster [ts] is illegal in syllable onset position, but legal (as in *cats*) in coda position. Firth argues that this is because there are two different prosodies, the illegal *i*tsV and the legal Vts*f*. Firth and his followers proposed a series of the following types of prosodies: sentence prosodies such as intonation; word prosodies such as vowel harmony; syllable prosodies such as nasalization, labialization and velarization; syllable-part prosodies such as aspiration.

Prosodic analysis has been successfully employed in describing **vowel harmony** (see Lass 1984: 239ff. for further details). It seems to capture generalities missed by segmental analyses. Consider the following words from Turkish (1) /sonunda/, (2) /syrerec/ and (3) /kutu/. In all three words, a feature attached to the initial vowel spreads across the word and mandates that the following vowels must have an identical value for the feature. In (1) the initial vowel mandates the feature setting [+back] while in (2) it mandates the feature setting [+front] and in (3) it mandates the feature setting [+round, +back].

A major drawback with Firthian phonology, however, is the lack of a standard notation, such as association lines employed in autosegmental phonology. This makes Firthian phonology hard to employ even as a descriptive device. For instance, the Turkish data described above would be notated along the following, rather reader-unfriendly lines[1]:

/sonunda/ = [+Back] svnv^{h}dv^{l}
/syɾeɾec/ = [+Front] sv^{hr}rvrvc
/kutu/ = [+Back, +Round, +High] kvkv

Flap

A flap is a term used to refer to the classification of a **consonant** on the basis of its manner of **articulation**. Flaps are produced by a single very rapid contact between the **articulators**. The IPA symbolizes **alveolar** and **retroflex** flaps. There is some dispute in the literature as to whether flaps and **taps** refer to the same manner of **articulation**. Ladefoged (2001: 150ff.) distinguishes between taps and flaps by claiming that flaps are typically retroflex articulations, where the tip of the tongue is curled up prior to making brief contact with the roof of the mouth. Taps, he claims, are made by a brief contact between the roof of the mouth and the tip of the tongue (see also Abercrombie 1967: 49; Catford 2001; Laver 1994: 224). However, other scholars do not distinguish between flaps and taps, for instance O'Connor (1973: 48); Collins and Mees (2008: 43–4); and Lodge (2009: 44).

Flaps do not form part of the phonemic sound system of English but flapped **allophonic** sounds may be heard in many American accents as allophones of /t/ in words such as *dirty* ['dɪɾiː] and *sorting* ['sɔɾɪŋ], which have an r-coloured vowel in the stressed syllable (Ladefoged 2001: 150). In upper **received pronunciation** an intervocalic <r>, in words such as *very*, may be pronounced as a flap, thus ['vɛɾi]. It is worth noting that Gimson (2008), who does not discuss flaps, labels this articulation as a tap.

Foot

A foot is a rhythmical unit of speech that consists of one stressed syllable and optional unstressed syllables. The term is an extension of the use of the term from poetics, where there has been more than two millennia of study into the patterning of **stressed** and unstressed syllables in verse. A foot consisting of a single pair of an unstressed syllable followed by a stressed syllable is an iambic foot. For example, /bɪ'kʌm/ contrasts with a trochaic foot, which consists of a single pair of a stressed syllables followed by an unstressed one, as in /'gɜːlfrɛnd/. **metrical** phonologists label feet that exhibit iambic rhythm as right-dominated and those that exhibit trochaic rhythm as left-dominated, and use the notation s for stressed and w for weak. Thus:

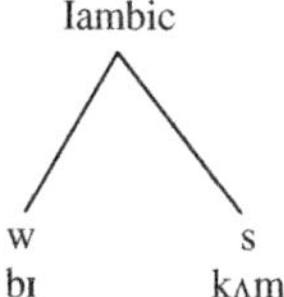

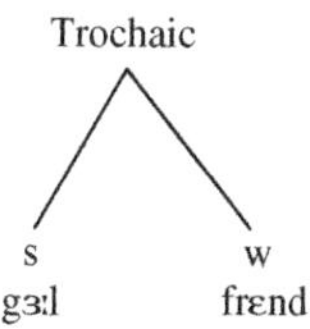

A slightly different use of the term is found in the work of Halliday (1994) who argues that different types of languages have different types of feet. Spoken utterances in stress-timed languages such as English are formed from trochaic or descending feet, while spoken utterances in syllable-timed languages such as French are formed from ascending or iambic feet – see **timing**. As many English words begin with unstressed syllables that will not be **accented** in speech, theorists such as Halliday, and Abercrombie (1967), argue that such feet begin with a silent ictus, which is notated by a caret ^. In (a) and (b) foot boundaries are notated with a slash.

(a) man is/happy
(b) ^ a/man is/happy

In example (a) there are two feet consisting of an accented syllable followed by an unaccented one, while in example (b) there are three feet with the first foot consisting of a silent ictus followed by an unaccented syllable.

Formant

A formant is a term used in **acoustic phonetics** to describe a concentration of acoustic energy found when a speaker produces a periodic sound such as a vowel. A formant is a reflection of the manner in which the air vibrates within the mouth. For any vowel the air is simultaneously vibrating at numerous different frequencies within the mouth. But the most dominant frequencies cluster together into formants, which show up clearly on spectrographs as thick black lines. The clustering of the vibrating air molecules is determined by the degree of lip-rounding, the height of the tongue and whether or not the tongue is in the front or the back of the mouth. While all vowels have numerous formants, only the first three formants are necessary to identify vowels (except the retroflexed American English vowel in *bird* [ɝ]). The *r colouring* of a vowel results in a reduction in the first formant value, which means that it cannot be accurately plotted on a two-dimensional formant chart.

Numerous studies have shown that the value of the first formant increases as the vowel becomes more open. In English [æ] has a higher first formant value than [iː], with [ɛ] intermediate between the two. Similarly, the degree of backness of a vowel correlates loosely with the second formant frequency value. Table 14 shows formant 1 and 2 values for nine English vowels produced by a male speaker. Using this information, the vowels can be plotted on a formant chart, which roughly corresponds to the traditional plotting of vowels on a vowel quadrilateral.[2] For further details see Ladefoged (2001: ch. 9).

F

Table 14 Formant values for nine English Vowels

Vowel	Formant 1 value (Hz)	Formant 2 value (Hz)
iː	275	2250
ɪ	400	2000
ɛ	575	1800
æ	725	1500
ɑː	700	1100
ɒ	600	500
ɔː	450	200
ʊ	400	1100
uː	300	1250

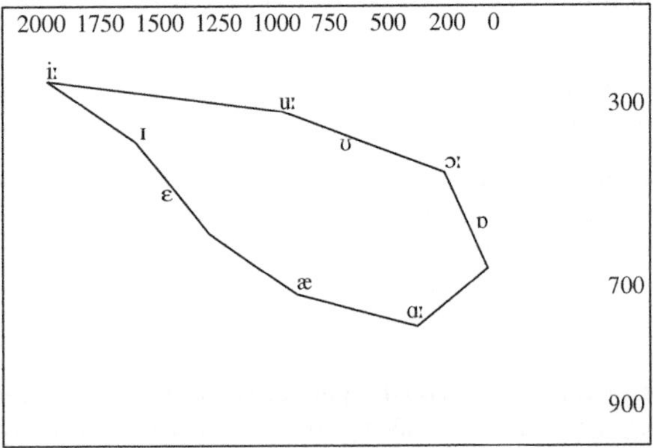

Figure 5 A formant chart of ten English vowels

Figure 5 plots the formant values on a chart with the vertical and horizontal axes representing the traditional features of height and front/backness, respectively. While there are some differences between this formant chart and a traditional vowel quadrilateral, especially in relation to the back vowels, it is clear that the traditional articulatory descriptions of vowels are in fact grounded in phonetic reality. What generations of phoneticians have concretized as being caused by the height of the tongue is actually determined by the first formant frequency. What they have described as being caused by the fronting or the backing of the tongue in the mouth is actually determined by the difference between the first and second formant frequencies.

The discussion to date has been somewhat overly simplified in that it assumes that speakers produce and hearers perceive vowels in isolation. Of course, this is not the case. In **connected speech**, vowel formants are influenced by preceding or following consonants found within the same **syllable**. Acoustically, in connected speech a vowel may consist of formant transitions out of a preceding consonant, a short steady state consisting of vowel formants, equivalent to those which would have been produced had the vowel been produced in isolation, and formant transitions into the following consonant.

In an innovative experiment Jenkins, Strange and Edman (1983) recorded a speaker producing CVC syllables that begin and ended with [b] but contained nine different vowels in the syllable nucleus. They edited the syllables by splicing them into three components: the initial onset [b], the vowel nucleus and the final coda [b]. This enabled them to present the syllables to groups of subjects in a number of different forms as (1) the unmodified original syllable; (2) 'silent center syllables' with the central vocalic steady state formants removed and replaced by silence but the formant transitions preserved; (3) 'variable-center syllables' with only the vocalic steady-state formants remaining; (4) 'fixed-center syllables' with only the vocalic steady-state formants remaining but the steady state clipped to match the duration of the shortest target vowel; (5) 'abutted syllables' that were similar to 'silent center syllables' but did not contain the formant transitions from and to the adjacent consonants. Their results indicated that their subjects were as accurate in identifying the vowel nuclei correctly when presented with the 'silent center syllable' stimuli as when they were presented with the original unmodified syllables. This indicates that, in connected speech, formant transitions are an important perceptual cue in identifying vowels.

All **sonorants** and not only vowels contain clear formant structures. **nasal** consonants and **nasalized** vowels have different resonances to their **oral** counterparts, because in nasals and nasalized sounds the **soft palate** is lowered and the air is free to vibrate in the nasal passage as well as the oral passage. The bands of resonating frequencies found in the nasal passage are known as anti-formants and show up in spectrographs as bands of white space that can be used to identify nasalized vowels (Figure 6).

Fortis

Fortis is a phonetic term that classifies **consonants** according to the strength of muscular effort and the amount of breath force used to articulate the sound. Fortis sounds contrast with **lenis** sounds. Fortis consonants are apparently articulated with greater muscular effort and a higher amount of breath force. It is argued that in phonetic environments where the sound has been devoiced it is the degree of muscular effort and breath force that is used to maintain a contrast between **phonemes** – see also **tense**. In English, voiceless sounds (especially **stops**) are often classified as fortis in text books, such as Collins and Mees (2008: 52), Gimson (2008: 159), Roach (2009: 44) and Rogerson-Revell (2011: 51). Laver (1994: 344), however, cautioned that the fortis/lenis distinction has yet to be confirmed empirically and suggests that, until it is, phoneticians should be cautious in describing sound contrasts in terms of fortis/lenis distinctions. Indeed, the only empirical support for a fortis/lenis distinction existing in languages is found in studies of Korean, such as in Cho, Jun and Ladefoged (2002) who reported a systematic difference between Korean stops in terms of whether they were fortis, lenis or aspirated.

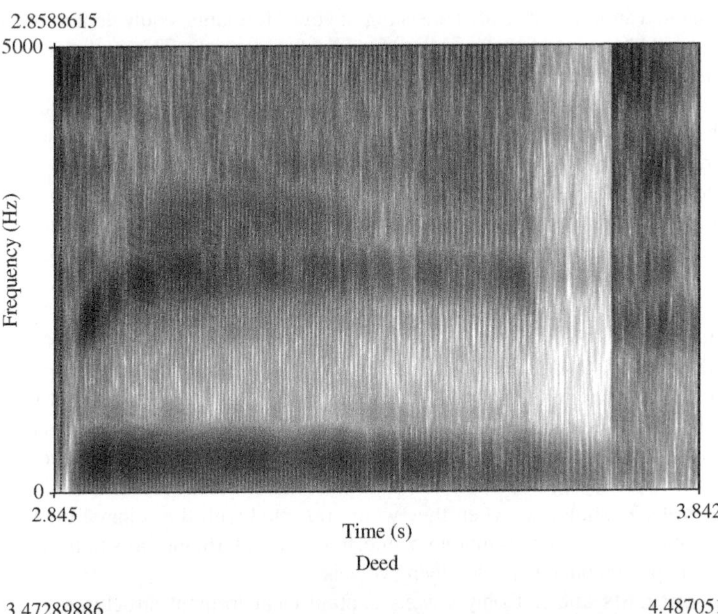

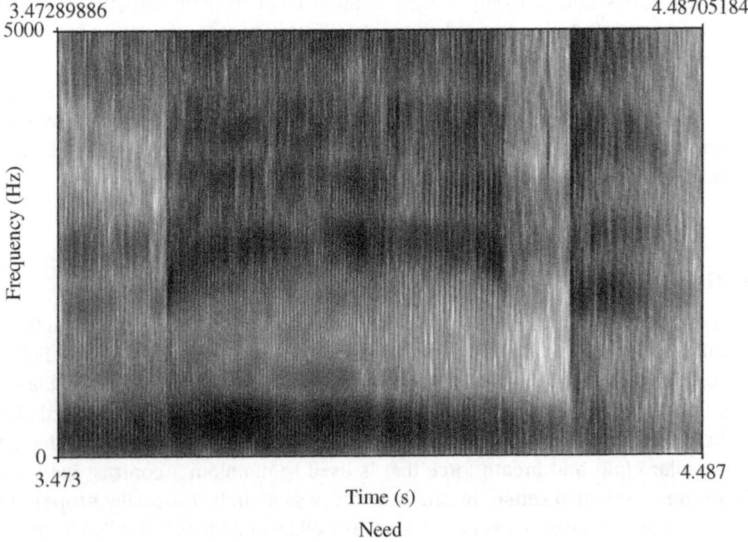

Figure 6 Spectrograms of *deed* and *need*

Fortition

Fortition is a phonological term that refers to a sound change in which a sound becomes stronger. It is the opposite of **lenition**, which is the process that refers to the weakening of a sound. The terms fortition and lenition may be used to describe historical sound change or synchronically to describe an **accent** or idiolect. Lass

(1984: 178) states that the most effective method of schematizing fortition/lenition is in terms of two strength scales: the first of openness of articulation and the second of sonority. Sounds made with a more open articulation are weaker than those made with a less open articulation. Sounds that are less sonorous are stronger than those that are more sonorous. Thus we have the following scale:

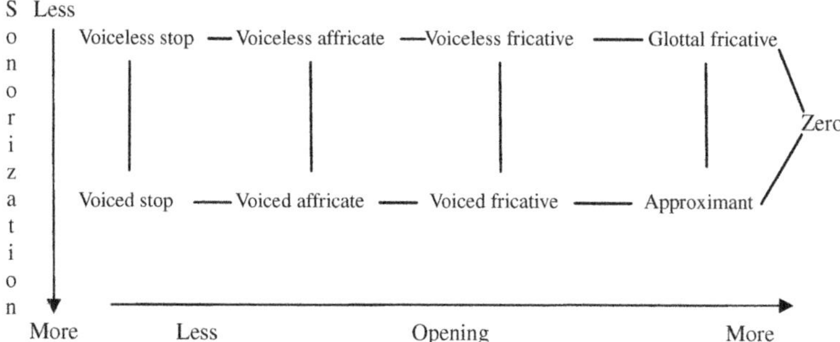

Figure 7 Fortition/lenition scale for oral consonants

To illustrate, a voiced affricate can be strengthened either by being articulated with a less open articulation as a voiced stop or by being made less sonorant and being articulated as a voiceless affricate. In German and Dutch, voiced obstruents are not found in syllable codas, for example, the Dutch and German words for Northwind, *noordenwind* and *Nordwind*, respectively, are pronounced with final [t] and not [d]. The historic final voiced obstruent has undergone a process of fortition and become voiceless. Lenition, however, is a more common sound change. In Celtic languages, initial mutation represents an oft quoted example of lenition, as in Lass (1984: 177), for example:

Root noun		His Noun		Lenition
/pɛn/	→	[ibɛn]	head	[p] → [b]
/braud/	→	[ivraud]	brother	[b] → [v]
/ɬɔŋ/	→	[ilɔŋ]	ship	[ɬ] → [l]

In Liverpool English, which has been strongly influenced by Celtic speakers from Ireland and Wales, the lenition of final stops is common, resulting in /p/, /t/, /k/ being realized as [ɸ], [s], [x], respectively (see Hughes, Trudgill and Watt 2005: 98). A further example of lenition widely heard in English is the realization of an intervocalic /t/ or /d/ as a **tap** /ɾ/. In basilectal London English, dark <L> may undergo lenition and be realized as a short back unrounded vowel [ɤ].

Free variation

Free variation is a phonological term that refers to the substitutability of one phone for another in a particular environment that does not result in a change in the word's meaning. Strictly speaking, in words such as *either* and *economic* the phonemes /iː/ and /aɪ/, and the phonemes /ɛ/ and /iː/ are in complementary distribution as /ˈiːðə/ and /ˈaɪðə/, and /ˌɛkəˈnɒmɪk/ and /ˌiːkəˈnɒmɪk/ realize identical lexical units. Wells (2000: 252 and 249) reports 1988 poll panel results which indicate that 88 per cent of UK speakers prefer /ˈaɪðə/ while conversely 84 per cent of US speakers prefer /ˈiːðə/; 62 per cent of British speakers prefer /ˌiːkəˈnɒmɪk/ and 38 per cent prefer /ˌɛkəˈnɒmɪk/.

However, as numerous sociolinguistic studies have demonstrated (Blom and Gumperz 2000; Trudgill 1974), overtly stated preferences are not always a reliable indicator of actual behaviour. People often produce pronunciations that they themselves claim not to prefer. While phonemically variations such as /ˈiːðə/ and /ˈaɪðə/ or even /bʌt/ and [bəʔ] may be free variation in the sense that it does not lead to new meaning, urban dialectologists have convincingly demonstrated that such variation is not actually free. Rather it is constrained by social and/or linguistic factors (see Chambers and Trudgill 1998: 49–50 for further information).

Frequency

Frequency is a term deriving from the study of the physics of sound and is used in **acoustic phonetics** to refer to the number of cycles of **vocal fold** vibration per second. It is measured in hertz with 1 Hz equalling 1 cycle per second (cps). The frequency of vocal fold vibration is perceived as **pitch**. The faster the vocal fold vibration, the higher the pitch is perceived as. On average, adult male speakers have lower pitch than adult females, who have lower pitch than prepubescent children. In other words, the rate of vibration of the vocal folds is lower for adult males than for adult females or prepubescent children – See **fundamental frequency**.

Fricative

A fricative is a term used to refer to the classification of a **consonant** on the basis of its manner of **articulation**. Fricatives are produced by a narrowing of the opening through which the airstream occurs. The two **articulators** approach so closely that the air moving between them produces audible friction. Fricatives may be **voiced** or **voiceless**. Fricatives can be articulated at the following places of **articulation**: **bilabial**, **labiodental**, **alveolar**, **dental**, **post-alveolar**, **retroflex**, **palatal**, **velar**, **uvular**, **pharygneal** and **glottal**. Fricatives are found in the vast majority of extant languages. Maddieson (2008a) reports that out of a survey of 567 languages only 49 did not contain a fricative phoneme. The absence of fricatives is a feature of Australian languages. Even the minority of Australian languages that have fricatives contain only a small number of **marked** fricatives such as a velar fricative in Tiwi, a language that in 1996 was spoken by around 1800 'non-fluent' speakers in the Northern Territory.

English contains a large number of fricatives all of which, with the exception of the glottal fricative, contrast for voicing. The English fricative **phonemes** are /f/, /v/, /s/, /z/, /θ/, /ð/, /ʃ/, /ʒ/ and /h/. The dental fricatives /θ/ and /ð/ are very rare cross-linguistically. Maddieson (2008b) reports that only 43 out of 567 languages surveyed contained dental fricative phonemes.

While there are few significant regional variants of the English fricative phonemes, the most significant dialectal features are listed below.

- In traditional West-Country speech word initial /f/, /s/, /θ/ and /ʃ/ may be replaced by their voiced counterparts /v/, /z/, /ð/ and /ʒ/. Wells (1982b: 343) provides the following examples: *farm, thimble, seven* and *shepherd* realized as [vɑːɹm], [ˈðɪmbəl], [ˈzɛvɛn] and [ˈʒɛpəɹd], though he notes that such pronunciations are 'sharply regressive' and presently more stereotypical than authentic (also see Altendorf and Watt 2008: 219).
- In present day Southern Irish speech /θ/ and /ð/ are often pronounced as **dental stops**.
- In basilectal London speech /θ/ and /ð/ may be fronted and replaced with [f] and [v]. A pronunciation such as [fɪŋk] could represent a homophonous realization of *fink* or *think* for non-Cockney speakers. However, despite this, Cockney speakers still maintain an underlying phonemic distinction between the four fricatives /f/, /v/, /θ/ and /ð/. The fronting of the dental fricatives remains socially stigmatized and has traditionally been absent from the accents of middle-class speakers. However, recent surveys have found evidence that the labiodental fricative may be replacing the dental fricative even in the speech of middle-class speakers of both genders (Williams and Kerswill 1999: 160).
- In the Southern states of the US labiodental fricatives are reported as replacing dental fricatives, as in Gimson (2008: 196). However, Wells (1982c: 553) claims that the fronting of dental fricatives only occurs in lower-class and particularly African American speech. Thomas (2008: 108) agrees with Wells that in African American speech /θ/ and /ð/ are often realized as [f] and [v] but adds that occasionally rural white speakers may realize /θ/ as [f]. Neither Tillery and Bailey (2008) nor Labov, Ash and Boberg (2006) in their description of the Urban Southern American accent discuss the substitution of dental fricatives by labiodental ones. Thus, we can conclude that it is not likely to be a widespread feature of the speech of Southern speakers. Conversely, Edwards (2008: 186) states that in African American vernacular English /θ/ and /ð/ may be realized by [f] and [v], though they are more likely to be realized by [t] and [d].
- Many basilectal urban accents of England, South Wales and Australia do not have the phoneme /h/.

As /ʒ/ has a relatively limited distribution within the English phonemic system, the pronunciation of words containing /ʒ/ sometimes varies. The cluster [zj] in word medial position and the **affricate** /dʒ/ in word initial position may be pronounced instead of /ʒ/. The following variant pronunciations are possible:

genre	[ˈʒɛnɹə]	[ˈdʒɛnɹə]
azure	[ˈæʒə]	[ˈæzjə]

In words of Gaelic or Scots origin, Scottish English contains an extra phoneme /x/ that allows the Scottish speakers to distinguish *lock* /lɒk/ and *Loch* /lɒx/. These words are homophonous in other accents of English.

Frictionless continuant

A frictionless continuant is a term used to refer to the classification of a **consonant** on the basis of its manner of **articulation**. See **approximant**.

Fundamental frequency

Fundamental frequency is a term used in **acoustic phonetics** to refer to the rate of vocal fold vibration and is notated as (F_0). It is measured in hertz. In a periodic sound such as a vowel, F_0 is the lowest harmonic in the sound wave. The higher harmonics will be whole-number multiples of the F_0 value. Thus, if F_0 is 100 Hz, the first harmonic will be 200 Hz, the second 300 Hz and so on. If the F_0 is 300 Hz, the first harmonic will be 600 Hz and the second 900 Hz, etc. The combination of F_0 and the amplitude of its various harmonics combine to give an individual sound its particular spectral quality. In other words, regardless of the actual F_0 value, the individual sound will have a consistent spectral shape that hearers can identify. F_0 is central to the study of **intonation** where changes in F_0 value correlate with perceived changes in pitch movement.

Generative phonology

Generative phonology is a hugely influential model of phonology that is closely associated with the work of Noam Chomsky and Morris Halle. Their joint views are most fully described in Chomsky and Halle (1968), hereinafter **spe**. Today, generative phonology as practised in **spe** has become outmoded, but the influence and spirit of **spe** remains as an important underpinning of modern schools of generative phonology such as **autosegmental phonology** and **optimality theory**, and see **distinctive feature theory**. This section sketches the approach set out in **spe** in order to illustrate the underpinnings of modern generative theory.

Generative phonology began as a reaction to the then prevailing structuralist paradigm. It forms part of the Chomskyan revolution in linguistics (for further information see Lyons 1991, which argued for a model that could satisfactorily generate all possible utterances in natural language). Generative grammar, including phonology, is a model of linguistic competence. It is concerned with the set of rules inside speakers' heads that allow them to transform the stored mental entities into instructions into how to pronounce the segments that make up their speech. Figure 8 details a model of a generative grammar and illustrates the role of phonology in the wider grammar.

Deep structure is generated by the base component that in the original model did not have a phonological or semantic component. Later models, as indicated by the dashed arrow, linked the semantic component, logical form, directly to the base component. A series of rules transform the deep structure representations into surface structures, which are then passed on to the semantic and phonological components prior to being uttered. In all generative models, phonological structures are fed by the syntactic component and fulfil the role of spelling out the intended utterance.

The phonetic representation component of the grammar is itself formed of a series of underlying forms that are generated through the operation of a series of linearly ordered rules. Phonological rules may be ordered in either a *bleeding* or *feeding* manner. In a bleeding order, the application of an earlier rule constrains the operation of a later rule. In a feeding order, the operation of an earlier rule enlarges the contexts in which a later rule can operate. For instance some languages, including English, have a rule of the form that **velars** are palatalized before front vowels. Thus, the insertion by an earlier rule of a front vowel between a consonant and velar consonant feeds the rule that palatalizes velars.

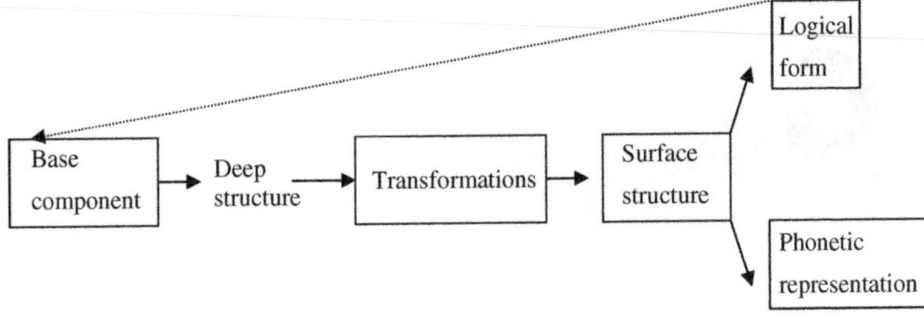

Figure 8 A generative model of grammar adapted from Chomsky (1990: 165)

The following example describes two languages, one of which palatalizes and one that doesn't:

Language A		**Language B**	
Input	C K[1]	Input	CK
Front vowel epenthesis	CVK	Palatalization	CK (Rule cannot operate)
Palatalization	CVX	Front vowel epenthesis	CVK

The different output in both languages is caused solely by the sequencing of the rules.

The minimal unit in *phonetic representation* is the distinctive feature. Distinctive features are stored at the level of underlying lexical representations as a series of phonological matrices. For example:

Egg	ɛ	g
Consonantal	–	+
Vocalic	+	–
Tense	–	–
Voice	+	+
High	–	+
Low	–	–
Continuant	+	–

The phonological matrices stored as underlying lexical forms pass through a series of linearly ordered rules that derive a phonetic representation, which is sent as neural instructions to the articulators and then pronounced as speech sounds. The following data illustrates the complexity of explicating the underlying representations of a form, in this case the Indonesian prefix that transforms nouns into verbs.

When we consider the data, one of the most obvious points is that the form of the prefix in numbers 10–17 is affected by the place of **articulation** of the following consonant. Thus:

Table 15 Indonesian prefixed data

	Noun	**Verb**	**Meaning**
1.	lempar	məlempar	'throw'
2.	rasa	mərasa	'feel'
3.	wakil	məwakil	'represent'
4.	jakin	məjakin	'convince'
5.	masak	məmasak	'cook'
6.	nikah	mənikah	'marry'
7.	ŋaco	məŋaco	'chat'
8.	ɲaɲi	məɲaɲi	'sing'
9.	hituŋ	məŋhituŋ	'count'
10.	gambar	məŋgambar	'draw a picture'
11.	kirim	məŋirim	'send'
12.	dəŋar	məndəŋar	'hear'
13.	tulis	mənulis	'write'
14.	bantu	məmbantu	'help'
15.	pukul	məmukul	'hit'
16.	d͡ʒahit	məɲd͡ʒahit	'sew'
17.	t͡ʃatat	məɲt͡ʃatat	'note down'
18.	ambil	məŋambil	'take'
19.	isi	məŋisi	'fill up'
20.	undaŋ	məŋundaŋ	'invite'

Initial consonant of the stem	**Final consonant of the prefix**	**For example**
bilabial	bilabial	məmbantu
alveolar	alveolar	məndəjar
palato-alveolar	palatal	məɲd͡ʒahit
velar	velar	məŋgambar

These facts allow us to propose an anticipatory assimilation rule, which states that the final nasal of the prefix assimilates to the place of **articulation** of the initial consonant of the stem. If we look at examples 11, 13 and 15 we note that the initial consonant of the stem is elided in the prefixed verbal form. To account for these facts we can propose a deletion rule in which the initial consonant of the stem is deleted if it is voiceless. Examples one to eight in Table 15 are of interest in that in each case the prefix does not contain a nasal. To account for these facts we can propose a second deletion rule, which states that if the initial consonant of the nominal base is [+ Sonorant] the final nasal of the prefix is deleted. This leaves us with only five examples and in each case the prefix is [məŋ], which represents the underlying lexical form. To summarize the relevant rules:

(1) An assimilation rule: assimilate the final nasal consonant of the prefix to the place of **articulation** of the following consonant.

(2) Deletion rule A: delete voiceless stops after the final nasal consonant of the prefix.

(3) Deletion rule B: delete the final nasal consonant of the prefix before a non-vocalic sonorant.

Thus, the data can be explained as follows:

Input [məŋ]

Noun →	Verb →	Rule 1 →	Rule 2 →	Rule 3
lempar →	məŋ lempar →	. . . . →	. . . . →	məlempar
rasa →	məŋ rasa →	. . . . →	. . . . →	mərasa
wakil →	məŋ wakil →	. . . . →	. . . . →	məwakil
jakin →	məŋ jakin →	. . . . →	. . . . →	məjakin
masak →	məŋ masak →	. . . . →	. . . . →	məŋ masak
nikah →	məŋ nikah →	. . . . →	. . . . →	mənikah
ŋaco →	məŋ ŋaco →	. . . . →	. . . . →	məŋaco
ɲaɲi →	məŋ ɲaɲi →	. . . . →	. . . . →	məɲaɲi
hituŋ→	məŋ hituŋ→	. . . . →	. . . . →	. . . .
gambar →	məŋgambar →	. . . . →	. . . . →	. . . .
kirim →	məŋ kirim →	. . . . →	məŋirim →	. . . .
dəŋar →	məŋ dəŋar →	mən dəŋar →	. . . . →	. . . .
tulis →	məŋ tulis →	mən tulis →	mənulis →	. . . .
bantu →	məŋ bantu →	məmbantu →	. . . . →	. . . .
pukul →	məŋ pukul →	məmpukul →	məmukul →	. . . .
d͡ʒahit →	məŋ d͡ʒahit →	məɲ d͡ʒahit →	. . . . →	. . . .
t͡ʃatat →	məŋ t͡ʃatat →	məɲ t͡ʃatat →	. . . . →	. . . .
ambil →	məŋ ambil →	. . . . →	. . . . →	. . . .
isi →	məŋ isi →	. . . . →	. . . . →	. . . .
undaŋ→	məŋ undaŋ→	. . . . →	. . . . →	. . . .

While there is no doubt that **spe** succeeds in elegantly capturing many of the facts of how language is pronounced, it has fallen out of favour for a number of reasons. The first and most serious is that while the blind phonological component in an **spe** generative grammar produces a well-formed word by taking an input string generated by the prior morphosyntactic component and applying linearly phonological rules, which result in a well-formed word, it is unable to specify why some nonsense words such as *strit*, but not *sftit, ftsit, stfti* or *tfsit*, are **phonotactically** legal words in English.

In addition, many of the proposed underlying forms seem unnatural and counterintuitive to native speakers. Chomsky and Halle (ibid.: 191–2) propose that the underlying form of *coin* contains not the expected **diphthong** /ɔɪ/ but rather the vowel /œ/, which never surfaces in any form of English. They further propose (ibid.: 233–5) that /x/ is found in the underlying representation of the word *right*. Their argument is partly based on the following set of examples, with both the verb and the stem of the derived adjectival or nominal element sharing the same underlying representation[2]:

expedite /ˈɛkspədaɪt/	expedit+ious	/ˌɛkspədɪʃ + əs/
ignite /ɪgˈnaɪt/	ignit+ion	/ɪgˈnɪʃ + ən/
delight /dɪˈlaɪt/	delic+ious	/dɪˈlɪʃ + əs/

The addition of the stem creates a phonetic context that allows for the operation of, first, the *spirantization* rule, which changes the stem final /t/ to /s/ and, second, the *palatalization* rule, which changes the /s/ to /ʃ/ (ibid.: 229–30). It is clear that the lexical items *right* and the derived form *righteous* share the same underlying form. But if the shared underlying form is /ɹɪt/ the derived form after the operation of the spirantization and palatalization rules should be the incorrect form /ɹaɪʃ + əs/ when in fact it is /ɹaɪtʃ + əs/. To account for these facts, they propose that the underlying form of *right* is /ɹɪxt/. The presence of the fricative /x/ blocks the spirantization of /t/. Instead /t/ is palatalized and becomes /tʃ/. A later rule deletes the velar fricative /x/. The resulting underlying form /ɹɪxt/, Chomsky and Halle concede, is unpronounceable for English speakers, though they do not see any reason why underlying forms should be naturally pronounceable.

Glide

A glide is a phonetic term for the audible transition from one sound to another. If the sound is a transition to a following sound it is known as an on-glide. If it is a transition away from a preceding sound it is known as an off-glide. In English, [w] and [j] in the words *will* /wɪl/ and *tune* /tjuːn/ are on-glides. Some scholars include only consonants under the term glide and restrict the glides to /w/ and /j/, as in Lodge (2009). However, others such as Collins and Mees (2008) use the term to refer to the second element of **diphthongs**. In /aɪ/, /ɔɪ/, /eɪ/, /ɑʊ/ /əʊ/ the second element of the vowel represents an off-glide.

Glottal

The term **glottal** refers to the classification of a **consonant** sound on the basis of the place of **articulation** of the sound. Glottal consonants are made in the larynx due to the closure or the narrowing of the **glottis.** Physiologically, only the glottal stop /ʔ/ and **voiceless** and **voiced fricatives** /h, ɦ/ are possible. The voiceless fricative /h/ is phonemic in English. Between vowels in words such as *ahead* or *ahoy* the /h/ is realized as the voiced [ɦ]. While it is theoretically possible for a language to have both voiced and voiceless glottal fricatives, there does not seem to be any language that contrasts words by substituting voiced and voiceless glottal fricatives. Glottal fricatives are relatively common across languages, with the voiceless fricative being the most common option. Languages such as Czech and Dutch, however, contain voiced glottal fricative phonemes.

Ladefoged (2001: 254) argues that [h] and [ɦ] represent transitions into a syllable. Accordingly there is little or no friction produced at the glottis. He proposes that [h] and [ɦ] should be considered to be consonants produced by a state of the glottis rather than consonants produced at the glottis (see also Laver 1994: 267, who does not include the place glottal in his list of possible fricatives).

G

In English /h/ has a highly restricted distribution. It can only appear syllable initially. It does not appear in any consonant clusters, with the possible exception of the relic form /hw/ as in older pronunciations of *whine*, which are not homophonous with *wine* – but see **labialvelar**. Perhaps because of its restricted distribution /h/ is lost in most basilectal forms of accents in England, South Wales and Australia, though not in America, Canada – though Wells (1982c: 501) reports <h> dropping in Newfoundland – Ireland and Scotland. Mugglestone (2003: ch. 4) is an enlightening account of the use of [h] as a marker of social differentiation from the 1600s to the present day. She notes, for instance, widespread views held even by renowned nineteenth-century phoneticians that the pronunciation of [h] was 'an almost infallible test of education and refinement' (ibid.: 95). Even today, Upton (2008b: 279) notes that <h> dropping is generally taken to be a marker of working-class speech.

Numerous languages from unrelated language families such as Arabic, German, Hausa, Hebrew, Persian and Thai have a glottal stop phoneme. A glottal stop is produced by bringing the vocal folds together and cutting off the airstream from the lungs. We make glottal stops when we cough or hold our breath. English does not contain a glottal stop phoneme, though glottal stops are commonly heard as allophones for /t/ in all accents of English. Despite this, the use of glottal stops has traditionally been pilloried as vulgar, though with the more recent fashionability of **estuary english** glottal stops are, in Wells's words, 'becoming respectable' (1994: 201). It is worth noting that, since Wells's comment, the UK has had a prime minister notorious for his (ab)use of glottal stops (Altendorf n.d.).

Traditionally there have been a number of separate types of glottal stop usage in **received pronunciation**. The first is labelled *regular glottal reinforcement* (Gimson 2008: 179). The glottal stop functions as a marker of a syllable boundary between vowels. For instance, in the word *reactor* some speakers may produce a glottal stop to reinforce the syllable boundary, thus: ['ɹiːʔætə]. In syllables beginning with an **accented** vowel a glottal may be inserted to reinforce the new syllable, for instance in the utterances *I haven't been anywhere* and *Her cooking is inedible* the words *anywhere* and *inedible* may be pronounced as ['ʔɛniweə] and [ɪn'ʔɛdəbəl]. A further common form of glottal reinforcement, thought one not found among Upper RP speakers, is where a voiceless stop or voiceless affricate may be reinforced by a glottal stop, as in *ripe, right, bank* and *preach* pronounced as [ɹaɪʔp], [ɹaɪʔt], [bænʔk] and [pɹiːʔtʃ]. Wells (1982a: 260) notes that the glottal reinforcement of a voiceless stop or affricate is more commonly associated with accents from the North rather than the South of England. Trudgill (2008: 189) notes that in many accents of South East England intervocalic and word final /p/ and /k/ may be glottalized. Speakers make simultaneous oral and glottal closures, and inaudibly release the oral closure prior to audibly releasing the glottal closure. Thus, we have the following pronunciations *rap* [ɹæpʔ], *pepper* ['pʰɛpʔə], *bake* [beɪkʔ] and *baker* [beɪkʔə].

In many urban accents of British English and rural accents in the South of England before a consonant or word boundary or **syllabic nasal**, and in GA before a syllabic nasal, glottal stops often replace [t]. Thus we may find the following pronunciations: *bright moon* ['bɹaɪʔmuːn], *bright light* ['bɹaɪʔlaɪt] *buttress* ['bʌʔɹəs], *fights* [faɪʔs] and *mutton* ['mʌʔn̩]. Traditional basilectal London speech goes further and allows [ʔ] to replace [t] when the stop is followed within the same word by a vowel, as in *butter* ['bʌʔə].

Glottalic

The term glottalic refers to an **airstream mechanism** that originates in the **glottis**. For a sound to be produced by a glottalic airstream mechanism there can be no respiratory activity. The flow of air originating in the glottis can be either **egressive** or **ingressive**. The larynx with the glottis closed is the initiator of the airstream. The larynx that is equipped with its own muscles can move upwards or downwards in the throat. With the glottis closed, the movement of the larynx is akin to that of a plunger. When moved downwards it draws air inwards and when moved upwards it pushes air outwards. Sounds produced with air pushed outwards are known as **ejectives**. Useful and readable descriptions of the glottalic airstream mechanism can be found in Abercrombie (1967: 28–9) and Laver (1994: 171–3).

Glottis

The glottis is the space or aperture between the **vocal folds**. There are five commonly described ways in which the size and shape of the glottis can be altered. If the vocal folds are far apart the glottis is open and **egressive** air is able to travel unimpeded into the lungs. This results in the production of a **voiceless** sound. If the vocal folds are shut tightly together, the glottis is closed and air is blocked from entering the mouth as in a glottal stop. The glottis may be partially closed in three different ways. First, the vocal folds may be held closely together though not close enough to block the airstream mechanism. This results in the production of a **voiced** sound. Second, the vocal folds may be held more tightly together than for the production of a **voiced** sound but not sufficiently close together to stop the airstream mechanism. This results in the production of a **breathy voice**. Finally, the vocal folds may be held tightly together at one end but are free to vibrate at the other end. This results in the production of a **creaky voice**.

Grave

This term has three distinct meanings. The first is slightly old-fashioned and is used in descriptions of **tone languages** to refer to a falling lexical tone. The second meaning is used in some accounts of **intonation** to describe a falling tone movement. The third meaning refers to one of the features of a sound in a version of **distinctive feature** theory (see Jakobson and Halle 1956). It involves an articulation made in the peripheries of the mouth, which has a concentration of acoustic energy in the lower frequencies such as back vowels, and labial and velar consonants.

Great Vowel Shift

The Great Vowel Shift (GVS) refers to a series of **sound changes** that led to a restructuring of the English long **vowel** system. It occurred between the fifteenth and eighteenth centuries. There is some controversy in the literature as to whether the GVS can be described as a single unified event or whether the vowel changes that occurred represented a series of unrelated changes. See Lass (1976) for an argument supporting the former position, and Stockwell and Minkova (1988) for an argument supporting the latter position. McMahon (2006) is a useful summary of both positions.

The changes to the English vowel system resulted in English having a particularly opaque relationship between the written spelling of a word and its pronunciation. For instance, the letters <ea> in words such as *tea, speak* and *mean* are pronounced with an /iː/ vowel, but in words such as *tear* and *spear* they are pronounced with an /ɪə/ vowel, while in words such as *great* and *steak* they are pronounced with an /eɪ/ vowel. This disjunction is a direct result of the changes that took place in the English vowel system between the fifteenth and eighteenth centuries. Table 16 contrasts the Middle English long vowel system with the Modern English one.

It is clear that the vowel system has changed as a result of a chain shift. The change has resulted in [+ high] vowels being diphthongized and the other vowels as a consequence becoming closer. Figure 9 illustrates.

While the overall direction of change is apparent, it is by no means clear why and how the GVS started. The two most common theories aiming to describe how the GVS occurred are the *pull chain* and the *push chain* theories. The pull chain theory claims that the initial vowels that changed were /iː/ and /uː/, which were diphthongized. The vacant high vowel spaces were filled by [eː] and [oː], which became [iː] and [uː]. The movement of the mid-high vowels pulled up the remaining long vowels and [ɛː] became [eː], [ɔː] became [oː] and [aː] became [ɛː]. The alternate theory, the push chain, argues that the mid-high vowels [eː] and [oː] shifted upwards and became [iː] and [uː], respectively. The original [+ High]

Table 16 Middle vs. Modern English vowel system, from McMahon (2006: 155)

	Middle English	**Modern English**
time	/tiːm/	/taɪm/
green	/gɹeːn/	/gɹiːn/
break	/bɹɛːk/	/bɹeɪk/
name	/naːmə/	/neɪm/
day	/deː/	/deɪ/
loud	/luːd/	/laud/
boot	/boːt/	/buːt/
boat	/bɔːt/	/bəʊt/
law	/lau/	/lɔː/

G

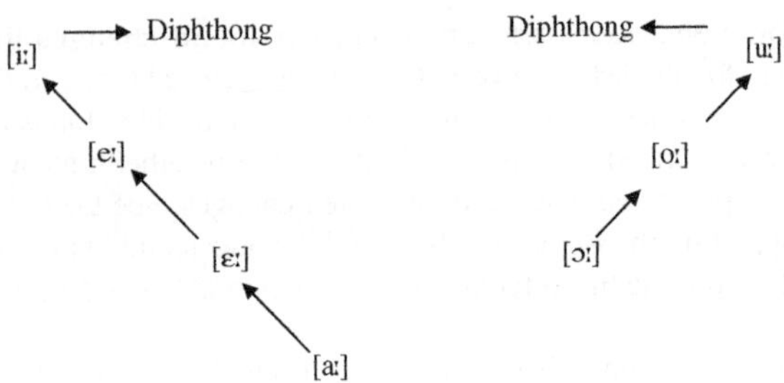

Figure 9 The Great Vowel Shift

vowels diphthongized in order to maintain the sound contrast. The vowels below the mid-high vowels were pushed up into the higher slot, for example, [ɛː] → [eː], [aː] → [ɛː] and [ɔː] → [oː].

Both theories are necessarily based on scant written data, which means that little if anything can be said about (1) what may have caused the vowel system to shift; (2) what order the shift may have taken; (3) whether or not the vowel shift occurred in a regular manner in different dialects.

One known fact of modern day English that is of probable relevance to the workings of the GVS is that in present day Scottish English the expected GVS diphthongization of /iː/ to /aɪ/ has occurred, for instance *time*, is pronounced as /taɪm/ and not /tɪːm/, but the expected diphthongization of /uː/ to /aʊ/ has not occurred, for example, *house* is pronounced as /huːs/ and not /haʊs/. This indicates that it is highly unlikely that the GVS operated in an identical manner in all varieties of English. In the case of Scottish English it is likely that the [oː] vowel had been previously fronted and was not operating as part of the long back vowel system. In its absence there was no non-high back vowel to move towards high back position and trigger the diphthongization of [uː]. This data is evidence, at least for [+ back] monophthongs in Scottish English, against the *pull chain* theory as the presence or absence of [oː] should be immaterial as a trigger for the diphthongization of [uː].

Harmony

Harmony is a phonological term that is used to refer to the way the articulation of one phonological unit is influenced by the presence of another unit in the same word or phrase – see **assimilation**. There are three kinds of harmony: **vowel** harmony, **consonant** harmony and **tone** harmony. Many African languages belonging to one of the major language families, *Niger-Congo, Nilo-Saharan* and *Afro-Asiatic* are known as harmony languages because the vowels within words including prefixes and suffixes have to agree with one another in terms of certain **features** (Maddieson 2008d). Other languages that contain vowel harmony are *Finnish* and *Turkish*. For instance, Lodge (2009: 151ff.) gives the following example of Turkish vowel harmony:

1. [i] or [e] must by followed by [i] or [e] within the same lexical item, for instance, /kibɾitleɾ/, /deɾcen/, /veɾdileɾ/ and /biɾbirleɾinden/.
2. [ɯ] or [a] must be followed by [ɯ] or [a] within the same lexical item, as in /atʃtɯ/, daha/, /kɯbɾɯs/ and /kɯbɾɯsta/.
3. [y] or [œ] must be followed by [y] or [e] within the same lexical item, for example, /tytyn/, /tytyndʒe/, /bœjledʒe/ and /œksyrmek/.
4. [u] or [o] must be followed by [u] or [a] within the same lexical item, as in /hukukdʒu/, /sonunda/ and /pojɾazala/.

In Turkish, with the exception of words borrowed from other languages, the presence of a vowel constrains the presence of all following vowels within the same lexical item. Unrounded front close or close-mid vowels can only be followed within the word by other vowels that are also unrounded close or close-mid and front. Back, close unrounded vowels and front, open unrounded vowels can only be followed by either a close unrounded vowel or a front open unrounded vowel. Front rounded vowels can only be followed by either a close front rounded vowel or a close-mid unrounded vowel. Back rounded vowels can only be followed by either a close back rounded vowel or a front open unrounded vowel. No other combination of vowels is allowable in words that are of native Turkish origin.

Consonant harmony appears to be far rarer than vowel harmony though Laver (1994: 388) suggests that the fact that vowel harmony is more recognized may simply be the result of the greater perceptual salience of vowels as compared with consonants. In languages that have consonant harmony, the presence of a type of consonant constrains the type of consonant that can appear later in the word. For instance, Laver (ibid.) argues that in the Niger-Congo language *Etsako* (or *Yekhee*), spoken by around 275,000 speakers in Nigeria,[1] consonants form into three sets: those that are **tense** /w m v z r ñ k g/, those that are **lax**[2] /wh mh vh zh rh ñh kh gh/ and those that are neither /p b f t d s l n j ɥ k͡p g͡b/. With a very small number of exceptions, tense consonants can only be followed by non-lax consonants and lax consonants can only be followed by non-tense consonants. Thus, Laver reports that, with a very small number of exceptions, a morpheme may only contain consonants from the tense and neutral sets or the lax and neutral sets. Consonants from the lax and tense sets are prohibited within the same morpheme.

Among the world's **tone** languages tone harmony, known as *downstep* or *downdrift*, is quite common in African tone languages. The presence of a low tone perseveres and influences the phonetic realization of any following high tones. Yip (2002: 149) provides the following example taken from *Efik*, a Niger-Congo language spoken predominately in Nigeria by around 400,000 people:

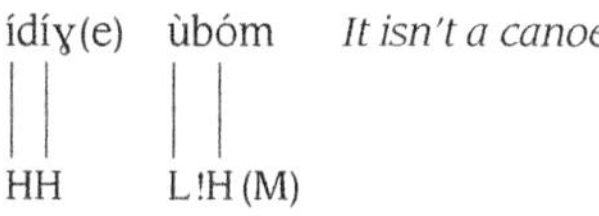

The final phonological high tone is lowered and realized phonetically as a mid tone – intermediate between a high and a low tone. The opposite (and far rarer) phenomena is known as *upstep*; the presence of a later low tone causes an earlier high tone to be phonetically realized higher than normal. Downstep is notated in the literature by '!' and upstep by '↑'. The following example from Yip (ibid.: 150) illustrates:

/únwónì/ → [ú↑nwónì] *mouth*

H↑ H L

In the example taken from *Engenni*, a Niger-Congo language spoken by around 20,000 people in Nigeria, the presence of the final low tone raises the high tone in a preceding syllable.

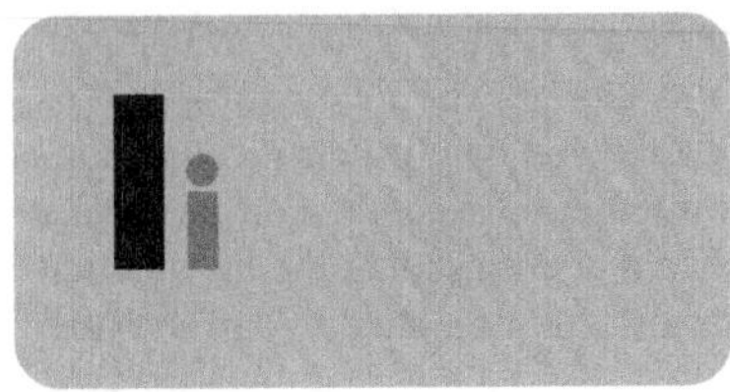

Implosive

An implosive is a **stop** that is produced by a flow of air initiated by an **ingressive airstream mechanism**. Implosives are produced when a closure is made in the vocal tract as with any stop, for example, /b/, /d/ or /g/. In the usual case the **glottis** is simultaneously closed. However, the air behind the closure is not compressed. Instead the larynx moves down, which results in a lowering of the pressure for the air trapped in the mouth. Upon release of the closure, air rushes into the mouth to equalize the air pressure inside and outside the body. It is the combination of the inrushing air and eggressive air produced by the opening of the glottis that results in the articulation of the implosive.

While voiced implosives are classified as being made on an ingressive airstream mechanism, the air that is pushing up through the glottis may be sufficiently great to prevent an ingressive flow occurring after the release of the stop closure. This has led many scholars, such as O'Connor (1973), Laver (1994) and Lodge (2009) to state that voiced implosives are powered by a complex airstream mechanism combining a glottalic ingressive mechanism with a pulmonic egressive mechanism. Yet there seems to be unanimity within the literature that the ingressive airstream is the distinguishing feature of voiced implosives. Hence voiced implosives can be classified as ingressive stops.

Ladefoged and Maddieson (1996: 82) report that implosive stops occur in around 10 per cent of the world's languages and are a feature of West African languages. For many years it was believed that implosives and **ejective** stops did not contrast in any language at the place of articulation. However, Uduk, a Nilo-Saharan language, is reported to have **bilabial** and **alveolar** contrasts of implosive and ejective stops. Implosives are symbolized by a special symbol formed by adding a hook to the symbol for the corresponding oral stop symbol. For example:

/ɓ/	/ɗ/	/ɠ/
bilabial implosive	alveolar implosive	velar implosive

The most common type of implosive stop found cross-linguistically is the bilabial. Implosives formed in the back of the mouth are much rarer. It was commonly believed that implosives must be voiced, but Ladefoged (2005: 150) reports the existence of a few languages that have both voiced and voiceless implosives, including the Owerri dialect of Igbo. The CD attached to his book is a very useful resource for readers interested in hearing how implosives differ from **aspirated** and **unaspirated** stops. Ladefoged notes the following range of contrasts between bilabial stops and bilabial implosives found in Owerri Igbo (ibid.: 151) – see also **phonation**.

Voiced	íba	*(to get rich)*
Voiceless unaspirated	ípa	*(to carry)*
Aspirated	ípʰà	*(to squeeze)*
Breathy voiced	íbʱà	*(to peel)*
Voiceless implosive	íɓ̥a	*(to gather)*
Voiced implosive	iɓa	*(to dance)*

It is worth noticing that because of the acoustic similarity between the voiced and voiceless implosives a more significant phonemic contrast between the lexical items *to gather* and *to dance* seems to be the difference in **lexical tone**.

Ingressive

An ingressive is a speech sound that is articulated using an inwards moving **airstream mechanism**. There are only two types of ingressive sounds that are part of the **phonemic** systems of some languages, namely **implosives** and **clicks**. Yet, speech powered by an ingressive mechanism is relatively common though incidental. People engaged in strenuous physical activity may produce ingressive speech. More interestingly, people produce ingressive speech that signals paralinguistic meaning. Speakers in the Western Isles may signal agreement by producing the syllable [ja] with an ingressive airstream. Their use of the ingressive airstream signals that their agreement is both summative and empathetic (T. Bartlett, personal communication). Laver (1994: 169ff.) reports similar paralinguistic uses of ingressive speech in numerous languages including Norwegian and Danish, and states that an ingressive [ja], depending on the context, projects sympathy or consideration. An ingressive [nɑɪ] signals sympathy.

Catford (1977: 68) notes that an ingressive **pulmonic** airstream is a less efficient mode of **phonation** than an egressive pulmonic airstream. It results in 'a croaking type' of voiced stop. Dieth (1950) (reported in Catford 1977) describes the 'Swiss-German custom of Fensterle', whereby a village boy speaking to his sweetheart disguises his voice from her parents by speaking with an ingressive airstream mechanism. Catford reports personally hearing Greek-speaking mummers, celebrating feast days in Cyprus, producing speech with an ingressive airstream mechanism to disguise their voices (Catford 2001: 30). The same custom exists in Greece among mummers celebrating the carnival immediately prior to Lent. The present author has heard juvenile mummers in Athens disguising their voices through the use of an ingressive airstream mechanism.

Initiator

An initiator is a term used in **articulatory phonetics** to refer to a **vocal organ** that is the source of the air movement used to power speech. Theoretically, any vocal organ can initiate a speech sound but, in practice, the lungs are the usual initiators of speech. In addition, the larynx and the tongue function as the initiators of some major classes of speech sounds in language. See **airstream mechanism**, **pulmonic**, **glottalic** and **velaric**.

Intensity

The intensity of a sound is the amount of energy transferred through the air at a particular point. It is related to **amplitude** in the following way. If a molecule is vibrating at 100 Hz around its place of rest and the amplitude is subsequently doubled, the molecule must travel a distance that is twice as far in both directions in order to complete a cycle from place of rest to place of rest. If the frequency is held constant, the air molecule must complete the cycle in the same amount of time. Hence it must move faster and the amount of energy expended in completing a cycle is increased. The relationship between an increased amplitude and increased intensity is that the intensity of a sound is proportional to the square of the amplitude. Doubling the amplitude increases the intensity by four times, while trebling the amplitude increases the intensity by nine times.

The range of energy used in producing a speech sound is very large. It is not uncommon for a very quiet sound to be a billion or 10^{10} times quieter than a shout. It is therefore impractical to measure the intensity of sounds on an absolute scale. Instead, the intensity of one sound is compared with the intensity of another sound using a logarithmic scale, the decibel scale. The decibel scale works as follows. If there are two sounds and the second sound is 100 times more intense than the previous one the ratio of intensity between the sounds is $1{:}10^2$. The difference of intensity – in this case the power^2 – is multiplied by 10, the deci of the decibel scale, resulting in a difference between the sounds of 20 db.

Interdental

Interdental is a term used in the **phonetic** classification of **consonants**. It refers to a **fricative** made with the tip of the tongue protruding between the teeth. Within languages, interdentals and **dentals** are in complementary distribution. American pronunciations of /θ/ and /ð/ tend to be interdental while British pronunciations tend to be dental.

Intonation

Intonation refers to the linguistic patterning of **pitch**, which rises and falls in spoken discourse. Intonation functions to (1) organize information, (2) realize communicative function, (3) express speaker's attitudes towards a proposition, (4) disambiguate syntactic structure, (5) create paragraph structure and (6) identify some spoken genres (see Tench 1996 for a full description). Intonation is usefully described in terms of tonality, tonicity and tone (Halliday 1967; Halliday 1970; Halliday and Greaves 2008).

Tonality refers to the speaker's segmentation of the speech signal into tone units. Each tone unit realizes a single quantum of information and in the unmarked case is coterminous with a clause. Thus, we would expect that a speaker would divide the following utterances as:

|| I'll get up soon ||
|| I'll get up soon || and leave my bed unmade ||

Crystal (1969: 170), who found that 60 per cent of all pauses in the speech stream occurred at clause boundaries or between elements of clause structure, offers some statistical support for the coterminosity of tone units and clauses. Many occurrences of marked tonality are, however, relatively predictable and involve the placing of an adverbial or circumstantial element into its own tone unit, for example:

|| I'm going to visit my sister || this week ||

The circumstance seems to have been projected as an afterthought. It is incidental information subservient to the significant information that the speaker visited their sister.

|| This week || I'm going to visit my sister ||

The circumstance has been projected as being of more significance. Perhaps the speaker has been promising to visit their sister for an extended period and is finally about to do so. Cruttenden (1997) notes that clause-modifying viewpoint adjuncts such as *officially, technically, fortunately* and *incidentally* are often placed in their own tone units where they project a minor addition to the clause. Other instances of marked tonality realize more unpredictable meaning, for example:

|| I'll get up soon || and leave my bed || unmade ||.

The placement of *unmade* into its own tone unit projects an ambiguous context. It is not clear if it is the speaker or the bed that is unmade.

Tone units tend to be short pieces of information with a duration of less than two seconds. They tend to be bounded by pauses and usually contain between one and three **accented** syllables, though tone units with five or six accented syllables are possible. The last accented syllable within the tone unit is known as the tonic syllable or nucleus. It serves as the focus of the new information within the tone/information unit. The tonic syllable is identifiable as the syllable that is perceived as the most prominent one within the tone/information unit by the combination of pitch, volume and length. A tonic placement on the final lexical item in the tone unit is an example of unmarked tonicity while a tonic placement on any other lexical item is marked. For example:

|| he was looking through the WINdow || (unmarked tonicity);
|| he was TELLing me || (unmarked tonicity);
|| allowed his WIFE to drive the car || (marked tonicity).
Examples from Crystal and Davy (1975: 44)

The lexical items that follow the tonic syllable are projected by the speaker as given information. They are recoverable from the previous text, the context of situation or the wider context of culture. The lexical items preceding the tone unit may be projected as new or given, depending on whether or not they are recoverable. If the entire tone unit is projected as containing only new information the tonic placement signals broad focus. Otherwise the tonic placement signals narrow focus.

The tonic syllable functions as the locus of the main pitch movement within the tone unit. The primary opposition is between falling and rising tones. Falling tones that are subdivided into falls and rise-falls are the unmarked choice in declarative mood. Rising tones are subdivided into fall-rises and rises. A further tone is the level tone that may be realized phonetically as a low-rise. It signals the speaker's disengagement from the message (see Brazil 1997: ch. 8). Falling tones signal that the content of the speaker's tone unit is projected as representing major information. Rises, if followed by falls, project that the speaker's utterance is not complete. An utterance final rise projects that the tone unit represents a gloss or an afterthought (see Tench 1996 for a fuller description). Examples (a) to (f) illustrate some of the systemic possibilities:

(a) || i went to the /SHOP || and bought some \BREAD ||
(b) || i went to the \SHOP || and bought some /BREAD ||
(c) || i went to the \SHOP || and bought some \BREAD ||
(d) || i went to the \SHOP || and bought some /\BREAD ||
(e) || i went to the \/SHOP || and bought some \BREAD ||
(f) || i went to the \/SHOP ||

In (a) the speaker's selection of a rise in the initial tone unit projects an expectation of incompleteness. The hearers are informed that the speaker is not yet ready to give up the floor. They are primed for the hearer to inform them as to why he/she went to the shop. In (b) the final rising tone signals that the purchase of the bread is merely a gloss that follows the major information. The important thing is that the speaker went to the shop and not what he/she bought. In (c) both tone units contain falling tones and hence both tone units are projected as major information. The utterance projects a sequence of equally important events. First, the speaker went to the shop; second, the speaker bought some bread. The rise-fall on the second tone unit in (d) projects the *buying of the bread* as somehow more intensified. Contextually, for example, this could project the speaker's definite commitment to the truth expressed by the proposition, or signal that the speaker is somehow impressed that she/he managed to purchase bread! The initial fall-rise in (e) projects a meaning very similar to that projected by the initial rise in (a). The fall-rise in (f), which is known as an independent fall-rise, projects an unspoken implication or contrast. Perhaps the bread in the particular shop is known to be expensive or of poor quality.

Speakers further employ the system of tone to signal communicative function. Falling tones that are used to project major information are speaker orientated in that they purport to tell the hearer something. In contrast, rising tones signal deference to the hearer. Thus:

|| Turn on the \HEATer || signals a command; whereas
|| Turn on the /HEATer || signals a request.

The fall expresses that the speaker believes him/herself to be in a position of dominance, while the rise projects the perhaps fictitious presupposition that the hearer has the final say on whether or not the heater will be turned on.

Similarly, in declarative mood utterances the choice between fall and rise signals a differing communicative function. The fall projects the tone unit as an act of telling, while the rise signals that the assertion is incomplete and invites the hearer to complete it.

|| James passed the \TEST || (a statement)
|| James passed the /TEST || (a query)

However, it is not the case that there is a one-to-one correlation between a speech act and a tone movement (O'Grady 2010: 63–4). For instance, regardless of tone selection, the utterance *I apologize for being late* is what speech-act theorists label an expressive speech act: an illocutionary act that expresses the speaker's sincerity (Searle 1998: 146–50).

Intonation is used to express speaker's attitudes or emotions. It is commonly claimed that the more involved or committed a speaker is to the discourse he/she is engaging in, the higher the speaker's pitch will be. Conversely the more detached the speaker is, the lower their pitch will be. Speakers may signal boredom or detachment through their selection of low pitch. However, it is vital to remember that speakers always speak within the confines of a particular context and, hence, in formal environments low pitch may not signal boredom but rather detached professionalism. Intonation is only one of the linguistic and paralinguistic resources that speakers use to convey attitude. It is used simultaneously with lexical choices, paralinguistic vocal effects, sniggers, facial and body gestures, eye contact and loudness to project the speaker's attitude to the communicative act he/she is engaging in.

Speakers' tonality selections realize syntactic meaning which, in writing, is signalled by punctuation. For example:

|| I washed and ironed the clothes ||.

The speaker signals that *clothes* is the object of both verbs.

|| I washed || and ironed the clothes ||.

The speaker signals ambiguity as to whether he/she washed him/herself or the clothes. The difference in tonality in the following examples signals in the first example that the speaker has only one sister, while in the second example the speaker is likely to have more than one sister: one who lives in Paris and others who live somewhere else.

|| my sister who lives in Paris || = a defining relative clause
|| my sister || who lives in Paris || = a non-defining relative clause.

In example (a) below, Jim is a doctor but in example (b) the differing tonality selection signals that Jim is the object of the unnamed doctor's attentions:

(a) || they sent Jim || a doctor || to help him ||
(b) || they sent Jim a doctor || to help him ||

Intonation functions – especially in pre-planned and scripted discourse such as radio and television news broadcasts – to segment longer stretches of speech into paragraph-like structures labelled in the literature as paratones, phonological paragraphs and pitch sequences (Brazil 1997; O'Grady 2010; Tench 1996;Wichmann 2000). Paratones start with a high pitch on the initial accented syllable (the onset) and continue until the speaker produces a very low pitch. The low pitch is usually followed by an extended pause. The speaker then resets his/her pitch to signal the beginning of a new paratone. A high pitched onset signals maximum disjunction while a low onset signals that the new paratone is projected as containing information equivalent to that in the previous one. A mid onset signals that the speaker intends to produce new information that develops what has been told previously.

The final function of intonation is the identification of speech styles. This function of intonation has to date (with the major exception of Tench 1990: ch. 7) been relatively poorly explored. Tench found that phonological paragraphing was more prevalent in certain genres such as news-reading, spoken anecdotes and bible-reading but less prevalent in other genres, notably informal conversation. Certain genres tend to be intoned with limited tone variation (for example, individual and group prayer) while news-reading and informal conversation have much more tone variation. In informal conversation there was a higher percentage of falling tones found than in planned scripted discourse. Tone units tend to more closely approximate to full clauses in pre-planned genres such as news-reading, but they tend to be shorter in unplanned genres such as informal conversation.

This brief description of intonation has unfortunately focused exclusively on intonation in English. This is because English intonation is the most fully explored, though the description is still by no means complete. There remains much work to be done in describing the intonation of other languages. The major works that survey the intonation of other languages include: Hirst and Di Cristo (1998) an edited collection which surveys the intonation of 21 languages including English; Jun (2005), an edited collection that surveys the intonation of 13 languages including English. Gussenhoven (2004) includes descriptions of the intonation of Basque, Japanese, French and the Scandinavian languages as well as English. Ladd (2008) includes numerous examples from languages that are not English. For an alternate description of intonation see ToBI.

Juncture

Juncture is a phonological term that is used to refer to the phonetic features that are used to demarcate a stream of speech into grammatical units such as morphemes and words. The most obvious junctural feature is silence, which signals separation between two units. In fast connected speech, however, speakers rarely pause. Hearers are required to employ other phonetic cues in order to mark morpheme or word boundaries. To illustrate, if a speaker produced the following phonemic sequence [kiːpstɪkɪŋ] the utterance would be theoretically ambiguous between the phrases *keep sticking* or *keeps ticking*. Yet, in practice, a hearer would in all probability have little difficulty in distinguishing between the two phrases, which would more than likely be pronounced as follows: *keep sticking* → [kʰiːp̚ stɪkɪŋ] and *keeps ticking* → [kʰiːp̚s tʰɪkiŋ]. In *keep sticking* the phonemic sequence [st] is found within the same word. The [t] is not in syllable onset initial position and so is not **aspirated**. In contrast, in the *keeps ticking* example, the phonemic string [st] is not found within the same word. The [t] is in syllable onset initial position and thus aspirated. Hearers can use the aspiration as a cue enabling them to separate the phonemic stream into morphemes and words.

If successive sound segments occur within the same syllable they are said to be in *close juncture*. If they are within different syllables they are said to be in *open juncture*. The presence of open juncture blocks the operation of a number of predictable phonetic processes such as aspiration, devoicing, **clear** or **dark** <L>, and **vowel** reduction. The following examples, originally from Gimson (2008: 307), illustrate:

Aspiration and Vowel Reduction

(a) I scream [aɪ skɹiːm] (b) icecream [aɪs kʰɹiːm]

The vowel [aɪ] in (b) because of the presence of a **fortis fricative** in **close juncture** is shorter than the [aɪ] vowel in (a). As the phonemic sequence [sk] is in close juncture in (a) [k] is not aspirated.

Devoicing and Vowel reduction

(c) nitrate [naɪˈtʰɹ̥eɪt] (d) night rate [naɪt̚ ɹeɪt]

In (c) the phonemic sequence [tɹ] is in close juncture in the onset position of the stressed syllable: hence [t] is aspirated and the following [ɹ] is as a consequence devoiced. In (d) the open juncture between the [tɹ] blocks the voicelessness of the [t] from persevering and devoicing the [ɹ], which remains voiced. In addition, as the /t/ is in syllable final coda position it may be unreleased or more exceptionally replaced by a glottal.

Dark and clear <L>

(e) illegal [ɪˈliːgəl] (f) ill eagle [ɪɫ iːgəl]

In (e) the open juncture between the phonemic sequence [ɪl] ensures that the /l/ is in onset position and hence clear, while in (f) the close junction between the /ɪ/ and the /l/ ensures that the /l/ will be dark. In addition, some speakers may insert a glottal stop between the /l/ and /iː/ both to aid the transition between the consonant in coda position and the following vowel, and to explicitly demarcate the open juncture between the segments.

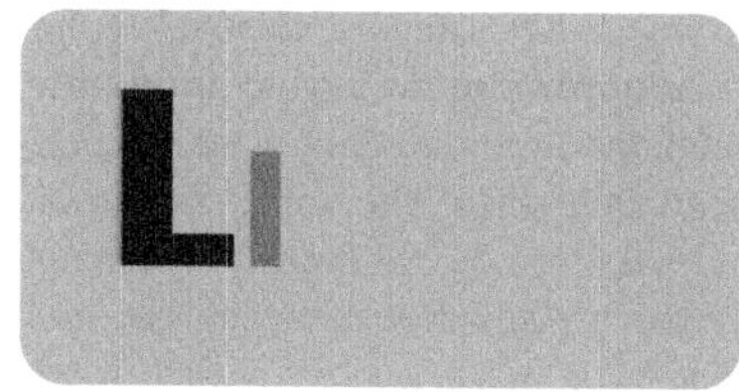

Labialization

Labialization is a type of **secondary articulation**. It occurs when a speaker produces a consonant with a simultaneous rounding of the lips. It is symbolized by 'ʷ'. Labialization is the most commonly found type of secondary articulation both in regard to the number of segments and the number of languages in which labialized consonants occur with **phonemic** status. For instance, Ladefoged and Maddieson (1996: 356) report the following data, originally in Grubb (1977), from Kwakw'ala (Kwakiutl) an Amerindian language spoken in British Columbia (Table 17).

Table 17 Labialized and non-labialized consonants in Kwakiutl

	LABIALIZED		LABIALIZED	
	VELAR	VELAR	UVULAR	UVULAR
Voiceless plosive	['kasa]	[kʷe'sa]	[qe'sa]	[qʷe'sa]
	beat soft	*splashing*	*coiling*	*peeling*
Voiced plosive	['gisgas]	[gʷe'su]	[ɢaɢas]	[ɢʷalas]
	incest	*pig*	*grandparent*	*lizard*
Voiceless ejective	[xe'sa]	['xʷasa]	['χasa]	['χʷat'a]
	Lost	*a dance*	*rotten*	*sparrow*
Ejective stop	['k'ata]	[kʷ'esa]	['q'asa]	['qʷ'asa]
	writing	*light*	*sea otter*	*crying*

In English, phonemes may be labialized if they precede back rounded vowels, as in *coop, goo* and *shoe*, which may be pronounced as [kʷu:p], [gʷu:] and [ʃʷu:]. There do not appear to be any English accents that can be distinguished by the presence or absence of labialization, though Painter (1963: 30–2) reports that in Black Country English all consonants are slightly labialized before the stressed THOUGHT, NORTH, FORCE, LOT and GOAT vowels. Devonish and Harry (2008: 282) report that some Jamaican speakers produce labialized **bilabial plosives** before the CHOICE vowel.

Labial-velar

The term labial-velar refers to the classification of a **consonant** sound on the basis of the **place of articulation** of the sound. Labial-velar consonants are produced at the **velum** or **soft palate** and are simultaneously accompanied by lip-rounding.

Labial-velar sounds may be voiceless [ʍ] or voiced [w]. They are relatively common sounds cross-linguistically with the voiced **approximant** having **phonemic** status in languages including the Semitic language Amharic, Cantonese, French, the African languages Hausa and Igbo, as well as English. The voiceless variant [ʍ] is rarer, though it was part of the sound structure of Old English. For most modern speakers of English there is no longer a distinction between [w] and [ʍ] words, so that the following pairs *whine/wine, whales/Wales, which/witch* are homophonous. The [w] and [ʍ] merger has not yet, however, occurred in all forms of English. The distinction between [w] and [ʍ] words is preserved in Scottish Standard English, though studies such as Macafee (2003) and Johnson (1997) suggest that among speakers of Urban Scots [ʍ] is being lost.

The situation is quite similar in Irish English where, in what Hickey (2008: 98) labels *Supraregional Southern Irish English*, [ʍ] and [w] are merging, resulting in homophonous realizations of pairs such as *which* and *witch*. Traditionally, perhaps because of Scottish influence, New Zealand English has been said to retain a distinction between [w] and [ʍ] words. Wells (1982c) reports that in the 1960s half of an intake of undergraduate students retained the distinction between [w] and [ʍ] words. However, more recent research indicates that the distinction is being lost and only conservative speakers retain the distinction between [w] and [ʍ] words (Bauer and Warren 2004).

Within the minority of speakers in the UK who speak **received pronunciation**, a number speak what has been dubbed Upper Received Pronunciation; the type of speech produced by a public figure such as Noël Coward – (see Wells 1982b: 282–3 and Upton 2008a: 239ff.). Such speakers may retain a distinction between [w] and [ʍ] words. However, for the majority of RP speakers the decline in the popularity of elocution and the increasingly less conscious awareness of prescriptive rules has resulted in the phonemic merger of [w] and [ʍ].

The position in the US appears to be slightly more complicated. Gimson (2008: 231) notes that [ʍ] is presented as the norm for the pronunciation of *wh* words in the US. However, as he notes, Wells (1982a: 229–30) had previously commented that the distinction between [w] and [ʍ] words is widely maintained, though decreasing in some of the larger US metropolitan areas. More recently Labov, Ash and Boberg (2006: 49) state that, 'while in the middle of the twentieth century only a few costal areas showed the [w] and [ʍ] merger. At the end of the century only a few areas show the distinction.' A YouTube clip from the popular US cartoon *Family Guy* reveals, at least among the intended audience of the TV programme, that speakers who maintain the distinction between [w] and [ʍ] are ridiculed as older and less hip. The relevant clip is available at http://www.youtube.com/watch?v=lich59xsjik. Further evidence for the merger of [w] and [ʍ] can be found in both the broad and narrow transcription of American English presented in Ladefoged (1999: 44) where *which* is transcribed as /wɪtʃ/. On balance, it seems that while the distinction may be retained prescriptively for American English (such as in teaching handbooks) it is rapidly being lost, or has already been lost by actual American speakers.

In English /w/ is found only in syllable onset position. In words that contain <w> after the vowel such as *bow* /bəʊ/, *bow/* /bəʊl/, *towel*/'taʊəl/, *tower* /'taʊə and *town* /taʊn/ the <w> represents the second part of the **diphthong**.

Labiodental

The term labiodental refers to the classification of a **consonant** sound on the basis of the **place of articulation** of the sound. Labiodental consonants are produced by contact or close proximity between the teeth and the lips. The usual articulation is made by the lower lips and the upper teeth. Assuming a normal **pulmonic egressive airstream mechanism** the following classes of consonants are classified by the IPA as labiodental: **nasal** [ɱ] **fricatives** [f, v] and approximant [ʋ]. As can be seen from Table 18, labiodental fricatives, especially the voiceless fricative, are common across languages. In British English some scholars such as Kerswill (2003) have noted that there appears to be an ongoing merger in popular British urban speech between **dental** fricatives and their labiodental counterparts.

Table 18 List of labiodental phonemes found in 25 language

Language	Nasal	Fricatives	Approximants
Amharic		f	
Arabic		f	
Bulgarian		f v	
Cantonese		f	
Czech		f v	
Dutch		f v	ʋ
English		f v	
French		f v	
German		f v	
Greek		f v	
Hausa			
Hebrew		f v	
Hindi		f	ʋ
Hungarian		f v	
Igbo		f	
Italian	ɱ	f v	
Japanese			
Korean			
Mandarin		f	
Persian		f v	
Portuguese		f v	
Russian		f v	
Spanish		f	
Swedish		f v	
Thai		f	
Welsh		f v	

Lateral

A lateral is an **approximant, fricative** or **affricate** consonant articulated in such a way that air flows past one or both sides of the tongue. Laterals may be **voiced** or **voiceless**. The IPA recognizes laterals produced at the following places of **articulation: alveolar, retroflex, palatal** and **velar**. In English, the lateral /l/ is voiced and alveolar. Maddieson (2008c) reports that around three-quarters of the languages he surveyed contained a voiced alveolar approximant. While most languages contain only one lateral consonant, a minority of languages (such as Welsh) have two. In addition to the voiced lateral approximant [l], Welsh contains the voiceless alveolar lateral fricative [ɬ], the initial sound in Welsh words spelt with a <ll>. It should be noted, however, that English speakers substitute either a clear <L> /l/ or one of the following clusters /θl/, /fl/ or /kl/ when pronouncing words that begin with the <ll> spelling.

Lax

This is a phonetic term used to classify sounds that are supposedly produced with less muscular effort and movement. It contrasts with **tense**. Chomsky and Halle (1968) classify the vowels in KIT and FOOT as [– Tense] or [+ Lax] and the vowels in FLEECE and GOOSE as [+ Tense] or [– Lax]. Chomsky and Halle note that during the articulation of [– Tense] vowels the width of the pharynx is not relatively stable and is liable to change. They claim that this is a result of a lower articulatory effort, which results in lower muscular tension in the vocal tract above the **glottis**.

Lenis

This is a phonetic term that classifies **consonants** which are apparently articulated with weaker muscular effort and a lower amount of breath force. Lenis sounds contrast with **fortis** ones. In English, voiced sounds – especially **stops** – are classified as lenis. In phonetic environments, where the voiced sound has been devoiced, it is the degree of muscular effort and breath force that is used to maintain a contrast between voiced and voiceless **phonemes** – see **lax**.

Liaison

Liaison is a phonological term used to refer to a transition between sounds where a sound is introduced at the end of a word if the following syllable commences with a vowel. A very common type of liaison found in non-rhotic forms of English involves the insertion of [ɹ] in connected speech, where the [ɹ] has no basis in the pronunciation of the syllable or word in citation form. Traditionally this has been classified in two ways. The first linking <r> occurs when there is a word final <r> in the spelling and the word is immediately followed by a word beginning with a vowel. For instance:

Citation form	**connected speech**
car /kɑː/, park /pɑːk/ →	car park ['k^{h}ɑːpɑːk]
car /kɑː/, engine /'ɛndʒɪn/ →	car engine [ˌk^{h}ɑːɹ' ɛndʒɪn]

far /fɑː/, distant /ˈdɪstənt/ →far distant place [ˌfɑːdɪstəntˈpleɪs]
far /fɑː/, away /əˈweɪ/ → far away [ˌfɑːɹəˈweɪ]

The orthographic <r> is pronounced only when immediately followed by a word beginning with a vowel.

The second type of epenthetic <r> is known as the intrusive <r>. It occurs where [r] is pronounced between the vowels /ɑː/ /ɔː/ /ɜː/ /ɪə/ /ɛə/ /ə/ and any another vowel. Unlike linking <r> there is no historic justification in the English spelling system for the insertion of an <r>, for example:

law and order → [lɑːrənˈɔːdə]
India and Pakistan → [ˈɪndɪəɹənˌpɑːkɪˈstɑːn]

Traditionally the use of the intrusive <r> has been stigmatized, (Gimson 2008: 305 n11). Older speakers in order to block an intrusive [ɹ] may produce a **glottal** stop or a pause between the vowels, for example, [lɑːʔənˈɔːdə] or [lɑː ənˈɔːdə]. Hughes, Trudgill and Watt (2005: 65) report, however, that among speakers of English with a South East-type accent the use of intrusive <r>, especially after /ə/ and /ɪə/, has become so prevalent that failure to produce an intrusive <r> is itself an indicator of a non-native accent! Younger RP speakers appear to be comfortable even with inserting [ɹ] within words before a suffix, for instance *sawing* → [sɔːrɪŋ]. Such usage tends to be stigmatized by older and more conservative speakers. Regardless of whether the [ɹ] links or intrudes, speakers produce it naturally in order to smoothen the transitions between a low vowel and a following one.

In French, liaison occurs in a manner analogous to linking <r> in English. Final orthographic consonants are predictably inserted within an immediate sense unit if the following word begins with a vowel. Otherwise the orthographic consonant, which in the examples below is /z/, is not realized, for example:

les enfants [lezɑ̃fɑ̃]	(the children)
les femmes [lefɑm]	(the women)
les amis [lezami]	(the friends)
les whiskeys [lewiski]	(the whiskys)

[z] is only pronounced where it liaises between the two vowels and smooths the phonetic transition from the first vowel to the second one.

Liquid

A liquid is a cover term in phonetics used to refer to all [l] and [r] type sounds. The two English liquid phonemes are /ɹ/ and /l/. This term is useful in **phonology** as it allows for the formation of general rules in **rhotic** forms of English such as 'liquids are syllabic at the end of a word when immediately after a consonant' (Ladefoged 2005: 58). See **approximant**.

Markedness

Markedness is a phonological term that refers to the expectedness or unexpectedness of a feature in the sound system. Within the literature the term is used in two similar but subtly different ways. For some scholars, an unmarked feature refers to a feature that is statistically probable. A marked feature refers to one that is statistically improbable. The English *Th sounds* are marked phonemes as they occur in few extant languages. Maddieson (2008b) surveyed 567 languages and reports that *Th* sounds are present in less than 40 of them. Other statistically marked classes of phonemes are **clicks** and **pharyngeals**, which are chiefly found in Semitic languages. Similarly, the absence of a common class of consonants within a language – such as **bilabials** reported by Maddieson (2008a) to be missing in only four of the surveyed languages, nasals absent in ten languages and fricatives in 48 – is considered to be marked.

Scholars working in the **generative** tradition equate unmarked features with those features that are more natural. Unmarked features represent the neutral state of the relevant articulator. Hence unmarked sounds are easier to pronounce than marked ones. Rocca and Johnson (1999: 585–6) list 17 markedness features apparently found across languages. They note that if a language contained only the unmarked features it could contain only the phonemes /t/ /a/ /i/ /u/. This strongly suggests that in the process of learning a language speakers must learn to produce culturally appropriate marked features (Stampe 1979) (and see **optimality theory**).

Metrical phonology

Metrical phonology is an influential **generative** model of phonology that was developed by Mark Liberman in his 1975 PhD dissertation, subsequently published as Liberman (1985). Metrical phonology originated as a theory of **stress** but has presently expanded to become a more general theory of the **syllable** and phonological boundaries above the syllable. The central insight of metrical phonology is that stress patterns are represented in a hierarchical string. Individual segments form into syllables, which form into **feet**, which form into words. The underlying relationship between adjoining constituents is that they are related to each other in terms of their relative strength. A particular syllable is strong only in the sense that it is stronger than its neighbouring syllables. Similarly, an individual foot is stronger than its immediately neighbouring feet. These insights allowed metrical phonologists to formalize both the stress patterns of individual words and the **rhythm** of words produced in connected speech. Thus:

```
                                   *        phrase level
      *      *              *  <-- *        foot level
    *  *    *  *            *  *   *  *     syllable level
   antique  table          antique-table
```

The word *antique* contains two syllables with the ult stronger than the penult. The position is reversed for *table*, which has a stronger penult syllable. Both *antique* and *table* are single foot words. When the words are combined together into the phrase *antique table*, the final foot is stronger. This results in a change of strength relations in the earlier foot, with the strength relations being reversed to avoid the stress clash. Metrical phonologists argue that the tendency for English stresses (strong syllables) to avoid one another is rule governed.

Consider the following noun phrase:

```
               *        phrase level
         *     *  *     foot level
   *     *     *  *     syllable level
   a   great  record
```

The first two words *a* and *great* form into a single foot **phonological word** with the ult syllable stronger. In the second word, which is also a single foot, the penult is the stronger syllable. When the words are combined together into the phrase *a great record*, the final foot is stronger. As in the previous example, this results in a stress clash. However, unlike the earlier example the strength relations cannot be reversed. The English Rhythm rule only allows stresses to move to the left within the same foot to avoid a clash. In the initial foot, the stress cannot move on to the weak clitic *a*. Nor can the strength relations be reversed in the final foot as that would involve a stress moving rightwards within the same syllable.

In recent years, scholars have combined the insights of metrical phonology with those of **autosegmental** phonology, as in Goldsmith (1990), in order to explicate a more natural phonetic underpinning to segmental phonology and in order to reduce the number of language-specific rules that generate the phonetic form of a language. Ladd (2008) adopts an autosegmental-metrical (AM) approach in analysing **intonation**. He proposes that some syllables in the stream of speech are perceived as being relatively stronger than their neighbouring syllables. These rhythmically prominent syllables form into prosodic constituents known as intonation phrases, which themselves form into compound contours formed out of relatively weak and relatively strong intonation phrases (see ToBI).

Mora

A mora is a unit of rhythm that represents the minimal unit of metrical time. In some schools of **phonology**, notably **autosegmental** and **metrical**, moras are notated as a separate level of phonological representation. The analysis of segments into moras, which is important in describing the **timing** of language, is applied only to **syllable** rhymes. For instance, a long vowel or a diphthong consists of two moras while a short vowel consists of one mora. So, when measuring out the beat of a language, a rhyme consisting of a long vowel, and a rhyme consisting of a short vowel plus a consonant, would each be classified as weighing two moras.

Nasal

A nasal is a term used to refer to the classification of a **consonant** on the basis of its manner of **articulation**. Nasals are produced by a complete closure of the oral cavity. Simultaneously the soft palate is lowered so that the airstream trapped in the oral cavity is free to escape through the nasal passage. The classification nasal is a subdivision of **stop** where it contrasts with **plosive**.

The IPA symbolizes nasal stops made at the following places of **articulation**: **bilabial** /m/, **labiodental** /ɱ/, **alveolar** /n/, **retroflex** /ɳ/, **palatal** /ɲ/, **velar** /ŋ/ and **uvular** /ɴ/. Nasal consonants are extremely common throughout the languages of the world. It appears that, with very few possible exceptions, the overwhelming majority of languages contain at least a single nasal consonant. In a survey of 567 languages Maddieson (2008a) lists just 12 or 13 known languages[1] that do not apparently contain a nasal phoneme. Of these languages Maddieson goes on to say that even among the few languages which have no nasal phonemes, nasal phones may be heard in most of them as **allophones**, for instance Eyak where [m] and [n] are allophones of /w/ and /l/, respectively. Nasal stops are usually voiced, as they are in English, but some languages (for instance, Welsh) has three voiceless nasal phonemes /m̥/, /n̥/ and /ŋ̊/ while Icelandic contains four voiceless nasal phonemes /m̥/, /n̥/, /ŋ̊/ and /ɲ̊/. There is a useful discussion on voiced and voiceless nasals in Ladefoged and Maddieson (1996: 110–16).

English contains three nasal **phonemes** with the same place of **articulation** as the three pairs of **voiced** and **voiceless** plosives: /m/, /n/ and /ŋ/. It is worth noting that in English the distribution of the nasal phoneme, at least to a certain extent, is predictable. When the nasal is followed by a plosive it has the same place of **articulation** as the following sound, for instance *limp* /lɪmp/ – bilabial, *bent* /bɛnt/ – alveolar, *sink* /sɪŋk/ – velar. In careful speech, speakers of most accents pronounce word final unstressed <ing> as [ɪŋ] but in casual speech there is a tendency for speakers to pronounce it as [ɪn].

Within English, the velar nasal /ŋ/ has a restricted distribution. It can only appear in post-vocalic position. The extent of the resistance English speakers have in pronouncing pre-vocalic /ŋ/ can be seen in New Zealand English, in which English speakers substitute /n/ for /ŋ/ when pronouncing words of Maori provenance with pre-vocalic /ŋ/ but pronounce the /ŋ/ when it is post-vocalic. The restricted distribution of /ŋ/ is by no means universal, as the following examples illustrate:

/ŋâ/ 'we' in Burmese, a language spoken in Burma.
/ŋú/ 'drink' in Igbo, a language spoken in Nigeria.

/ŋil/ 'relative' in Irish, a language spoken chiefly in some Western regions of Ireland.
/ŋan/ 'sun' in Taba, a language spoken in Indonesia.

There is only one regional variant of the English nasal phonemes, namely the relic pronunciation of /ŋ/ in parts of the North West Midlands in England. Speakers traditionally retained [g] in the pronunciation of words such as *sing, tongue, hung,* which were pronounced as follows: [sɪŋg], [tʌŋg] and [hʌŋg].[2] Recent sociolinguistic surveys such as Chinn and Thorne (2001) and Mathisen (1999) indicate that the realization of [ŋg] for /ŋ/ remains prevalent in the North West Midlands.

Nasalization

Nasalization is a type of **secondary articulation**. It occurs when a speaker produces a speech sound, usually a **vowel**, with a lowered soft palate. Unlike in the pronunciation of **oral** vowels some of the air escapes out of the nasal passage. This results in a very different vowel quality. Nasalized vowels are notated by a ˜ diacritic over the vowel. In English, which has only oral vowel phonemes, nasalized **allophones** may be heard if the vowel is immediately followed by a **nasal**. For instance, consider the difference in vowel quality between the following pairs of words, *beet/bean* [bi:t]/[bĩ:n], *site/sign* [saɪt]/[saĩn] and *suit/soon* [su:t]/[sũ:n]. The difference is most noticeable if the words are said slowly and the vowel purposefully lengthened. Wells (1982c: 541) reports that some speakers from the South of the US substitute a nasalized vowel for a nasal, which is followed within the same syllable by a **voiceless** consonant, for example words such as *lump, pint* and *drink* may be pronounced as follows: [lʌ̃ə̃p], [pã̃ĩt], [dɪ̃ɪk].

Nasalized vowels are a feature of Romance languages such as Portuguese and French, which has four nasalized vowels [ɑ̃], [ɔ̃], [ɛ̃] and [œ̃], though Fougeron and Smith (1999: 79) claim that for many speakers [œ̃] has been replaced by [ɛ̃] (see also Harris 1988: 210). Some examples of French nasalized vowels are:

sans	*without*	[sɑ̃]
bon	*good*	[bɔ̃]
saint	*saint*	[sɛ̃]
brun	*brown*	[bʁœ̃]

Maddieson (1984) reports that the nasalization of vowels is common across languages, with around 20 per cent of known languages employing this feature. In contrast, nasalized consonants are far rarer though still possible. For instance, Ladefoged and Maddieson (1996: 132) report the presence of an African language, Kwangali, which contrasts nasalized and non-nasalized [h].

Obligatory Contour Principle

The Obligatory Contour Principle (OCP) is a phonological principle that prohibits adjacent identical elements. However, because of the existence of numerous exceptions to the OCP it is better considered to be a tendency rather than a rule. The OCP was first developed during the study of **tone** languages (see **autosegmental phonology**) and used to motivate a mapping of a lexical unit that contained only low tones as (a) rather than (b):

The presence of the low tone across all three syllables is caused by the spreading of an underlying low tone rather than by the presence of three separate low tones. In more recent years it has become apparent that the OCP acts not only to constrain tones but also **features**. For instance, the usual English plural marker is either /s/ or /z/, for example, /kæts/ or /dɒgz/, but the English plural marker of *face* [feɪs] and *phase* [feɪz] is /ɪz/. The insertion of the vowel ensures that identical elements are not adjacent to one another. Similarly in English the following list of consonant clusters in the onset are disfavoured because of the presence of adjacent features: /pw/, /bw/, /pf/, /bv/, /pm/, /bm/ (adjacent labial features), /tn/, /dn/, /ts/, /dz/ adjacent coronal features and /gw/[1] (adjacent dorsal features). However, the OCP does not operate as stringently in coda position, for example, /klæmp/, /kæts/, /diːdz/, etc.

Obstruent

An obstruent is a phonetic term that classifies **consonant** sounds on the basis of the degree of constriction. Sounds that are made with a constriction which impedes the passage of air through the mouth such as **plosives, fricatives** and **affricates** are obstruents.

Optimality theory

Optimality theory (OT) is an influential **generative** model of phonology that was developed in the early 1990s in a series of conference papers and technical reports by Alan Prince and Paul Smolensky. This work has subsequently been published as Prince and Smolensky (2004). Archangeli and Langendoen (1997) is an accessible overview of OT. Gussenhoven and Jacobs (2005), a general survey of phonological theory, is an accessible introduction to the workings of OT. A fuller but more challenging introduction to OT can be found in McCarthy (2004), a collection of key writings produced by leading OT theorists, which includes in chapter 1 a reduced version of Prince and Smolensky (2004). McCarthy (2008) assumes no previous experience with OT and illustrates how to produce an OT analysis. Finally there is an extensive OT online archive that is searchable by keyword available at http://roa.rutgers.edu/.

Unlike other generative models OT is not a rule-based approach. Rather it posits that phonological outputs result from the ranking of constraints. In OT there are two types of constraint families or groupings: faithfulness and **markedness**, which are posited as being universal or common to all languages. The faithfulness constraints demand that the output form preserves the input form. They serve to, for example, block **elision** and **epenthesis**. The markedness constraints demand that the output corresponds with the general tendencies found across languages. They restrict more physically effortful or difficult pronunciations. The key insight afforded by OT is that all constraints are potentially violable. In other words, they are not absolute prohibitions but rather violable restrictions. Differences in output reflect differences in the relative rankings of the constraints.

OT has developed a detailed and transparent formalism that has enabled analysts to successfully deploy it in the phonological analysis of tricky examples from numerous extant languages, and even to explain historical sound changes (see McMahon 2000b). The formal machinery of OT consists of an input that is identical to the notion of underlying representation found in **spe**. The input is fed into a generator (GEN) that generates all the possible pronunciations of the form. This results as a set of candidates, one of which will be selected as the optimal or most harmonious candidate. The competing candidates are evaluated by the set of constraints (CON) contained in the evaluator. The optimal or most harmonic candidate is selected as being the candidate that has the fewest violations of the highest ranked constraint(s). In the event that two candidates are tied, the winning candidate is the candidate with a lower number of violations of a lower ranked constraint.

O

OT analyses are usually presented visually in the form of violation tableaux. The following example, Table 19, illustrates a simplified tableau for the word *ape*. In the top left-hand corner of the table we find the word ape, which is the *lexical representation* or *input*. Below it we find four possible candidates with the optimal candidate indicated by ☞. Four constraints are shown in the very simplified tableau, with DEP and MAX being faithfulness constraints, and ONSET

Table 19 A toy OT analysis of ape

/eɪp/	DEP	MAX	ONSET	NO-CODA
☞eɪp			*	*
eɪpə	*!		*	
eɪ		*!	*	
peɪp	*!			*

and NO-CODA being markedness constraints. McCarthy (2008: 175) notes that: 'An OT constraint has one job: to assign some number of violation marks to a candidate based on its output structure or how it differs from the input.' Violation marks are notated by (*) with fatal ones indicated by (!). The four constraints can be worded as follows:

- DEP: Assign one violation mark (*) for every output element that isn't found in the lexical representation.
- MAX: Assign one violation mark (*) for every input element that isn't found in the output.
- ONSET: Assign one violation mark (*) for every syllable that does not contain an onset.
- NO-CODA: Assign one violation mark (*) for every consonant that is found in the coda of a syllable.

In the table, a solid line indicates that the constraint to the left dominates the constraint to the right. A broken line indicates that, either for the purpose of the present analysis or because it is presently unknown, the relative ranking of the candidates between themselves is unknown. In Table 19, DEP and MAX dominate or outrank ONSET and NO-CODA but are unranked relative to one another.

Native speakers of English know that the winning pronunciation is /eɪp/. The issue is how to formalize the analysis using the machinery of OT. The first thing to note is that violation of the markedness constraints ONSET and NO-CODA cannot be fatal as otherwise the most harmonic output would be restricted. Therefore, the faithfulness constraints MAX and DEP are ranked higher than ONSET and NO-CODA. The winning candidate [eɪp] does not violate either DEP or MAX. The losing candidates, [eɪpə] and [peɪp], contain a segment not found in the input and so violate DEP. The other losing candidate [eɪ] violates MAX as [p] has been deleted. It is important to note that even though all the candidates violated two constraints, selection of the most harmonic candidate rests only on constraint violation relative to the importance of the ranking of the constraints that have been violated. The constraints ONSET and MAX are not active in selecting [eɪp] ss the most harmonic candidate and this is indicated by their shading.

The following example, Table 20, illustrates a tableau from an imaginary language dubbed *Not-English*, where ONSET and NO-CODA constraints dominate DEP and MAX. The lexical representation remains /eɪp/.

Table 20 A toy OT analysis of ape in 'Not English'

/eɪp/	NO-CODA	ONSET	DEP	MAX
eɪp	*!	*		
eɪ.pə	*!	*	*	*
☞eɪ		*		*
peɪp	*!		*	
eɪ.əp	*!	**	*	

All of the candidates violate one or both of the two markedness constraints. The most harmonic candidate violates the ONSET constraint. Three of the losing candidates violate both the ONSET and the NO-CODA constraints, with [eɪ.əp] violating the Onset constraint twice. The symbol . indicates a syllable boundary. In the example above [eɪ.pə] is the sole non-monosyllabic candidate. The remaining candidate [peip] violates the NO-CODA constraint, but not ONSET. As we know that in *Not English* [eɪ] is the winning pronunciation, this entails that in *Not English* NO-CODA dominates ONSET.

The following example introduces two further markedness constraints: SON and #COMPLEX, which are worded as follows:

Table 21 A toy OT analysis of strew

/stɹuː/	SON	DEP	MAX	#COMPLEX
☞stɹuː				**
tsɹuː	*!			*
tɹuː			*!	*
stə.ɹuː		*!		*

- SON: assign one violation mark (*) for every onset or coda cluster that contains an inappropriate sonority profile – see **syllable**.
- #COMPLEX: assign one violation mark (*) for every tautosyllabic consonant cluster in the specified position.

All the candidates violate #COMPLEX, with the most harmonious candidate violating it twice. However, as the shading indicates, #COMPLEX is not active in selecting the most harmonic candidate and consequently violations of #COMPLEX are not fatal. In the losing candidate [tɹuː] /s/ has been deleted and this fatally violates MAX. A /ə/ vowel has been inserted into the losing candidate [stə.ɹuː] resulting in a fatal violation of DEP. The SON constraint has been violated in [tsɹuː]. Thus, in this example a violation of any of the highest three ranking constraints is fatal. The broken line indicates that, from the data presented in the example, we cannot rank the three constraints relative to one another.

O

OT analyses have been successfully deployed above the segment to describe the division of speech into tone units (see **intonation**). Unlike earlier generative approaches such as Chomsky and Halle (1968), OT does not posit a normal intonational pattern with the tone being expected to attach to the accented syllable of the final lexical item in the tone unit. Instead it recognizes that different inputs will result in different outputs. The input is ultimately a pragmatic decision based on the speaker's assumption of the state of speaker/hearer common ground. In the following example, Table 22, based on example 40 from Gussenhoven (2004: 161), the input, based on the accenting of the final lexical item *sister*, indicates that the speaker's intention was to signal that the entire utterance comprised new information.

The constraints in the example are alignment constraints, a subdivision of the markedness constraint family. They can be worded as follows:

- ALIGN FOC: assign one violation mark (*) for every occasion where the focus constituent does not right align with a major phrase boundary – notated as ι.
- WRAP XP: assign one violation mark (*) for every occasion where an XP is not contained in a single major phrase.
- ALIGN XP: assign one violation mark (*) for every occasion where a right-hand XP boundary fails to coincide with a major phrase boundary – notated as ι.
- BIN MAP: assign one violation mark (*) for every occasion where a major phrase does not consist of exactly two minor phrases.

Gussenhoven (ibid.: 160), as indicated in the table, has demonstrated elsewhere that the constraints are ranked in the following manner: ALIGN FOC dominates WRAP XP and ALIGN XP, which both dominate BIN MAP.

Table 22 An OT analysis of tonality

She [[lóaned] [her róllerblades]np [to Róbin's síster] pp] vp	**ALIGN FOC**	**ALIGN XP**	**WRAP XP**	**BIN MAP**
a (she lóaned her róllerblades to Róbin's síster)ι		*		*!
☞ b (she lóaned her róllerblades)ι (to Róbin's síster)ι			*	
c (she lóaned)ι (her róllerblades)ι (to Róbin's síster)ι			*	*!
d (she lóaned)ι (her róllerblades to Róbin's síster)ι		*!	*	

None of the competing candidates violate the highest ranked constraint ALIGN FOC, as the focused constituent *sister* (see **tonic**) right aligns with a major phrase boundary. Hence, in order to discover the most harmonic candidate we need to examine the next two highest ranking constraints, ALIGN XP and WRAP XP, where we find that all of the candidates violate one or both of the constraints. Candidates 'a' and 'd' violate ALIGN XP as rollerblades does not coincide with a major phrase boundary while candidates 'b', 'c' and 'd' all violate Wrap XP because the entire XP is not coterminous with a single major phrase.[2]

Of the four candidates, 'd' is penalized because it alone violates the two equally highly ranked constraints. Hence, as indicated by the shading, for 'd' the application of the lower ranked constraint BIN MAP is immaterial. However, for the remaining three candidates it is the constraint BIN MAP that selects the most harmonious candidate: in this case 'b'. Candidate 'a' fatally violates the constraint by not dividing the major phrase into two minor phrases, while candidate 'c' violates it by breaking the major phrase into more than two minor phrases.

To summarize, OT has a rigorous formal notation system that has allowed analysts to employ it successfully in describing (1) the phonological patterns of numerous languages, (2) sound change, (3) language development and (4) language variation. It has been criticized, however, for being too powerful, for employing constraints that are language specific rather than universal, and for being unable to account for cases, such as the interaction between vowel epenthesis and velar deletion (elision) in Turkish, where the application of the phonological processes is not apparent or opaque from the surface form. This is because, as originally stipulated (see constraint wording above), OT constraints are input/output correspondences with no information on losing candidates available. A possible solution to this problem is Stratal OT (see McCarthy 2008). A final criticism is that as **gen** generates an infinite number of pronounceable candidates that OT theory is not easy to accommodate within a processing module of language.

Oral

Oral sounds are sounds that are produced with the soft palate raised, sealing off access to the nasal tract. The term contrasts with **nasal**. In English, all vowel phonemes and all consonant phonemes except /m/, /n/ and /ŋ/ are oral.

Palatal

The term palatal refers to the classification of a **consonant** sound on the basis of the place of **articulation** of the sound. Palatal consonants are produced by contact or close proximity between the front of the tongue and the hard palate. Assuming a normal **pulmonic egressive airstream mechanism** the following classes of consonants are classified by the IPA as palatal: **plosives** [c, ɟ], **nasals** [ɲ], **fricatives** [ç, ʝ], **approximants** [j] and **lateral fricatives** [ʎ̝].

The sole English palatal phoneme is the **semi vowel** /j/, which, as Table 23 indicates, is a sound common to many languages. In English, /j/ is restricted in its distribution and can only appear before a vowel. If it is the final element in an accented cluster it can only be followed by /uː/ and either /ʊə/ in older and more conservative accents or /ɔː/ in younger accents. In unaccented clusters it also can be followed by /ʊ/ and /ə/. Table 23 illustrates the possibilities.

Traditionally /j/ as been found in prevocalic accented clusters after any consonant except /ɹ/ and /ʃ/. However, in many accents including **received pronunciation** there are an increasing number of pronunciations where the /j/ is deleted if it immediately follows /l/, /s/ and for some speakers /n/. Wells (2000: 450) reports that while 58 per cent of British speakers pronounced *lure* with a prevocalic /j/ 42 per cent did not do so. He further reports (ibid.: 748) that only 28 per cent of British speakers pronounced *suit* with a prevocalic /j/ but 72 per cent did not do so. It seems that in the UK speakers from East Anglia are the most likely to drop /j/. They may drop it after any of the following consonants: /l, s, n, t, d, θ, m, p, b, f, k and h/ (Trudgill 2008: 192–3). In General American, /j/ is regularly absent in accented clusters following /t, d, θ, ð and n/. Wells (2000: 510) reports that 86 per cent of American speakers deleted /j/ when pronouncing the word *news*.

In Standard English, the cluster /j/ following /h/ is often realized as the voiceless palatal fricative /ç/ (see Table 23). Thus, we have the following pronunciations: *hew* [çuː], *huge* [çuːdʒ] and *human* [ˈçuːmən]. However, because of the paucity of words containing the voiceless palatal fricative and its restricted distribution [ç] is not treated as an English **phoneme** but rather as an **allophone** of /h/. In English, the **velar stops** /k/ and /g/ may be fronted when they immediately follow a **front vowel** such as /iː/ and some speakers may as a result pronounce *key* and geese with an initial palatal stop. Thus [cʰiː] and [ɟiːs] not [kʰiː] and [giːs].

Palatal consonants are a noted feature of both Southern Irish and Ulster English. Wells (1982b) reports Ulster pronunciations of *car* and *back* as [caːɹ] and [bac] and a Southern Irish pronunciation of *bark* as [baːɹc]. It seems likely that the

Table 23 List of palatal phonemes found in 25 languages

Language	Plosive	Nasal	Fricatives	Approximants	Lateral approximants
Amharic		ɲ		j	
Arabic				j	
Bulgarian				j	
Cantonese				j	
Czech	c ɟ	ɲ		j	
Dutch				j	
English				j	
French		ɲ		j (ɥ)[1]	
German			ç	j	
Greek	c ɟ	ɲ	ç ʝ	j	ʎ
Hausa				j	
Hebrew				j	
Hindi				j	
Hungarian		ɲ		j	
Igbo		ɲ		j	
Italian		ɲ		j	ʎ
Japanese				j	
Korean				j	
Mandarin					
Persian				j	
Portuguese		ɲ			ʎ
Russian	c		ç ʝ	j	
Spanish		ɲ	ʝ		
Swedish			ʝ		
Thai				j	
Welsh			j		

[1]French is unusual in that it contains /ɥ/ which is a labialized palatal approximant /tɥe/ *tuer* (to kill).

Table 24 The distribution of /j/ in Standard British English

Accented Clusters		Unaccented clusters	
Before /uː/	*pew* /pjuː/ *beauty* /ˈbjuːti/	Before /uː/ Before /ʊ/	*argue* /ˈɑːgjuː/ *opulence* /ˈɒpjʊlens/
Before /ʊə/ Or /ɔː/	*pure* /pjʊə/ /pjɔː/	Before /ʊə/ Before /ə/	*tenture* /ˈtɛnjʊə/ or *tenure* /ˈtɛnjə/

presence of palatal(ized) consonants in Irish English is the result of the influence of Irish Gaelic, which like Russian contrasts palatal and velar consonants (Ní Chasaide 1999: 112). This leads to what is commonly known as a distinction between slender (palatal) and broad (velar) consonants. For instance, Stenson (1991) reports that seven bilingual speakers in North West Ireland transferred Irish palatal approximants into their English. This resulted in a pronunciation of *million* as [ˈmɪʎən] and not /ˈmɪljən/.

Palatalization

Palatalization is a type of **secondary articulation**. It occurs when a speaker produces a consonant with the front of their tongue raised. It is symbolized by ʻʲʼ. Some languages such as Russian distinguish palatalized consonants, known informally as *soft consonants* from nonpalatalized consonants, known informally as *hard consonants.* For instance, the Russian word [pʲotr] *Peter* commences with a soft consonant while the word [pjot] *rink* begins with a hard consonant.

Palatalized consonants may be heard, usually before **front vowels**, in some English dialects. The **velar plosives** /k/ and /g/ are palatalized in the following realization of *cake*, produced on the Shetland Islands, [tʲeək], Melchers (2008: 46). Velar plosives preceding [a] are palatalized and are a noted feature of Ulster English, for instance *Cavan* [ˈkʲavən] and *Gavin* [ˈgʲavɪn], (Milroy 1981: 25–6). It seems likely that the palatalization of velar plosives before /a/ is a relic pronunciation remaining from the transient popularity of palatalized consonants in fashionable London speech in the seventeenth century when the plantation of Ulster occurred. The palatalization of velar plosives before /a/ also occurs in the English creoles spoken in Suriname, where the palatalized velar plosives have phonemic status.

Palato-alveolar

The term palato-alveolar refers to the classification of a **consonant** sound on the basis of the place of **articulation** of the sound. Palato-alveolar consonants are produced by contact or close proximity between the blade (or possibly the tip) of the tongue and the area between the alveolar ridge and the hard palate. Assuming a normal **pulmonic egressive airstream mechanism** the following classes of consonants are classified by the IPA as palato-alveolar: **fricatives** [ʃ, ʒ]. In addition, Ibo realizes the approximants /ɹ/ and /l/ between the alveolar ridge and the hard palate. An unusual sound is [ɽ] **flap** (intermediate between /ɹ/ and /l/, which is articulated between the alveolar ridge and the hard palate).

As Table 25 indicates, the most common palato-alveolar sound is the **voiceless fricative**, which is found across numerous languages including English. In Japanese, which does not contain a /ʃ/ phoneme, the sound exists as an **allophone** of /s/ when followed by the vowel [i]. Thus, Japanese speakers pronounce the following words *shimasu* /simasɯ/, *sushi* /sɯsi/ and *sensei* /sense/ as [ʃimasɯ], [sɯʃi] and [sense], respectively.

There are no major regional differences in the pronunciation of /ʃ/ and /ʒ/ within English. Gimson (2008: 202) reports that medially /ʃ, ʒ/ are not used by all

P

Table 25 List of palato-alveolar phonemes found in 25 languages

Language	Flap	Fricatives	Approximants	Lateral approximants
Amharic		ʃ ʒ		
Arabic				
Bulgarian		ʃ ʒ		
Cantonese				
Czech		ʃ ʒ		
Dutch				
English		ʃ ʒ		
French		ʃ ʒ		
German		ʃ ʒ		
Greek				
Hausa		ʃ		
Hebrew		ʃ ʒ		
Hindi		ʃ		
Hungarian		ʃ ʒ		
Igbo		ʃ ʒ	ɹ	l
Italian		ʃ		
Japanese	ɽ			
Korean				
Mandarin				
Persian		ʃ ʒ		
Portuguese		ʃ ʒ		
Russian				
Spanish				
Swedish				
Thai				
Welsh		ʃ		

British speakers. In words before /uː/ and /ʊ/ there is often variation between /ʃ, ʒ/ and /s, z/ + /j/. Thus, *issue* and *casual* may be pronounced in the following ways. The percentage figures are from Wells (2000) and refer to a 1988 British English panel poll. It appears that American speakers would produce /ʃ/ and /ʒ/ in these words.

Issue	/ˈɪʃuː/49%	/ˈɪʃjuː/30%	/ˈɪsjuː/ 21%
Casual	/ˈkæʒuəl/ 77%		/ˈkæzjuəl/ 23%

/ʒ/ is a relatively recent phonemic entry of French origin into the English sound system and as such has a limited distribution. For some speakers, it exists word initially in French loan words such as *genre* /ˈʒɒnɹə/ and *gigolo* /ˈʒɪɡələʊ/ though others (including the author) tend at times to pronounce these words as /ˈdʒɒnɹə/

and /ˈdʒɪɡələʊ/. Because of the lack of words that are distinguished by the substitution of /ʃ/ and /ʒ/, words such as *Asia* can be pronounced either as /ˈeɪʃə/ (49 per cent) or /ˈeɪʒə/ (51 per cent).

Parametric speech

Transcriptions of connected speech may give the erroneous impression that speech is formed out of a chain of discrete targets. For instance, in order to pronounce the phrase *she cooks well* /ʃiː kʊks wɛl/ the speaker first ensures that the soft palate is raised, then moves the tongue towards the alveolar ridge until a light contact is made. With the tongue at rest /ʃ/ is articulated. Next the tongue is pushed slightly more forward while also raising it until it approaches closely to the alveolar ridge before coming to rest. The side rims of the tongue make a firm contact with the upper teeth and the speaker articulates /iː/. Then the front of the tongue is moved back while simultaneously moving the back of the tongue upwards until it forms a closure with the soft palate. The speaker releases the closure and produces /k/. Once more the tongue is at rest before it begins to move again.

In fact nothing is further from the truth! While speaking, our tongue never returns to the place of rest. Sometimes it never reaches the desired target before it begins to move in pursuit of a following desired target. Following sounds influence the articulation of earlier sounds and vice versa. In a possible articulation of the phrase, [ʃiː k̠ʰʷʊk̚s wɛʷɫ] it is probable that the initial /k/ would be retracted and rounded in anticipation of the following vowel /ʊ/ and that the second /k/ would be unreleased with the front of the tongue having moved in anticipation of the following fricative prior to the release of the stop. The vowel /ɛ/ is likely to be partly rounded because of the presence of the previous consonant /w/ – see **assimilation, harmony** and **epenthesis**.

Pharyngeal

The term pharyngeal refers to the classification of a **consonant** sound on the basis of the place of **articulation** of the sound. Pharyngeal consonants are articulated by the root of the tongue or the epiglottis against the pharynx, which is the tube behind the mouth and above the larynx. Many scholars (for example, Catford 2001) distinguish between pharyngeal and epiglottal articulations on the basis of whether the articulation is made in the part of the pharynx just behind the mouth or in the lower part of the pharynx just above the larynx. Sounds made just behind the mouth are pharyngeal while those made above the larynx are epiglottal. The IPA has symbols for **voiceless** and **voiced** pharyngeal **fricatives**, namely: [ħ, ʕ].

These sounds are claimed to be characteristic of Semitic languages such as Arabic and Hebrew, with [ħ] representing the Arabic letter ح and [ʕ] representing the Arabic letter ع. There is, however, some dispute in the literature as to the classification of these Arabic sounds. Catford himself notes that the voiced fricative [ʕ] has no turbulence, though the voiceless sound [ħ] is followed by an audible hiss. Thelwall and Akram Sa'adeddin (1999: 53) argue that [ʕ] is not a pharyngeal fricative but rather a **retracted tongue root** glottal stop. Ladefoged

Table 26 Pharyngeal and epiglottal consonants in Agul

Voiced pharyngeal fricative	muʕ	*bridge*	muʕar	*bridges*
Voiceless pharyngeal fricative	muħ	*barn*	muħar	*barns*
Voiceless epiglottal fricative	mɛʜ	*whey*	mɛʜɛr	*whey*
Voiceless epiglottal stop	jaʡ sɛʡ	*centre* *measure*	jaʡar sɛʡɛr	*centres* *measures*

and Maddieson (1996: 167) argue that what are called pharyngeal fricatives are actually epiglottal [ʜ] and [ʢ]. Catford (1988: 96) recognizes that in a few varieties of Arabic the sound represented by ع is produced by a complete closure formed by folding back the epiglottis. This view does not seem too dissimilar to that expressed by Thelwall and Akram Sa'adeddin (1999). Thus, the jury appears to be still out as to how best to classify these sounds: a pair of pharyngeal fricatives? A pair of epiglottal fricatives? Or a voiceless pharyngeal fricative and voiced epiglottal stop?

It is generally recognized that among non-oriental speakers of modern Hebrew the voiceless pharyngeal fricative [ħ] is replaced by either a voiceless **velar** [x] or **uvular** [χ] fricative and that [ʕ] is replaced by a glottal stop [ʔ]. However, it is worth remembering that Oriental Hebrew was chosen in Israel as the prestigious form to be used for broadcasting, etc., and is therefore in some sense analogous to RP in the UK (Laufer 1999: 96). Laufer (ibid.) classifies the pharyngeal consonants of Hebrew as a voiceless fricative [ħ] and a voiced approximant [ʕ], which further illustrates the uncertainty in the literature about the actual status of pharyngeal consonants in Semitic languages. One language that apparently contains both pharyngeal and epiglottal fricatives is Agul, a non-Semitic language spoken in Southern Dagestan by approximately 12,000 speakers (Table 5.9 in Ladegoged and Maddieson 1996: 168; and see http://www.phonetics.ucla.edu/appendix/languages/agul/agul.html for further details). See also Table 26.

Pharyngealization

Pharyngealization is a type of **secondary articulation** that is heard as adding a throatiness to the articulation of a sound. It occurs when a speaker produces a consonant or a vowel while simultaneously retracting the root of the tongue. The IPA symbol for pharyngealization is the same as that for **velarization**. No language is known to distinguish between these two secondary articulations. Pharyngealized **allophones** are not reported as occurring in any English dialect, with the sole exception of Welsh English speakers from traditional Welsh-speaking regions. Penhallurick (2008: 116 and 118) reports that some pronunciations of **dark** <L> produced especially in Gwynedd, and all Welsh English vowels other than the most open, may be pharyngealized.

Phonation

Phonation is a phonetic term used to refer to any vocal activity in the larynx, the role of which is neither to initiate an **airstream mechanism** nor to

articulate a speech sound. The main phonation types are **voice, voicelessness, creaky voice** and **breathy voice**. Most languages, including English, contrast **phonemes** solely on the basis of voicelessness versus voiced, though some languages, chiefly from the Indian subcontinent, contain phonemes that are distinguished by the other phonatory settings.

Phone

A phone is a phonetic term for the smallest perceptible discrete segment of sound in a speech signal. A phone is the physical correlate of a **phoneme**. However, a phoneme may be realized by a range of audibly distinct phones known as **allophones**.

Phoneme

A Phoneme is a phonological term that refers to the minimal unit of meaning in the sound system of a language. All words in any language can be described as a series of phonemes, though no two languages have exactly the same phonemic system. Some scholars argue that phonemes are psychologically real and that we store lexical units as phonemes in our mental lexicons. Other scholars deny that phonemes are stored in the mental lexicon and argue that they are merely bundles of oppositions or **distinctive features**. In any case phonemes, with the marginal exception of **free variation**, are identified as not occurring in the same environment within words. In other words, they are not in *complementary distribution*. Sounds that are in complementary distribution are **allophones**. Phonemes are abstract units of meaning. They do not represent a specific sound and instead consist of a range of allophones (see Jones 1967: 7ff.). For instance, the English phoneme /p/, at least in some dialects, is realized by the actual sounds [pʰ] for example in *pet*, [p] *spot*, [p̚] in tap. The three phones in English never contrast; substitution of one for the other does not result in a meaningful distinction. Conversely, the distribution of /p/ and /b/ overlaps and the overlap leads to a meaningful distinction, for example, /pɛt/, /bɛt/ and /kæp/, /kæb/. The existence of such minimal pairs automatically grants phonemic status to /p/ and /b/. The phonemes of a language can be established through a set of minimal pairs in a particular phonetic context. For instance in the contexts /iː/, /ɪn/ /ɛn/ /əʊ/ and /ɪə/ we can establish the following consonant phonemes in English:

Table 27 Consonants: minimal pairs in onset position

Context /_iː/	Context /_ɪn/	Context /_ɛn/	Context /_əʊ/	Context /_ɪə/
/piː/*pea*	/pɪn/ *pin*	/pɛn/ *pen*	/pəʊ/ *Po*	/pɪə/ *pier*
/biː/*bee*	/bɪn/ *bin*	/bɛn/ *Ben*	/bəʊ/ *bow*	/bɪə/ *beer*
/tiː/ *tea*	/tɪn/ *tin*	/tɛn/ *ten*	/təʊ/ *toe*	/tɪə/ *tear*
....	/dɪn/ *din*	/dɛn/ *den*	/dəʊ/ *doe*	/dɪə/ *deer*
/kiː/ *key*	/kɪn/ *kin*	/kɛn/ *Ken*	....	....
/giː/ ghee	....	....	/gəʊ/ *go*	/gɪə/ *gear*

P

Table 27 (Continued)

Context /_iː/	Context /_ɪn/	Context /_ɛn/	Context /_əʊ/	Context /_ɪə/
/fiː/ *fee*	/fɪn/ *fin*	fɛn/ *fen*	fəʊ/ *foe*	/fɪə/ *fear*
....	....	/vɛn/ *Venn*	....	/vɪə/ *veer*
/θiː/ tea	/θɪn/ *thin*	....	....	....
....	....	/ðɛn/ *then*	....	....
/siː/ *sea*	/sɪn/ *sin*	....	/səʊ/ *so*	/sɪə/ *sear*
....	....	/zɛn/ Zen	....	....
/ʃiː/ *she*	/ʃɪn/ *shin*	....	/ʃəʊ/ *show*	/ʃɪə/ *shear*
/hiː/ *he*	....	/hɛn/ *hen*	/həʊ/ *how*	/hɪə/ *hear*
....	....	....	....	/tʃɪə/ *cheer*
/dʒiː/ *gee*	/dʒɪn/ *gin*	....	/dʒəʊ/ *Joe*	/dʒɪə/ *jeer*
/wiː/ *we*	/wɪn/ *win*	/wɛn/ *when*	/wəʊ/ *woe*	/wɪə/ *weir*
....	....	/jɛn/ *Yen*	/jəʊ/ *yo*	/jɪə/ *year*

Table 28 Nasals: minimal pairs in coda position

Context /sɪ_/	Context /hʌ_/	Context /hæ_/
/sɪm/ sim	/hʌm/ *hum*	/hæm/ *ham*
/sɪn/ sin	/hʌn/ *Hun*	/hæn/ *Han*
/sɪŋ/ *sing*	/hʌŋ/ *hung*	/hæŋ/ *hang*

Only two English consonant phonemes have not been identified in the five contexts given above: namely /ŋ/ and /ʒ/. In English, /ŋ/ is restricted in its distribution to syllable coda position and so must be examined in that context – but see **archiphoneme**.

/ʒ/ is considered to be the newest member of the English consonant phoneme system and, according to Fry (1947), is the least common consonant used by speakers. It seems to have two independent etymologies (Gimson 2008: 203): one a borrowing from French as in some pronunciations of words such as *prestige* /ˌpɹəˈstɪʒ/ and *beige* /beɪʒ/; the other resulting from the **coalescence** of /z/ + /j/ in words such as *occasion* /əˈkeɪʒən/ and *treasure* /ˈtɹɛʒə/. It is noteworthy that /ʒ/ is restricted in its distribution in that for some speakers it only exists in word non-initial position. For other speakers it is found in a limited subset of French loan words in initial position, as in *genre* /ˈʒɛnɹə/, and names and brands such as *Giselle* /ʒɪˈzɛl/ and Givenchy /ʒiːˈvɒnʃi/. Because of the paucity of occurrence it is difficult to find contexts where the phonemic status of /ʒ/ can be satisfactorily demonstrated. Some relevant examples are:

Contrast between /ʒ/ and /dʒ/
/ˈlɛʒə/ *leisure* /ˈlɛdʒə/ *ledger*

Contrast between /ʃ/ and /ʒ/
/kənˈfjuːʃən/ *Confucian* /kənˈfjuːʒən *confusion*
/əˈljuːʃən/ *Aleutian* /əˈluːʒən/ *allusion*

P

The English **vowel** phonemes of any particular accent can be similarly distinguished by examining their distributions and by establishing minimal pairs within contexts. Phonemes have proved to be an adequate means of describing the systems of individual dialects. The presence or absence of a phoneme has been used by dialectologists to demarcate dialectal boundaries or isoglosses. However, phonemes are far less useful in generalizing sound change or in describing the processes of connected speech. For instance, T-voicing – a well-known feature of American and increasingly New Zealand speech – involves the realization of /t/, /d/ or /n/ as [ɾ], for example, *city* ⟶ [ˈsɪɾi] *leader* ⟶ [ˈliːɾɚ] and *winner* ⟶ [ˈwɪɾɚ]. Attempting to explain in phonemic terms why [ɾ] is realized instead of /t/, /d/ or /n/ when they immediately follow a stressed vowel and are themselves immediately followed by an unstressed vowel would lead to an analyst having to propose three independent rules for each phoneme. Instead, if each phoneme is considered to be a bundle of **distinct features** the commonalties between the three phonemes can be explicated and a single rule can be written. For example:

[+ stress V]/[+ coronal]/[– stress V] → [+ sonorant]
[+ anterior] [– lateral]
[– continuant]

Phonetics

Phonetics is a science that studies the characteristics of human speech. It provides methods for the description, classification and the transcription of speech sounds. It is usually divided up into three related subdisciplines – **articulatory** phonetics, **acoustic** phonetics and **auditory** phonetics – which examine how speech sounds are made, the physical nature of the sound wave and how speech sounds are heard, respectively. Strictly speaking, as phonetics is concerned with the physical reality of speech and not with how speech sounds create meaning, phonetics is not a subdiscipline of linguistics but rather an autonomous though closely related discipline to linguistics.

Phonology

Phonology is a subdiscipline of linguistics, which studies the sound systems of languages. Phonologists are interested in how the sound system of a language patterns into a distinctive meaningful structure. Traditionally there have been two main branches of phonology: 1) segmental phonology, which analyses speech into discrete units such as the **phoneme** or the **distinctive feature**; 2) suprasegmental phonology, which analyses features that extend over more than one segment (for instance **autosegmental, firthian** and **metrical** phonology). While rule-based **generative** phonology has been by far the most influential school of phonology recently generative phonological theory has begun to eschew abstract rule-based models in favour of more natural models that stress the importance of phonetically plausible constraints – see **markedness** and **optimality theory**.

P

Phonological word

A phonological word is a phonological domain above the **foot**, which is usually but not always coterminous with a lexical word. A phonological word minimally must contain a strong **foot** and is notated with an Omega symbol ω – see **metrical phonology**. In the following example there are two phonological words, but three lexical words:

[[John's ω1] [bald ω2]]

John's – which represents two lexical words *John* and *is* – consists of a single foot. It is therefore a single phonological word. A very common type of phonological word in English is an unstressed definite article followed by a noun that is phonetically indistinguishable from an unstressed prefix, for example: *a foot/afoot, a head/ahead* and *a bet/abet*. Clark, Yallop and Fletcher (2007: 105) observe that the history of some English words indicates that the boundary between article and noun is very weak. They note that the words *adder* and *apron* are derived from the earlier forms *nadder* and *napron*, which were misanalysed as *an adder* and *an apron* rather than *a nadder* and *a napron*. Readers interested in an extended discussion of the status and extent of phonological words should consult Roca and Johnson (1999: 483–93), who argue that phonological words may on occasion be coterminous with units that are smaller than lexical words.

Phonotactics

Phonotactics refers to the sequential or tactic relations between **phonemes** in any given language. Speakers of all languages know which sequences of phonemes are valid within their language. For instance, in an English speaking community it is possible to imagine a newly coined word *strit* but not one pronounced *sftit, ftsit, stfti* or *tfsit*. This is because only the consonant cluster *str* is a legal phonotactic string in English.

English, like all languages, has strict rules licensing where in the **syllable** phonemes can be placed and in what types of syllables phonemes can be found. In English, a number of phonemes, /h/, /j/, /w/ have restricted distribution and can only be found in syllable onset position. Conversely /ŋ/ can only be found in coda position. In stressed open syllables only long vowels or diphthongs are legal. Thus, in Table 29 the words in column A are possible words in English while the words in column B are not.

P

Table 29 Possible and impossible nonsense words in English

Column A	Column B
tɑːv	tɪ
vəʊ	vɒ
huːl	luːh
ʃɑːn	ŋɑːʃ

Unlike the nonsense words in Table 29 the majority of English words contain consonant clusters. These too are tightly regulated. Only clusters that tend to comply with the *sonority scale* – see **syllable** – are allowed. A legitimate English word can consist only of a vowel with no onset or coda as long as the vowel is long or a diphthong, for example: *eye* /aɪ/, *oh* /əʊ/, or *awe* /ɔː/. However, in most cases the word will contain either an onset or a coda and more likely both. In initial position, the consonant may be realized by zero as in the following words: ape /eɪp/, up /ʌp/, egg /ɛg/, out /aʊt/. In single consonant onsets all English consonants except /ŋ/ can occur in this position, though /ʒ/ is rare except in loan words such as *genre* and *gigolo*, which however, do have alternate pronunciations, for example: /ˈʒɒnrɛ/ or /ˈdʒɒnrɛ/ and /ˈʒɪgələʊ/ or /ˈdʒɪgələʊ/.

There may be two consonants in the initial cluster and, if this is the case, there are two different types of cluster. In the first case, the initial consonant must be /s/ and the second consonant can be any of the **fortis plosives** or /m/ and /n/. Some examples are *speed* /spiːd/, *steel* /stiːl/, *sky* /skai/, *smark* /smɑːt/ and *sniff* /snɪf/. There are a few minor exceptions to the rule that the initial consonant must be /s/. In a very few words of German and Yiddish origin the initial consonant can be /ʃ/, as in the following words of *schmooze* /ʃmuːz/, *schmuck* /ʃmʌk/ and *schnapps* /ʃnæps/.

The second type of two-consonant cluster has a **liquid** or **glide** in second position. If the second consonant is /ɹ/, the initial consonant can be any plosive or voiceless fricative, though /v/ and /s/ are highly unusual. Thus we have the following types of words: *pray* /preɪ/, *bray* /breɪ/, *train* /treɪn/, *drain* /dreɪn/, *craze* /kreɪz/, *graze* /greɪz/, *frill* /frɪl/, *thrill* /θrɪl/, *shrill* /ʃrɪl/, *Sri Lanka* /sriːˈlæŋkə/[1] and *vroom* /vruːm/. If the second consonant is /l/, the initial consonant can be a **bilabial** or **velar** plosive or a fortis **labiodental** fricative or a fortis **alveolar** fricative. There are two marginal exceptions, notably in some words of Yiddish origin where the initial consonant can be /ʃ/, and in some words of Slavic origin where the initial consonant can be /v/. Thus, we have the following types of words: *play* /pleɪ/, *blade* /bleɪd/, *clay* /kleɪ/, *glade* /gleɪd/, *flay* /fleɪ/, *slay* /sleɪ/, *schlep* /ʃlɛp/[2] and *Vlach* /vlɑːk/. If the second consonant is /w/ the initial consonant can be an alveolar or velar plosive, or a fortis dental, or a fortis alveolar fricative. The **lenis** velar plosive is unusual and only appears in words of Welsh origin. Similarly, in words of German origin, the fortis **palato-alveolar** fricative may appear in consonant initial position. Some example words are *twin* /twɪn/, *dwell* /dwɛl/, *quit* /kwɪt/, *thwart* /θwɑːt/, *swim* /swɪm/, *Gwen* /gwɛn/, *schwa* /ʃwɑː/. If the second consonant is /j/ in **received pronunciation** any consonant other than /ŋ/, /ɹ/ or /ʃ/ can appear in cluster initial position. However, this is not the case in GA, where there is a widespread tendency for /j/ dropping, known as *yod dropping*, especially before plosive consonants, see **palatal** for further information.

In English, three-consonant clusters are legal. The initial consonant in all cases must be /s/. The middle consonant in the cluster must be a fortis plosive and the last consonant in the cluster must be a liquid or an approximant. However, because of the difficulty of articulating certain sequences not all potential combinations are available. The cluster beginning /sp/ cannot be followed by /w/ but can be followed by /l/, /r/ or /j/. Some examples are *split* /splɪt/, *spree* /spriː/

and *spew* /spjuː/. The cluster beginning /st/ cannot be followed by /l/ or /w/, but can be followed by /r/ or /j/. Some examples are *street* /striːt/ and *stew* /stjuː/. The /sk/ clusters can similarly be followed by /j or /ɹ/. Some examples are *skew* /skjuː/ and, *scream* /skɹiːm/. /sk/ clusters can also occur with a limited number of medical words that commence with the prefix *scler* /skliə/, from classical Greek, which means hard, as in *sclerosis* /slkəˈrəʊs/. The sole other skl initial cluster I have been able to locate in the literature is the word *sclaff* /sklæf/.[3] The only other three-consonant cluster beginning with <s> that I can locate in the literature is *smew* /smjuː/ which is the name of a small duck (Gimson 2008: 255). It will be noted that if the third consonant in the initial cluster is /j/ he following vowel must be /uː/ or /ʊə/, for example: *spurious* /ˈspjʊərɪəs/.

There can be between zero and four consonants in *coda* position. If the syllable is open the vowel cannot be any of the following /ɛ, æ, ʌ ɒ/. Gimson (ibid.: 254) notes that /ʊ/ appears in open syllables in some pronunciations of *to* when the word is followed by a word beginning with a vowel or by a pause. However, this view is not universally accepted, and others such as Wells (2001: 783) consider that these pronunciations of *to* actually contain the vowel /u/. There is unanimous agreement in the literature that if the open syllable is **stressed** only long vowels and diphthongs can occur.

The final coda can consist of a single consonant. All consonants except /ɹ, h, j, w/ can occur in this position in non-rhotic accents, /ɹ/ is found in codas in **rhotic** accents. There are far more permissible CC clusters in coda position than there are in onset position. There are two distinct types of cluster found. The first is where any permissable consonant is followed by one of the following: /t/, /d/, /s/, /z/ and θ/. These clusters usually arise because of suffixation indicating (1) past tense, such as *kicked* /kikt/, *smelled* /smɛld/; (2) plural marking; (3) third person; (4) a genitive such as *pets* /pɛts/, *trains* /treɪnz/, *hits* /hɪts/, *runs* /rʌnz/ , *Pete's* /piːts/ and *John's* /djɒnz/; and (5) suffixation that creates a noun such as *length* /lɛŋθ/ The second type of legal CC cluster coda consists of a nasal, either /m/, /n/ or /ŋ/; a lateral /l/ or /s/ in the position immediately following the vowel, which is itself followed by another consonant. In all cases, the second consonant will be of lower sonority than the initial one. Thus, the nasals and laterals can theoretically be followed by any **obstruent** and /s/ can be followed by any **affricate** or **plosive**. However, not all available possibilities are utilized. Some examples are *camp* /kæmp/, *paint*, /peɪnt/ *link*, /lɪŋk/ *weld* /wɛld/ and *list* /lɪst/.

There are two types of CCC consonant codas, the first of which results from the suffixation of the second type of CC consonant coda described above, for example: *camps* /kæmps/, *paints* /peɪnts/, *links*, /lɪŋks/ *welds* /wɛldz/ and *lists* /lɪsts/. Gimson (2008: 257) notes two unusual monomorphemic words that follow this pattern: *mulct* /mʌlkt/ and *calx* /kælks/.[4] The second type involves a further selection of /t/, /d/, /s/, /z/ and θ/ and is usually but not always connected with suffixed words, for instance *lengths* /lɛŋθs/, *products* /ˈprɒdʌkts/, seconds /səˈkɛnds/. There are two very common monomorphemic words with a CCC final cluster, notably *text* /tɛkst/ and *next* /nekst/.

Four consonant coda clusters are very rare in English. They are always the result of suffixication caused by the addition of /t/ or /s/ to a word that ends in a three-consonant cluster. The permissible final clusters are /mpts/ as in *prompts*; /mpst/ as in *glimpsed*; /lkts/ as in *mulcts*; /lpts/ s in sculpts; /lfθs/ as in *twelfths*; /ntθs/

as in *thousandths*; /ksts/ as in *texts* and /ksθs/ as in *sixths* (for further information see Gimson 2008: Section 10:10). Speakers (especially when speaking quickly) tend to elide the third consonant in a four-consonant coda cluster, though there is less likelihood of the elision of the third consonant in the clusters /ksts/ and /ksθs/ – see **elision**.

Pitch

Pitch is the perceptual correlate of the vibration of a speaker's **vocal folds** or the fundamental frequency F_0 of a sound. The relationship between the frequency of vibration of the vocal folds and the auditory sensation of pitch is indirect. But, in general, the faster the frequency of vibration the higher the perception of pitch will be. As adult males on average have longer and thicker vocal folds than adult females, adult males usually speak with lower pitch than adult females. However, it is clear that anatomical differences between males and females are not solely responsible for differences in the overall voice pitch of adult males and females in the languages of the world. In certain languages, such as Japanese, there is a far larger discrepancy – especially in formal settings between the pitches of adult males and adult females – than there is in other languages such as Greek or English. In Japanese, adult females tend to speak with disproportionally high-pitched voices while their male counterparts tend to speak with disproportionally low-pitched voices. It seems that pitch is modulated by cultural factors of which gendered stereotypes appear the most significant (see Yuasa 2008 for a fuller discussion).

Plosive

A plosive is a term used to refer to the classification of a **consonant** on the basis of its manner of **articulation**. Plosives are produced by a complete closure of the vocal tract and are, as a result, **stop** consonants. Simultaneously the soft palate is raised, thus ensuring that the airstream is unable to escape out of the **nasal** passage. Plosives are also known as **oral** stops. The IPA symbolizes plosives made at the following places of **articulation**: **bilabial** /p b/, **alveolar** /t d/, **retroflex**, /ʈ ɖ/ **palatal**, /c ɟ/ **velar** /k g/, **uvular** /q ɢ/ and **glottal** /ʔ/. The IPA recognizes the possibility of a language containing plosive **phonemes** made with either **labiodental** or **pharyngeal** articulation but does not symbolize them (see the discussion of **pharyngeal**). Ladefoged and Maddieson (1996: 17) report the presence of voiced and voiceless labiodental stops among languages found in Southern Africa.

English contains six plosive phonemes /p/, /b/, /t/, /d/, /k/ and /g/. The voiceless plosives are realized in different ways depending on where they are found in a **syllable**. If they are syllable initial they are usually **aspirated**, and if syllable final they are unaspirated. If they are word or morpheme final, and especially if followed by another consonant, they may have no audible release. Voiceless syllable initial plosives that follow /s/ are unaspirated. If the voiceless plosives are followed by either a **nasal** or /l/ as in *happen* [hæp^{n}n̩], *apple* ['æpl̩] and *please* [p^{hl}iːz] they have either nasal or **lateral** release.

The degree of voicing on a voiced plosive depends to a very large extent on its position within a word. They are only fully voiced if word medial and between two voiced sounds, for instance *husband* [ˈhʌzbənd̥], *symbol* [ˈsɪmbəl], *older* [ˈəʊldə], *leader* [ˈliːdə], *anger,* [ˈæŋgə] *meagre* [ˈmiːgə]. Word initially voiced plosives are at least partially devoiced – see **vot** – while word finally they tend to be partly or even fully devoiced. Devoicing is indicated by transcribing a small circle known as an *under-ring* or circle underneath the consonant, with the exception of /g/, where for ease of legibility a small circle known as an *over-ring* is placed above the consonant. Thus, the words *tab, tad* and *tag* may be pronounced as follows: [tʰæb̥], [tʰæd̥] and [tʰæg̊]. Like voiceless plosives, voiced plosives followed by a nasal or /l/ have nasal or lateral release.

There are few significant differences in how English speakers of different accents realize plosives. The most significant differences are listed below:

- While the vast majority of accents aspirate voiceless plosives, Celtic-influenced varieties are more strongly aspirated. Some speakers in Lancaster unusually do not aspirate voiceless plosives.
- Indian speakers of English tend not to aspirate voiceless plosives probably because of the influence of Indian languages that contrast aspirated and very strongly unaspirated plosives.
- For many speakers of British English in word medial positions /t/ is frequently replaced or re-enforced by a **glottal** stop – see **glottal**.
- For many speakers of American English, and increasingly for speakers of New Zealand English, an intervocalic /t/ or /d/ is realized as a **tap** – for instance, *butter and leader are* pronounced as [ˈbʌɾɚ] and [ˈliːɾɚ].
- Southern Irish speakers tend to palatalize velar plosives, especially when the plosive follows a **front vowel**. Thus *kick* may be realized as [kʰiːç]. It is worth noting that the final <k> is realized as a palatal fricative – see **palatal** and **lenition**.
- One of the most stereotypical features of the 'Irish brogue' is that dental fricatives are realized as dental stops. Thus *thin* is pronounced as [t̪ʰɪn] and not [θɪn] – see **dental**.

Prosody

P

Prosody is a collective term that is used to refer to any feature whose domain extends beyond the segment. It is similar to the term suprasegmental, but unlike suprasegmental it is restricted to features that are linguistically meaningful. The term includes variations in **pitch, tone**, **intonation** and **rhythm**. For some theorists, such as J. R. Firth, the term also includes features such as **labialization** and **nasalization** (See **firthian prosodic phonology**).

Pulmonic

The term pulmonic refers to an **airstream mechanism** that originates in the lungs. Air can be pushed out of the lungs to produce an **egressive** flow of air or **sucked** into the lungs to produce an **ingressive** flow. An egressive pulmonic airstream is the usual power source for speech.

Received pronunciation

Received pronunciation (RP) is the regionally neutral variant of British English that originated in the court and the public schools in the nineteenth century. It is informally known as BBC English. It is the accent of English that has been traditionally taught to foreign learners of 'British English'. The term 'received' signifies that it is the accent that was considered suitable for those who wished to be accepted in society. The accent is a prestigious social accent, though linguistically it is simply an accent of English that is no more privileged than any other. Mugglestone (2003) provides a useful discussion of how RP was adapted as a marker of class identity, cultural capital and social superiority by the upper classes in England.

Presently it is more useful to speak of RPs rather than a single monolithic prestigious accent. Wells (1982b: 280ff.) notes that, 'The accent popularly associated with a dowager duchess is not quite the same as Mainstream RP.' He distinguishes between U(pper) RP, which has connotations of the traditional aristocracy, and mainstream RP, favoured by some younger speakers, which as an accent is claimed to be neutral in terms of occupation and geographical origin. Wells (ibid.) describes a further accent Near RP as an accent that includes little in the way of regional pronunciation that could be used to identify a speaker's origin. He concedes that drawing an absolute boundary between mainstream RP and Near RP is subjective and contentious. Hence it makes more sense to classify RP as a set of related accents that operate along a cline extending in one direction to URP and in another to Near RP or perhaps even to more regionally marked varieties that have been dubbed Regional RP (see **estuary english**).

Retroflex

The term retroflex traditionally refers to the classification of a **consonant** sound on the basis of the place of **articulation** of the sound. Retroflex consonants are produced when the tip of the tongue is curled back in the direction of the front part of the hard palate. Ladefoged and Maddieson (1996: 25) argue that the shape of the tongue is as important in producing a retroflex articulation as the place of **articulation**. They describe sounds made with the tip curled, which form either an **alveolar** or **post-alveolar** articulation as retroflex-type articulations. However, the majority of scholars (such as Catford 1988; Laver 1990; Lodge 2009) disagree and only classify sounds made with a post-alveolar articulation as retroflex. The IPA symbolizes retroflex sounds by adding a tail curved to the right to the equivalent alveolar phone.

The IPA recognizes retroflex **stops** [ʈ, ɖ], **nasal** [ɳ], **flap** [ɽ], **fricatives** [ʂ, ʐ], **approximant** [ɻ] and **lateral approximant** [ɭ]. Retroflex sounds are characteristic of Indo-Aryan languages such as Hindi or Urdu, but they are also found in Dravidian languages such as Tamil, the African language *Ewe* (which contains a /ɖ/ phoneme) and various Amerindian and Australian languages. Hindi has four retroflex stop phonemes: voiceless aspirated, voiceless unaspirated, voiced and voiced with breathy voice – see **phonation** – which contrast with their **dental** equivalents. Ohala (1999: 100–1) presents the following contrasts (Table 30).

Table 30 Dental and retroflex stops in Hindi

	Dental	**Retroflex**
Voiceless	/t̪ɑl/ *beat*	/ʈɑl/ *postpone*
Voiceless aspirated	/t̪ʰɑl/ *platter*	/ʈʰɑl/ *lumber shop*
Voiced	/dɑl/ *lentil*	/ɖɑl/ *branch*
Voiced with breathy voice	/dʱɑɾ/ *knife edge*	/ɖʱɑl/ *shield*

Not surprisingly, Indian speakers of English may substitute retroflex stops for alveolar ones. Wells (1982c: 628) notes that retroflexion, 'remains a sure way for an impressionist to suggest an Indian accent'. Retroflexion is not absolute, sounds may be more or less retroflex depending on the extent to which the tongue is curled back. Wells (ibid.) notes that speakers from Southern India tend to produce more strongly retroflexed sounds than those from the North. This is to be as expected as it is likely that retroflex consonants on the Indian subcontinent emanate from the Dravidian languages of the South and have been borrowed by the Indo-Aryan languages of the North.

Retroflex sounds are not part of the **phonemic** inventory of any European language but can be commonly heard in Standard Swedish. Engstrand (1999: 141) reports that in Standard Swedish the following consonant clusters – /rt, rd, rn, rs, rl/ – are often produced as **allophonic** retroflex sounds [ʈ, ɖ, ɳ, ʂ, ɭ]. Thus, *nordan (north)* is pronounced [ˈnuːɖan]. In English, many speakers of rhotic accents such as Americans, Irish and West Country speakers produce a retroflexed <r>, a process that is also known as *r colouring*. Hickey (2008: 89–90) reports that the traditional realization of <r> in Southern Irish English is a velarized alveolar continuant [ɾˠ] – see **velarization**. He states that the retroflexed [ɻ] found in Ulster English is of Scottish origin. He also notes that in modern fashionable Dublin speech and among younger female speakers throughout Ireland [ɻ] is frequently found. He argues that the Southern [ɻ] is of independent sociolinguistic origin, namely a disassociation with the rural sounding traditional [ɾˠ]. Thus, in Dublin *card* is pronounced as [kʰæːɻd].

Stuart-Smith (2008: 65) reports that /r/ in Scotland is usually realized as a post-alveolar approximant [ɹ], a retroflex approximant [ɻ] or as an alveolar **tap** [ɾ]. She notes that retroflex approximants are more common among middle-class speakers. Wells (1982b: 342) notes that in the West Country retroflex [ɻ] is more frequent than post-alveolar [ɹ]. Speakers in Hampshire, Wiltshire, Dorset, Somerset, Devon and Cornwall traditionally produce both pre-vocalic and post-vocalic <r> as [ɻ].

Rhotic

Rhotic refers to accents that pronounce a variant of [r] in **syllable** coda position. Cross-linguistically rhoticity appears to be rare. R-coloured vowels exist only in 'less than one percent of the world's languages', Ladefoged and Maddieson (1996: 313). However, as two of the languages that have r-coloured vowels include some forms of English and Chinese, r-coloured vowels are familiar to most of us. Within the English language rhotic accents are found chiefly in South West England, Scotland, Ireland and in most American accents, excepting New York and the accent of the former Confederate states.

McMahon (2006: 152) notes that evidence from historical spelling indicates that from the fifteenth to the seventeenth centuries English writers had difficulty in accommodating post-vocalic <r> before a consonant, leading to spellings such as *moyning* for *morning*. However, some seventeenth-century orthoepists in England retained post-vocalic /r/ within their descriptions of the English vowel system, though it is not clear whether these descriptions were intended to be prescriptive or descriptive. In other words, we do not know whether they were describing the widespread and accepted pronunciation of post-vocalic /r/ or vainly fighting for its retention. Today within England the prestige accent, RP, is non-rhotic and consequently there has been both a continued loss of post-vocalic /r/ and a stigmatization of English speakers who pronounce post-vocalic /r/. Yet despite this, the loss of post-vocalic /r/ has been gradual. Upton (2006: 314) notes that it is only in the past 50 years that speakers in Reading (a town on the western outskirts of London) have stopped pronouncing post-vocalic /r/. Recent evidence indicates that within England the areas in which post-vocalic /r/ is spoken are continuing to decline. Younger speakers, even in traditional rhotic areas, are increasingly adopting non-rhotic pronunciations.

In America, the prestige accent is rhotic and so the situation is to some extent reversed. Labov's groundbreaking studies of New York speech in the 1960s demonstrated that r-coloured vowels were being introduced into New York speech by speakers who were mimicking the American rhotic standard (Labov 1966). More recent evidence (Labov, Ash and Boberg 2006: 47–8) indicates that r-coloured vowels are being increasingly pronounced by Southern American speakers whose traditional dialect was non-rhotic. For further information see **accent, diphthong, retroflex** and **vowel**.

Secondary articulation

Secondary articulation is the production of a sound that has two simultaneous articulations. Unlike **double articulation** one of the articulations is primary and the other secondary. Secondary articulations involve an additional **articulatory gesture** such as the raising of the front or back of the tongue. This results in an auditorily distinct **allophone**. Secondary articulations are classified as follows: **nasalization, labialization, palatalization, pharyngealization, uvularization** and **velarization**.

Semi-vowel

Semi-vowel is a term used in the classification of **consonant** sounds on the basis of their manner of **articulation**. Semi-vowels are sounds that **phonologically** function as consonants but **phonetically** are articulated without the usual characteristics associated with consonants such as **closure** and **friction**. The English semi-vowels are /j/ and /w/, (see **approximant**). They are shortened versions of the /iː/ FLEECE and GOOSE /uː/ **vowels**, respectively. Semi-vowels tend to have limited distributions, for instance /j/ and /w/ occur in English only prior to a vowel, as in *yet* /yɛt/, *wet* /wɛt/, *tune* /tjuːn/, *twain* /tweɪn/. Phonetically they represent a glide into a vowel but phonologically the presence of pre-vocalic /j/ and /w/ contrasts with other consonants, as in the formation of the words *yet, wet, bet, pet, set, met, net*. For a slightly different view see Ladefoged (2001: 215), who argues that semi-vowels are better classified as non-syllabic vocoids (also for an opposing view see: Lodge 2009: 49).

In American English, regardless of how /j/ is classified, it is clear that there is an increasing tendency to elide the /j/ in consonant clusters – a process labelled *yod dropping* by sociolinguists – unless the previous consonant is either **bilabial** or **velar**. Thus, the following are typical American pronunciations – *beauty* /ˈbjuːti/ *tune*, /tuːn/ *news* /nuːz/ and *cute* /kjuːt/. In the UK, with the exception of East Anglia where /j/ can be dropped after any consonant, /j/ tends to be retained after **plosives** and **nasals**, though as Gimson (2008: 229) notes, increasingly pronunciations such as /nuːz/ are being heard in the UK.

Sibilant

A sibilant is a phonetic term that is used to describe **fricatives** that are articulated with a grooved tongue in which the airstream is compressed into a narrow channel. As a result, the airstream becomes more turbulent. Sibilant fricatives are nosier and have more acoustic energy than non-sibilant fricatives, which are produced with a flat tongue. In English, the fricatives /s/, /z/, /ʃ/ and /ʒ/ are sibilants while /f/, /v/, /θ/, /ð/ are non-sibilants.

Sonorant

A sonorant is a phonetic term that classifies **vowel** and **consonant** sounds on the basis of the degree of constriction. Sounds that are made with a constriction which does not impede the passage of air through the **vocal tract** and have a **vocal fold** position which allows for spontaneous voicing such as **vowels, approximants, semi-vowels** and **nasals** are sonorants. Sonorant sounds are also known as resonant sounds.

Sound change

Sound change is a term that is used in historical linguistics to describe changes in the sound system of a language over an extended period. Changes can occur in either the **consonant** or the **vowel** systems, either through the merger of two **phonemes** into a single phoneme, or by the splitting of a phoneme into two. An example of a merger in English is the loss of a distinction between the initial **labal-velar** consonants in words such as *which/witch*, *whine/wine* and *whales/Wales*. An example of a split in English is the **alveolar** nasal /n/, which in Old English had two **allophonic** realizations in syllable coda position: [ŋ] if followed by a **velar** consonant and [n] if followed by a pause or an alveolar consonant. Presently there is a phonemic contrast between the nasal sounds in *sin* and *sing*.

Scholars in the nineteenth century devoted much energy to uncovering the laws that governed sound change. One of the best known examples is Grimm's law (see **fortition**), which explains how the consonants in the Germanic languages (including English) differ systematically from those found in cognate forms in other Indo-European languages. For instance, Grimm noticed a series of words that in Indo-European languages began with /p/ /t/ /k/ while the Germanic cognate words had /f/ /θ/ /x/. For instance:

Sanskrit	Greek	Latin	German	Old English	English
pada	pus	pes	fuß	fot	foot
trayas	treis	tres	drei[1]	thrie	three
kukkurra	Kion	Canis	Hund[2]	Hound	Hound (dog)

The overall change from Proto-Indo-European (PIE) to Proto-Germanic (PG) is schematized by Lass (1984: 130) and is as follows:

Proto-Indo-European					Proto-Germanic			
p	t	k	k^w		f	θ	x	x^w
b	d	g	g^w	→	p	t	k	k^w
b	d̤	g̈	$\ddot{g}^w$		b	d	g	g^w
	s					s		

It is clear that at some stage in the history of Proto-Germanic (PG) the consonant system underwent a series of sound changes that resulted in predictable differences between PG and PIE. The change, ignoring the invariant [s] is: PIE breathy voiced stops /d̤/ /g̈/ and /g̈ʷ/ underwent a process of lenition and became the PG voiced stops /d/ /g/ and /g̈/. The PIE voiced stops /b//d//g/ and /gʷ/ underwent a process of fortition by being devoiced and becoming /p/ /t/ /k/ /kʷ/. The PIE voiceless stops underwent a process of lenition and changed into the following fricatives /f/ /θ/ /x/ /xʷ/ (see **great vowel shift**).

Stop

A stop is a term used to refer to the classification of a **consonant** on the basis of its manner of **articulation**. Stops are produced by a complete closure of the oral cavity. There are two types of stops: (1) **plosives** or **oral** stops, which are produced with the **soft palate** raised; (2) **nasal** stops, which are produced with the soft palate lowered.

Stress

Stress is a phonological feature in which one syllable within a lexical item is heard as being louder or more prominent than the others. In all polysyllabic words, one syllable is perceived as being the most prominent. It receives the primary stress. In addition, another syllable that precedes the primary stressed syllable may be perceived as being more prominent than the remaining syllables.[3] In the citation form of polysyllable lexical items, primary stress is notated by a ˈ diacritic while the optional secondary stress is notated by a ˌ diacritic. For example:

perfume /ˈpɜːfjuːm/ a two-syllable word that has primary stress on the initial syllable;
conurbation /ˌkɒnɜːˈbeɪʃən/ a four-syllable word that has primary stress on the third syllable and secondary stress on the first syllable.

Stress is not an optional feature that a speaker can add to or subtract from a word (see **accenting**). It is an invariant part of the lexical item. If the stress pattern is altered, the lexical item itself is changed, as such the nominal element *record* has primary stress on the first syllable while the verbal element *record* has primary stress on the second syllable. The lexical items *below* and *billow* chiefly differ in terms of stress, with the former having primary stress on the second syllable (for example, /bəˈləʊ/) and the latter having primary stress on the first syllable (for example, /ˈbɪləʊ/).[4]

Lexical stress is signalled in English through four phonetic means, the first of which is the most significant: (1) higher or lower **pitch**; (2) longer **duration**; (3) more **intensity**; and (4) vowel quality with stressed vowels articulated towards the periphery of the **vowel** space. Unstressed vowels tend to be produced towards the centre of the vowel space. Stressed syllables tend to be longer, louder and lower than unstressed ones. Lass (1987: 108) commented that the sole 'universal' requirement needed to realize a stressed syllable is that the syllable be perceived as somehow standing out from the other syllables.

Cross-linguistically two types of languages can be identified: those with fixed lexical stress and those with variable lexical stress. In languages with fixed lexical stress, the position of the stressed syllable is invariant. In a survey of

444 languages Hyman (1977), reported in Laver (1994: 518–21), found that around 70 per cent of the surveyed languages had fixed lexical stress with the stressed syllable being predominantly located in the initial, penultimate or final syllable. This indicates, Laver suggests, that lexical stress serves to assist the hearer in demarcating word boundaries. Some examples of languages with fixed lexical stress are French (where the lexical stress is normally realized on the final syllable), Welsh and Polish (where it is normally realized on the penultimate syllable), and Finnish and Czech (where it is normally realized on the initial syllable).

English, as previously mentioned, along with languages such as Greek, has variable lexical stress. In Greek there are minimal pairs such as /ˈpoli/ *city* and /poˈli/ *much*, where the words are distinguished solely by stress placement. Variable stress does not mean that the placement of a stressed syllable within a lexical item is in the vast majority of cases anything other than entirely predictable. In English there are three main factors that need to be considered when examining the rules governing stress placement[5]:

1 **Syntactic information**
Stress placement is sensitive to which part of speech the lexical item is. There is a predictable difference in lexical stress placement in the following noun/verb pair: – *a* /ˈrɛkɔːd/ and *to* /rɪˈkɔːd/. In the noun/adjective/verb triad *a* /ˈpɹɛzənt/, /ˈpɹɛzənt/, /pɹəˈzɛnt/ the verb alone is stressed on the final syllable. It is impossible to know how to assign stress correctly to a string of **phonemes** such as [pɹɛzɛnt] without first knowing whether the lexical item formed from the string of phonemes is functioning as a noun, verb or adjective.

2 **Morphological information**
All lexical items must consist of a mandatory *root* or *base* such as *arm* and optional affixes. Prefixes attach before the word, as in *disarm*, and suffixes attach at the end of the word, as in *armful*. A word may contain both a prefix and a suffix, as in *disarming*. Some prefixes and suffixes preserve the word stress of the root, for instance: the suffix *hood* in the pair *brother* /ˈbɹʌðə/ and *brotherhood* /ˈbɹʌðəhʊd/. Others such as the suffix *#ette* alter the stress of the root by taking the stress, as in the pair *kitchen* /ˈkɪtʃən/ and *kitchenette* /ˌkɪtʃəˈnɛt/. Suffixes that are of Old English origin are known as *neutral suffixes*, when added to a root they do not alter the lexical stress pattern. Some of the most common suffixes of Old English origin are *#hood, #ly, #ness* and *#ing*. In contrast, other suffixes known as *tonic endings* have been borrowed from Modern French and alter the lexical stress pattern of the root by causing the stress to move on to the suffix. Some example suffixes are *#ee, # aire, #oon, #ese* and *#esque*. For a complete list see Kreidler (2004: 273–5). Neutral suffixes and tonic endings can attach to roots regardless of whether the root is itself derived from Old English or is a more recent borrowing. If they attach, regardless of the word's etymology they preserve or take the lexical stress. The word *absent* was borrowed from French in the fourteenth century and is the root in the pair *absenting* /æbˈsɛntɪŋ/ with stress preserved, and absentee /ˌæbsənˈtiː/ with stress taken by the suffix. Unlike suffixes, there is very little regularity and predictability in how prefixes affect stress. No prefix is itself stress-carrying

and, consequently, the best treatment of prefixes appears to be to ignore the presence of a prefix and assign the stress as if the word did not contain a prefix.

3 **Phonological information**
The exact placement of stress in a word depends in part on the nature of the last two syllables, which are known as the *ult(imate)* and the *penult(imate)*. Stress placement is sensitive to whether or not a **syllable** has a free or a checked vowel. If the vowel is checked, stress placement is sensitive to the number of consonants that form the syllable coda. Free vowels are those vowels that can occur in monosyllabic words that form open syllables, for example: the vowels /iː/, /eɪ/, /aɪ/, /uː/, /əʊ/, aʊ/, /ɑː/, /ɔː/ and /ɔɪ/. All other vowels are checked. If the ult or the penult syllable contains a free vowel then that syllable – all things being equal – is likely to receive the lexical stress. Examples of ult containing free vowels that are stressed are *remain* /ɹɪˈmeɪn/, *destroy* /dɪˈstɹɔɪ/ and *devout* /dɪˈvaʊt/. Examples where the penult contains a free vowel that is stressed are *diploma* /dɪˈpləʊmə/ *horizon* /həˈraɪzən/ and *arena* /əˈɹiːnə/. However, as we have seen, it is not possible in English to use phonological criteria alone to determine stress placement. So the following paragraphs consider the placement of stress in terms of nouns, verbs and adjectives.

In considering how English nouns are stressed it is first necessary to consider how many syllables the noun contains. If the answer is two we would expect that the penult will receive the stress. This is the case even if the ult contains a free vowel, as in *membrane* /ˈmɛmbɹeɪn/. If the noun contains more than two syllables, the initial point to consider is whether or not the ult contains a free vowel. If it does, as in words such as *appetite* /ˈæpɪteɪt/, the antepenult syllable receives the stress, but note the exception *apartheid* /əˈpɑːtheɪd. If on the other hand the ult contains a checked vowel, and the penult contains either a free vowel or a checked vowel that is followed by two or more consonants, the penult receives the stress, for example, with a free vowel in the penult *aroma* /əˈɹəʊma/, and with a checked vowel followed by two consonants in the coda *memorandum* /ˌmɛməˈrændəm/. Syllables containing a free vowel, or syllables containing a checked vowel followed by a coda that contains two or more consonants, are in Kreidler's terms 'stressable'. Finally, if the ult does not contain a free vowel and the penult is not a stressable syllable the antepenult is stressed, as in *citizen* /ˈsɪtɪzən/.

In assigning stress to a verb, the first point that must be considered is whether or not the ult is stressable. If it is not stressable the penult receives the stress, as in *solicit* /səˈlɪsɪt/ and *imagine* /ɪˈmædʒɪn/. If on the other hand the ult is stressable, then the number of syllables within the verb is of relevance to the stress placement. If the verb contains two syllables the ult receives the stress, as in *agree* /əˈgɹiː/ and *record* /ɹəˈkɔːd/. Verbs that contain more than two syllables and have a stressable ult are stressed on the antepenult, as in *solidify* /səˈlɪdɪfaɪ/ and *complement* /kɒmˈplɛmɛnt/. Historically, all verbs that had stressable ults were stressed on the ult. This remains the case in Caribbean varieties of English where, if the ult is stressable, it is stressed even in verbs that contain more than two syllables (Aceto 2008: 645).

When considering the stressing of adjectives no further rules are required. Some adjectives follow the verb stress rules while others are stressed like nouns. Adjectives that end with the suffixes *#al, #ant/ent, #ar* and *#ous* follow the noun stress rules. In words such as *fatal, present, solar* and *famous* the root is monosyllabic and it receives the stress. However, in words such as *accidental, magnificent, popular* and *momentous* either the penult or antepenult may be stressed. If the penult is stressable it receives the stress, for example, /ˌæksɪˈdɛntal/ and /məʊˈmɛntəs/, otherwise the antepenult receives the stress, as in /ˈpɒpjʊlə/ and /mægˈnɪfɪsənt/.

In addition to the rules set out below there are a number of cases of adjectives and verbs that end in open syllables containing vowels that are not easily classifiable as free or checked. For instance, it is debatable whether the words set out in Table 31 end with the free vowels /iː/, /uː/ and /əʊ/ or the checked vowels /ɪ/, /ʊ/ and /?/.[6]

Table 31 Words completed with either a checked or a free vowel, from Kreidler (2004: 168)

Copy envy marry worry easy happy ugly
Argue continue issue rescue
Borrow follow swallow hollow narrow yellow

However, while there does not seem to be any overall consensus on this matter, probably because there is no phonological distinction between minimal pairs contrasting checked and free vowels in final position, it is clear that for the operation of the stress rules the vowel in the ult is considered checked and the syllable is therefore non-stressable. The stress, in other words, falls on the penult syllable.

The rules given above are not entirely all encompassing, probably because English is a language that borrows lexis from fixed stress languages and this creates some uncertainty in how a particular lexical item should be stressed. For instance, many speakers pronounce the name of the rock band the *Libertines* with stress on the ult, though in fact, according to the English stress rules for nouns, it should be stressed on the antepenult. It has more than two syllables, has the free vowel /iː/ in the ult and the penult is not stressable, so the antepenult should receive the stress.

There are many words in the English language which, when written, end in <y>. Of these <y> words some contain a neutral suffix, as in *friendly, clearly, dirty, smithy* and *doggy*, where the base has the potential to stand alone as a word. When it does, the base receives the stress. Others contain the non-neutral *acy, ancy* or *ency* suffix, as in words such as *delicacy, decency, fallacy, pregnancy* and *emergency*. In these cases the stress rule is that if the syllable before the suffix is (a) the initial syllable of the word, as in *fallacy* /ˈfæləsi/ or (b) stressable, as in *diplomacy* /dɪˈpləʊməsiː/, then that syllable is stressed. If not, stress is placed on the second syllable before the suffix, as in *emergency* /ɪˈmɜːdʒənsi/ and *harmony* /ˈhɑːməni/. A noted exception is the lexical item *discrepancy* /dɪsˈkɹɛpənsi/, which has stress on the syllable immediately prior to the suffix despite the syllable not being stressable!

Nouns and adjectives that end with *ary* have three different stress patterns, as exemplified in the following words: (a) *complimentary*, (b) *contemporary* and (c) the rare case *veterinary*, where there are two weak syllables between the stressed syllable and the suffix. The rules for these three types of words are:

- If the syllable before the suffix is either initial or stressable it is stressed, as in (a) *compliment+ary* /ˌkɒmplɪˈmɛntəɹi/.
- Otherwise the penult syllable in the base is stressed, as in (b) *contempor+ary* /kɒnˈtɛmpəɹəɹi/. In the case of the lexical item *vocabul+ary* /vəʊˈkæbjʊləri/, as predicted the stress is on the penult syllable of the base, but this it must be noted results in a stress shift compared with the noun /ˈvəʊkæb/.
- In exceptional cases, where the ult and the penult of the base are not stressable, the stress appears on the antepenult syllable of the base, as in *veteran+ary* /ˈvɛtəɹənəɹi/.

Nouns and adjectives that end with the suffix *#ory* (with marginal exceptions) follow this rule: if there is only one syllable before the suffix, as in *mem+ory* /ˈmɛməɹi/, or the syllable before the suffix is stressable, as in *advis+ory* /ədˈvaɪsəɹi/, that syllable receives the stress – otherwise the stress goes on the penult of the base, for example, *derogate+ory* /dɪˈrɒgətəɹi/.

The final category of nouns to be considered are what Kreidler dubs abstract nouns of Greek and Latin origin that end with the suffixes #y, but not *#ary*, *#ory*, *#ology*, *#ometry*, *ography* and *opathy*. The stress rules are that if the word including the suffix contains three syllables the antepenult receives the stress, as in *energy* /ˈɛnəɹgi/ and *galaxy* /ˈgæləksi/. Otherwise, there are two possible patterns. In these abstract nouns with more than three syllables, if the penult of the entire word is stressable the preantepenult receives the stress, as in *patriarchy* /ˈpeɪtɹiːɑːki/. If the penult is not stressable, the stress is placed on the antepenult, as in *taxonomy* /tækˈsɒnəmi/ and *biology* /baɪˈɒlədʒi/.

To this point this book has only discussed the English lexical stress rules for lexical items that are single and not compound words. English, however, contains numerous lexical items that can be decomposed into two or more other words. Such lexical items are known as compound words. In written orthography there is much confusion about how to write compounds. Sometimes, as in the case of *armchair, sunset, blackbird*, compounds are written as single orthographic items. At other times they are written with a hyphen, as in *gear-change, fruit-cake, tea-cup*, and at other times as two separate words such as *apple tree, fire engine, desk lamp*. But in all cases they are compounds and follow the compound lexical stress rules.

The stress rules for compounds are relatively straightforward. If the compound consists of two nouns the stress normally goes on to the first element, for example *armchair* /ˈɑːmtʃeə/, *fruit-cake* /ˈfɹuːtkeɪk/ and *bus stop* /ˈbʌsstɒp/. In most other kinds of compounds the stress usually goes to the first syllable, for example: adjective+noun *blackbird* /ˈblækbɜːd/ and verb + preposition *cave-in* /ˈkævɪn/ and verb + adverb *a comeback* /ˈkʌmbæk/. There are, however, a number of exceptions to the general tendency for the initial element of a compound to receive stress.

- Compounds with an adjectival first element and a second element containing the *ed morpheme*. In these cases the stress is usually on the second element, as in *bad tempered* /bædˈtɛmpəd/ and *heavy-handed* /hɛviˈhændəd/.

- Compounds where the first element functions as a number. These compounds are usually stressed on the final element, as in *two wheeler* /tuːˈwiːlə/, *third class* /θɜːdˈkɑːs/ and *five fingers* /faɪvˈfŋgəs/.
- Compounds that function as adverbs are usually stressed on the final element, as in *head first* /ˌhɛdˈfɜːst/, *north east* /ˌnɔːθˈiːst/ and *downstream* /ˌdaʊnˈstɹiːm/.
- Compounds that function as a verb and have an adverbial element in initial position are normally stressed on the final element, as in *to downgrade* /ˌdaʊnˈgɹeɪd/,[7] *to back-pedal* /ˌbækˈpɛdəl/ and *to ill-treat* /ˌɪlˈtɹiːt/.

It is worth noting that there are words in which the stress pattern is in **free variation**. Some examples are set out in Table 32. The poll panel numbers are from Wells (2000).

Table 32 Free variation in the stressing of two words

controversy	/ˈkɒntɹəvɜːsi/	/kənˈtɹɒvəsi/
	UK40%/USA100%	UK60%
kilometre	/ˈkɪləmiːtə/	/kɪˈlɑːmətə/
	UK52%/USA16%	UK 48%/USA84%
formidable	/ˈfɔ;mɪdəbəl/	/fəˈmɪdəbəl/
	UK46%/USA68%	UK54%/USA32%

The final topic to be addressed is *phrasal stress* in English. In the absence of any over-riding pragmatic need, the stress of phrases can be largely determined through the application of a rhythm rule, which where possible tries to avoid stress clashes by dis-preferring the stressing of adjacent syllables. Stressed syllables tend to avoid close contact with one another. For instance, the word *Japanese* /dʒæpəˈniːz/ is stressed on the ult but the stress moves to the antepenult in the phrase *Japanese books*, where it functions as a secondary stress for the entire phrase /ˌdʒæpəniːz ˈbʊks/. Similarly, if we consider the phrase *North American modern art* it can be seen that in a stream of speech the lexical stresses tend to avoid one another. For example:

North /nɔːθ/
American /əˈmɜːɪkən/
North American /ˌnɔːθ əˈmɜːɪkən/

There is no change in the stressing of the individual lexical items, though the stress on *American* is primary and the preceding stress on *North* is secondary.

North American art /ˌnɔːθ əmɜːɪkən ˈaːt/

The lexical item *art* receives the primary stress and, to avoid the stress clash, the stress on *me* is downgraded. The secondary stress is placed on *North*.

North American modern art /nɔːθ əˌmɜːɪkən mɒdən ˈaːt/

The lexical item *art* retains the primary stress but, in this phrase, as the presence of the extra syllables *modern* avoids the possibility of the stress clash the secondary stress is on *me*. In **metrical** notation the potential stress class is avoided in North

S

American art by the secondary stress moving leftwards on to the next strongest syllable:

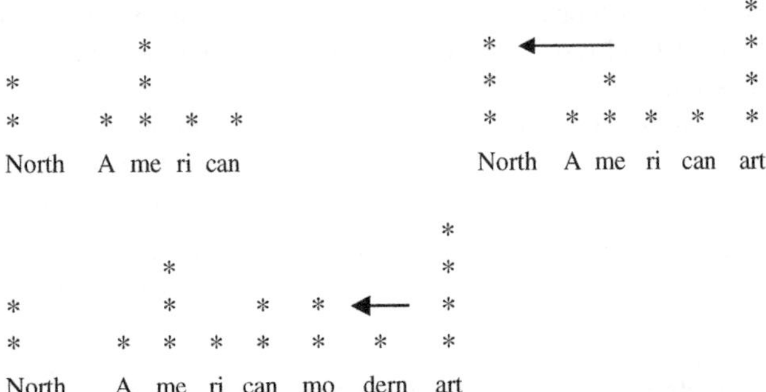

To avoid a potential stress clash with the primary stress on *art* the stress moves to the first syllable in *modern.* Because there is no potential stress clash between *me* and *art* the secondary stress for the phrase is on *me.*

Strong form

In connected speech, many function words such as pronouns, modals, auxiliary verbs, conjunctions and prepositions can be articulated either as strong or, more usually, as **weak** forms. The strong form is pronounced when the word receives a degree of **stress** indicating that the word remains an independent semantic unit. The function word realizes a textual or interpersonal meaning that the hearer needs to take account of. Thus, strong forms are preferred if: (1) the speaker wishes to contrast two function words, for example, The gift is [fɔː] John and not [frɒm] him; or (2) if the speaker wishes to emphasize his/her view of the likelihood, or necessity of a proposition, for example:

> Chelsea [wɪl] win the champions league this year.
> You [mʌst] attend the next training course.

Similarly, strong forms are used to highlight conjunction, for example:

> I'd like the sausage [ən], [n] mash = one named food item.
> I'd like the sausage [ænd] mash = two separate food items where mash represents a choice of a type of potato, and perhaps contrasts with chips.

Prepositions that are found at the end of utterances are realized as strong forms, for instance: *where are you all coming* /fɹɒm/.

Syllable

The syllable is a phonological unit that is far easier to identify than it is to define, though even in English it is not perhaps always as easy to identify as we first believe. Most people, without giving the matter much thought, believe that while they may not be able to define a syllable, they can count out the syllables in a word or phrase of their native language. However, experiments have shown that there is considerable disagreement among English speakers in where syllable boundaries actually lie. Roach (2009: 61) notes that native English speakers recognize that the word *extra* consists of two syllables but can disagree as to where the boundary between the syllables actually lies. There are five possibilities with the + diacritic indicating the potential syllable boundary:

1. ɛ+kstrə
2. ɛk+strə
3. ɛks+trə
4. ɛkst+rə
5. ɛkstr+ə̆

Of the five possibilities, a theoretical case can be made for either possibility 2 or 3. In fact, it is by no means clear which is the correct answer or even if there is a correct answer! Wells (2000: 279) and the majority of a class of undergraduate students I polled opted for possibility 3, though a sizeable minority of the native speaking students opted for possibility 2. What is clear is that the remaining three possibilities are not acceptable syllable divisions. Prior to examining theoretical explanations of how speech is divided into syllables it is first necessary to briefly review the literature in order to identify what a syllable is. Table 33, which collects some recent definitions of what a syllable is, shows that even though we can identify a syllable, what a syllable actually is remains somewhat vague.

Table 33 Some recent definitions of the syllable

A prosodic constituent made up of segments abstractly connected in sonority clusters (Rocca and Johnson 1999: 702).
A unit of speech which has one peak – usually a vowel – and may have an onset and a coda (Kriedler 2004: 294).
A phonological unit consisting of segments around the pivotal vowel or vowel-like (diphthong) sound, which is known as the *nucleus* (Yavas 2006: 20).
A linguistic unit larger than a phoneme and smaller than the word, usually containing a vowel as its nucleus (Collins and Meese 2008: 284).
The concept of a unit at a higher level than that of the phoneme or sound segment, yet distinct from that of the word or morpheme (Gimson 2008: 47).

It is not clear whether a syllable is best considered to be a linguistic unit, a prosodic constituent, a phonological unit or something vaguer. This reflects the fact that it is possible to develop a phonological theory of meaning that argues that **phonemes** group together and form into words. Such a theory sidetracks the presence of syllables in the proposed phonological hierarchy. However, ignoring the importance of syllables in word formation may simply reflect the fact that most languages such as English are written with letter symbols and not with logographs, for example: Chinese characters or syllabaries, as in Japanese Kana. Consideration of speech errors provides some evidence supporting a link between syllables and word formation. Consonants before a vowel swap only with consonants before a vowel, and consonants after a vowel swap only with consonants after a vowel (for further information see Shattuck-Hufnagel 1979). To illustrate, the following errors are attested by Fromkin (1973): *mell wade* instead of *well made*, and *tof shelp* instead of *top shelf*, but errors such as *mew lade* and *tosh felp* have not been attested. The conclusion seems to be that speakers have an internal representation of a word, which includes its syllable structure.

Syllables must contain an obligatory vowel or vowel-like sound and may have additional consonants both before and after the vowel-like sound. Consonants before the vowel are called the *onset*, those following the vowel are the *coda*. Collectively the vowel and coda are known as the rhyme.

Syllables in all languages have the following template:

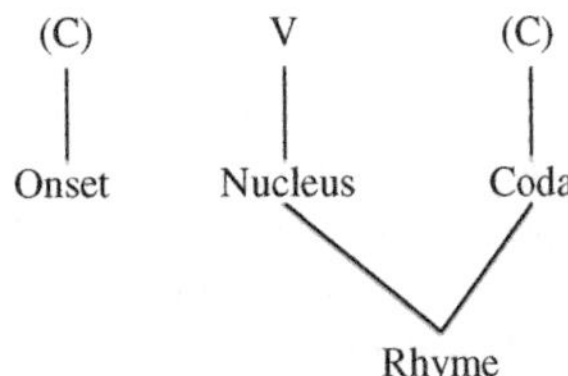

The brackets around the C indicate that the consonant, unlike the vowel, is optional. Depending on the language, there can be more than one consonant in onset and rhyme position but there can be only one vowel. The template above allows for two kinds of syllables: *open syllables* and *closed syllables*. Open syllables have no coda, while closed syllables do. Open syllables represent the unmarked syllable structure cross-linguistically. There are two theoretical bases for this claim. The first is that children produce open syllables prior to producing closed ones (see Berko Gleason and Bernstein Ratner 1998: 358). VC words such as *egg* emerge after CV words such as *gee*. The second is that many languages, including major ones such as Italian, Japanese and Mandarin, contain only open syllables.[8] Differences in syllable templates can lead to considerably different pronunciations and are one of the factors that learners of second languages have to overcome.

The list of words set out in Table 34, taken from Rocca and Johnson (1999: 238), represent English words that have been borrowed into Japanese and assimilated into the Japanese sound system. The most significant difference between the original English words and their reshaping according to the rules of the Japanese sound system is how the words are divided into syllables. The need to maintain an open CV structure results in – from an English-centred point of view – the introduction of epenthetic vowels to break up VC clusters. Thus, monosyllabic words such as *milk CVCC* are resyllabified with two extra vowels to comply with the permissible CVCVCV structure as *mi+ru+ku*. It is of interest that even though Japanese does allow CVN syllables – as in *Hon (book), Kon+ni+chi+wa (good day), sa+yon+na+ra (good bye)* – the word *sum* when borrowed into Japanese is resyllabified into a CVCVCV template as *su+ra+mu*, thus indicating Japanese speakers preferences for open syllables.

The conclusion that we can draw is that open syllables are core syllables in the sense that every language has open syllables, though many languages have other types of syllables as well. While it is relatively simple to delimit syllable

Table 34 The resyllabification of English borrowings into Japanese

English original	# of Syllables	Japanese borrowing	# of Syllables
Christ+mas	2	Ku+ri+su+mas+su	5
Text	1	Te+ki+su+to	5
Club	1	Ku+ra+bu	5
Dress	1	Do+re+su	5
Glass	1	Gu+ra+su	5
Disc	1	Di+su+ku	5
Sum	1	Su+ra+mu	5
Plus	1	Pu+ra+su	5
Bott+le	2	Bo+ru+to	5
Gro+tesque	2	Gu+ro+te+su+ku	5

boundaries in languages that contain only open syllables, as we saw with the word *extra* earlier, the position is not so straightforward in languages that contain both open and closed syllables.

Syllable boundaries are not identified using the same principles that writers use to split up words that owing to space problems cannot be written on the same line. Yavas (2006: 143–4) provides an excellent account of written syllabification. Basically, he argues that written syllabification seems to follow three principles:

1. If a word has prefixes or suffixes these cannot be divided.
2. If an orthographic vowel letter stands for a long vowel, the next letter in the written representation goes in the next 'written syllable'.
3. If the two principles clash, the first principle prevails.

Using Yavas's guidelines we would divide the following three written words like so:

- Ball-oon. Principle 1 prevails.
- Teach-ers. Principle 1 overrides Principle 2.
- Be-low. Principle 2 prevails.

The division of syllables in speech follows two different principles, the first of which is *onset maximalization*, which says that the maximal formation of onsets takes priority over the formation of codas. In other words, speakers put as many consonants as they can into the onset. Thus,

- Ba+loon /bə+ˈluːn/
- Tea+chers /ˈtiː+tʃəs/
- Be+low /bɪ+ˈləʊ/

If we syllabify according to onset maximalization only the spoken word *below* has the same syllable structure as its written counterpart. The second 'principle' is the *sonority hierarchy/scale* in which the most sonorous elements are assigned the greatest value. There are numerous competing numerical models of this, which assign different numerical values to different elements. But all that matters is that more sonorous elements have a higher numerical value than lower ones (Table 35).

Table 35 The sonority scale with English examples

Class	**Value**	**English phonemes**
Open vowels	11	ALWAYS FOUND IN THE NUCLEUS
Close vowels	10	
Glides[1]	9	SOMETIMES FOUND IN NUCLEUS
Liquids	8	
Nasals	7	
Voiced fricatives	6	ALWAYS FOUND IN ONSET/CODA
Voiceless fricatives	5	
Voiced affricates	4	
Voiceless affricates	3	
Voiced plosives	2	
Voiceless plosives	1	

[1] It will be remembered that, in English, glides cannot appear in coda position and hence cannot be syllabic.

The ideal syllable profile should have rising sonority in the onset, the peak of sonority in the nucleus and declining sonority in the coda. This can be schematized as:

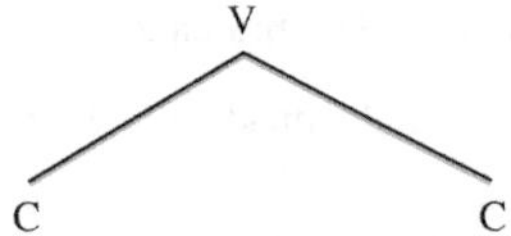

Using the number scale, we see that the three example words have the following sonority profiles:

- Balloon /b ə + ˈl uː n/
  2 10+8 10 7
- Teachers /ˈt iː + tʃ ə s/
  1 10+3 10 5
- Below /b ɪ + ˈl əʊ/
  2 10+8 10

In the three examples, the two principles do not conflict. Each proposed syllable division according to onset maximalization contains syllables with rising sonority in the onset and falling sonority in the coda. As a result, we can confidently identify the spoken syllable boundaries in these three words. However, if we consider the word *extra* we get different syllable divisions depending on which principle is applied.

According to onset maximalization

The word has the following syllable division: ɛk+strə. The consonant cluster *str* is a legal onset in English as can be demonstrated by the monosyllabic words *street, strict* and *stream*. Thus, if we maximize the onset of the second syllable, the division of the syllable will be between the /k/ and the /s/.

According to the sonority scale

The word *extra* has the following sonority profile:

ɛ	k	s	t	r	ə
10	1	5	1	8	10

Regardless of how the string of phonemes is segmented there must be a breach of the ideal sonority profile. If the division is between the /k/ and /s/ where will be a dip in the sonority profile of the onset of the second syllable, though the overall direction of the sonority profile will be a rise. On the other hand, if the division is between the /s/ and the /t/, there will be a rise in the coda of the initial syllable though the overall direction of the sonority profile will fall. In short, we can see that not all syllables will have an ideal sonority profile. This is part of the reason that we have difficulty in identifying syllable boundaries in all contexts. One entirely predictable deviation from the ideal sonority profile is caused by the plural marker or the third person agreement marker realized phonetically as either /s/ or /z/, for example:

k	æ	t	(s)		d	ɒ	g	(z)
1	11	1	(5)		2	11	2	(6)

Despite this, there is a strong tendency in English for syllables to follow the ideal sonority profile. The tendency for sonority to rise during the onset, reach a peak at the nucleus and fall during the coda is a useful way of entering the word of **phonotactics**, the licensing of legitimate consonant clusters before and after the vowel.

In recent times, some Chomskyan-inspired phonologists, in their pursuit of language universals, have proposed an alternate way of schematizing syllable templates. They have argued that there are in actuality, despite appearances, no complex codas in English or indeed in any other language. The prima facie counterintuitive claim is based on two facts about the English language. The first is that complex codas in English overwhelmingly appear in word or morpheme final position. This is quite different to the position of complex onsets that frequently appear word medially, for instance *su+blime, poul+try* and *di+stress*. Even in words where complex codas are found medially, as in *pump+kin, re+demp+tion*, there is a tendency for speakers to elide the second consonant in the coda, which will be noted is always a stop followed immediately by another stop. This results in common pronunciations of these words as [ˈpʌmkin] and [rɪˈdɛmʃən]. In some sense, the medial /p/ in *pumpkin* and in *redemption* is no more than an optional phonetic transition similar to the epenthetic [p] commonly added in the pronunciation of *ham[p]ster* [ˈhæmpstə]. The argument is that in all three words the [p] is an artefact resulting from the transition between the **bilabial nasal** and the following consonant sound – see **distinctive feature**. Therefore, the claim is that the [p] is different from the other phonemes that make up the word.

The second fact is that word internally, rhymes consisting of a long vowel or diphthong, and a sonorant, are not usually found, though this is very common in word final position, as in *blame* /bleɪm/, *moan* /məʊn/, *seen* /siːn/, *hall* /hɔːl/ and *howl* /haʊl/. At the same time, numerous English words consist of final rhymes made up of a short vowel, a sonorant and an obstruent, as in *camp* /kæmp/, *bent* /bɛnt/, *bend* /bɛnd/, *yelp* /jɛlp/ and *geld* /gɛld/.

The proposal based on these two facts is that rhymes in English consist of two timing slots known as **moras**, which can be filled either by a long vowel or diphthong, or a short vowel followed by a consonant. Any additional consonants that follow the rhyme do not form part of the rhyme but instead are licensed directly by the syllable itself. In the examples below, the nucleus in *seen* weighs two moras and the two timing slots are occupied by the long vowel /iː/. In the word *bent*, the nucleus that is occupied by the short vowel /ɛ/ only weighs one mora. The other mandatory timing slot is taken by the sonorant /n/ which is found in the coda. In the word *bit*, as in *bent*, the two mora are distributed in the rhyme across the nucleus, where the timing slot is occupied by the short vowel /ɪ/, and the coda, where it is occupied by the obstruent /t/. The extra consonants do not form part of the rhyme but are attached directly to the syllable head as follows[9]:

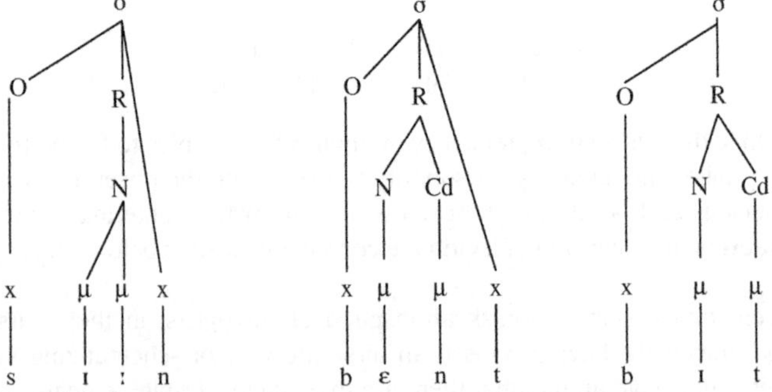

Figure 10 An alternate way of looking at a syllable template based on Roca and Johnson (1999).

While this is a rather counterintuitive construal it is, however, a useful means of describing rhythm in English. Extra consonants that are licensed directly from the syllable, as in the /n/ in *seen* and the /t/ in *bent*, have to borrow time from the onset of the following syllable. This results in a beat in English that is not syllable timed – see **timing**. Any readers who are interested in delving more deeply into the proposal that English does not have complex codas should look at Roca and Johnson (1999: 284–7).

It is widely accepted that a syllable functions as a unit of timing but there are some scholars, see for instance a recent account by MacNeilage (2008), who argue that words are not articulated phone by phone but rather syllable by syllable. However, the psychological status (if any) of a syllable remains in doubt, though the evidence from speech errors provides some support for the view that a syllable is a unit of articulation.

Tap

A tap is a term used to refer to the classification of a **consonant** on the basis of its manner of **articulation**. Taps are produced by a single very rapid contact between the tip of the tongue and the roof of the mouth. The IPA symbolizes taps and **flaps** on the same line of the IPA chart. Accordingly, some linguists consider taps and flaps to be identical while others maintain that taps have a more direct brief closure than flaps. Taps do not form part of the phonemic sound system of English, but tapped **allophonic** sounds may be heard in many American accents as allophones of /t/ where they are intervocalic and in stressed syllables, and where they are in a stressed syllable preceding a **syllabic** consonant, as in *butter* [ˈbʌɾəɹ], *atom*, [ˈæɾəm] *battle* [ˈbæɾl̩]. To British ears, the tapped sounds resembles a [d] and thus, theoretically at least, there is the potential for a British speaker perceiving an American pronunciation of *atom* as *Adam*.

Target

A target is a **phonetic** term that refers to an ideal articulation which a speaker aims for in the production of a phoneme. However, in connected speech, targets are often not fully realized. For instance, in the articulation of the word *key* the speaker aims to produce a **velar stop** prior to the **vowel** but it is likely, owing to the following vowel target, that the /k/ which is produced will be considerably fronted and may be articulated as a **palatal** [c]. Laver (1994: 106ff.) contrasts a linear description of speech, where each segment represents a discrete meaningful configuration of features, with a **parametric** description of speech, which more transparently reflects the dynamic unfolding of speech. However, a parametric approach, while more phonetically transparent and descriptively accurate of the speech signal, cannot be easily segmented into **phonemes** and is thus more phonemically opaque.

Scholars working on what have traditionally been referred to as register **tone** languages describe lexical tone in terms of high and low tonal targets, which speakers may not always fully realize. In other words, what appear to be tone movements are, they claim, better described and analysed in terms of transitions between idealized tonal targets (also see ToBI).

Tense

tense is a phonetic term used to classify sounds that are supposedly produced with more muscular effort. It contrasts with **lax**. Chomsky and Halle (1968) somewhat controversially include [+/– tense] as a **distinctive feature** in their universal classification of vowels. For them, [+ tense] sounds are produced with 'a deliberate, accurate, maximally distinct gesture that involves considerable muscular effort'. Thus, they classify the FLEECE and GOOSE vowels as [+ tense] and the KIT and FOOT vowels as [– tense] or [+ lax]. Drawing on earlier phonetic studies Chomsky and Halle argue that the behaviour of the pharynx correlates with tenseness; during the articulation of [+ tense] sounds the pharynx width remains constant, which suggests a negative correlation between the features [tense] and [**atr**].

Other scholars such as Gussenhoven and Jacobs (2005) note that, while somewhat phonetically different, the features [+/– tense] and [+/– **atr**] never co-occur within the same language and this raises the issue of a connection, if any, between the features [tense] and [**atr**]. Ladefoged and Maddieson (1996) reviewed numerous previous studies that had investigated the correlation between tongue position and the features [tense] and [**atr**], and tentatively concluded that in languages which contain the feature [**atr**] the advancement of the tongue root is a separate tongue gesture, but in Germanic languages, the advancement of the tongue root is merely one of the concomitants of tongue height. They went on to argue that the feature [tense] was unnecessary for the classification of vowels and that all English vowels can be distinguished in terms of height, backness, lip-rounding and length.

Timing

Speech, if we factor out dysfluencies and pauses, is perceived as being rhythmical in the sense that it is a recurrent movement of some kind that produces an expectation that the movement will be repeated. There appear to be two kinds of recurrences that create future expectancies, notably the movement between **syllables** and the movement between **stresses**. Traditional descriptions of rhythm have claimed that languages can be classified as either syllable-timed or stress-timed (Abercrombie 1967: 96–8). In syllable-timed languages such as French, Spanish, Greek, Turkish, Polish, Hindi and Guajarti all syllables are supposed to take roughly the same amount of time to utter. In stress-timed languages such as English, Dutch, German and Russian it is claimed that there is roughly the same amount of time between stressed syllables, regardless of how many intervening unstressed syllables there are.

In recent years there have been experimental attempts to demonstrate the physical differences between stress-timed languages such as English, and syllable-timed languages such as French. These experiments have largely consisted of digitalized corpora of conversational English and French speech being fed into machines that measured the time intervals between (a) stressed syllables and (b) syllables. Abercrombie (1967: 98) had claimed that in stress-timed languages there should be considerable variation in syllable length, while in syllable-timed languages the variation in syllable length should be much reduced. In stress-timed languages there should be little variation in timing between stresses, while in syllable-timed languages there should be much more variability in timing between stresses. Roach (1982) examined three putatively syllable-timed languages and three putatively stress-timed languages but was unable to find any evidence for either of Abercrombie's claims. However, he noted that – because of the difficulty of devising an objective test that can conclusively distinguish between stress-timing and syllable-timing – while his results were largely negative they remain inconclusive.

Beckman (1992: 458) has pointed out that simply comparing chunks of speech does not tend to control for phrase-final syllable lengthening, which make languages seem less rhythmical than they in fact are. As a result, she argues that experiments which have measured the speech signal and apparently not found any evidence supporting the division of languages into stress-timed and syllable-timed are inconclusive. She points out that, despite such inconclusive experimental evidence, the metaphor of syllable-timed and stress-timed languages remains very much alive and claims that, 'it must capture some fundamental mental fact about rhythmic patterns across languages'. More recently Ling, Grabe and Nolan (2000) have argued – on the basis of vowel duration measurements – that the Singapore accent of English is actually syllable-timed. They demonstrated that vowel durations in Singapore English are 'more nearly equal in duration' (ibid.: 397) than they are in British English, and argue that this results in both forms of English having different rhythms. For Ling et al. (2000) the presence of extra consonants in the onset and coda would appear to have the potential to obscure the regular rhythmic patterning of language – see **syllable** and below for a discussion of the contribution of Bolinger (1981).

Regardless of whether or not languages can be classified as either stress-timed or syllable-timed it is clear that poetry in some languages (such as French) rests upon a syllable-timed rhythm while poetry in other languages (such as English) rests upon a stress-timed rhythm (Abercrombie 1967: 98). In other words, at least in some genres of language the rhythm can be classified as either predominantly syllable-timed or predominantly stress-timed. Mitchell (1969), in a critical review of Abercrombie, argued that no language is totally syllable-timed or stress-timed, but accepted that each language has a tendency to be dominated by one particular rhythmical patterning. In a similar vein, Crystal (1969: 163) has argued that speakers of English produce stretches of more rhythmically regular speech inside stretches of less rhythmical speech in order to focus attention on a particularly important point.

Scholars, regardless of their position on whether languages can be classed as syllable-timed or stress-timed, acknowledge that rhythm and stress are perceptual and not physical categories. Hence their relation to the physical reality of a speech signal may not be one to one. It is possible that human beings may perceive speech as being more rhythmical than it actually is. We may perceive some speech as being predominantly syllable-timed and other speech as being predominantly stress-timed, though measurement of the physical speech wave does not exhibit compelling evidence of a physical difference between what is perceived as syllable-timed and what is perceived as stress-timed! Further experimental evidence on how people perceive rhythm in language is needed in order to resolve this issue.

Proponents of the view that English is a syllable-timed language argue that English contains a rhythmical unit – the **foot** – which contains one stressed syllable and optional unstressed syllables. Each English foot takes roughly the same amount of time to utter as another. The difference between syllable-timed and stress-timed languages is that in syllable-timed languages all syllables are roughly isochronous while in stress-timed languages it is the feet that are isochronous. Thus with foot boundaries notated by a slash:

/ walk/ down the/ path to the/ end of the ca/ nal
1 2 3 3 1
(Roach 1991: 120)

The division of the utterance into feet does not necessarily respect lexical divisions, as can be seen from *canal*, where the word's initial unaccented syllable is found in the fourth foot. A foot in English must start with a stressed syllable and can end either with zero as the first and fifth foot above, or with one or more unstressed syllables as in the second, third and fourth foot above. The first and the fifth foot consist of a single syllable, while the second foot consists of two syllables. The other feet have three syllables. The claim is that the articulation of each foot takes roughly the same amount of time to produce, so that the five accented syllables, as underlined above, are perceived as rhythmically regular intervals.

An alternate theory of rhythm is found in Bolinger (1981) who proposed a *borrowing rule*. He argued that the occurrence of full vowels is a better predictor of English rhythm. A full vowel in Bolinger's terms is any vowel other than schwa /ə/, the KIT vowel /ɪ/ and the FOOT vowel /ʊ/. The borrowing rule states that a syllable with a reduced vowel borrows time from any immediately preceding vowel containing a full vowel. The borrowing rule predicts that syllables containing full vowels that are not immediately followed by syllables containing reduced vowels will take approximately an equal length of time; though there will be some small differences in duration caused by the innate length of the vowel and whether any following consonant is **fortis** or **lenis**. A syllable containing a reduced vowel will be much shorter than one containing a full vowel. But as the borrowing rule states that a syllable containing a reduced vowel will borrow time from an immediately preceding syllable containing a fully voiced vowel, a syllable containing a full vowel that is immediately followed by a syllable with a reduced vowel will be shortened. Reduced vowels that borrow time from preceding syllables with full vowels will be longer than syllables with reduced vowels that follow other reduced syllables.

The following example, adapted from Gimson (2008: 265) illustrates how the rule works and contrasts it with a stress-timed description of the rhythm. In the example, the diacritic F stands for a full vowel, R for a reduced vowel, R+ for a reduced vowel that has borrowed from a preceding full vowel and F– for a shortened full vowel:

(a)	Those	wal	la	bies	are	dan	ger	ous
	F	F–	R+	R	R	F–	R+	R
	Those/wallabies are/dangerous							
(b)	Those	por	cu	pines	aren't	dan	ger	ous
	F	F	F	F–	R+	F–	R+	R
	Those/porcupines aren't/dangerous							

A stress-timed account of rhythm predicts that as both the (a) and the (b) utterances consist of three feet, that each foot should be perceived as taking roughly the same amount of time to utter. Thus, if a speaker produces the (a) and the (b) utterance with roughly the same tempo, the words *wallabies are* and *porcupines aren't* should be perceived as taking roughly the same amount of time. The borrowing rule predicts that *porcupines aren't*, which consists of two full vowels, one reduced full vowel and a lengthened reduced vowel, should be perceived as having longer duration than *wallabies are*, which consists of a shortened full vowel, a lengthened reduced vowel and two reduced vowels. Which (if either) of the two accounts of rhythm – the borrowing rule or stress-timing – is correct remains to be seen.

ToBI

ToBI, which is short for Tone and Break Index, is an **autosegemental** representation of **intonation**. The Tone (To) component was initially developed by Janet Pierrehumbert in her 1980 PhD dissertation. The Break Index (BI) component was codified following a series of prosodic transcription workshops in the early 1990s. Some of the key ToBI influenced publications are Pierrehumbert (1980), Pierrehumbert and Hirschberg (1990), Jun (2005) and Ladd (1996/2008). ToBI is a broad phonological transcription system, which has currently been adapted to describe the intonation not only of numerous dialects of English but also numerous other geographically diverse languages such as Italian, French, German, Japanese and Korean.

A ToBI description has three tiers: a lexical tier, a tonal tier and a break index. The tonal tier (To) consists of a string of High (H) and Low (L) tones which phonetically represent turning points in the intonation contour. Transitions between the tones are of no importance. In a more recent development, Ladd (1996/2008) has extended the theory by linking the sites of the tones with rhythmically stronger syllables, and in the process created an Autosegmental-Metrical (AM) account of intonation. Tones notated with a simple H and L are the equivalent of pre-tonic prominent syllables, while those notated by a * in addition to H or L are roughly equivalent to what have traditionally been described as tonic syllables. Tones after the starred tone represent either phrase tones notated by H- or L-, or boundary tones notated by H% or L%. L tones after the starred tone indicate an absence of a rising intonation contour, whereas H tones indicate the presence of a rising intonation contour.

The break index (BI) is notated from 0 to 4, in which 0 represents intra-word pauses, 1 breaks between words, 3 breaks between smaller phrases and 4 breaks between larger intonational phrases; 2 is a default category that is used to represent all other breaks or mismatches. A break of 3 is accompanied by a phrase tone while a break of 4 is accompanied by a boundary tone. The following examples illustrate:

(a) he went to the shop to buy milk and cheese
H L* H- L H* L- L% (Tonal Tier)
1 0 1 0 3 0 1 1 1 4 (Break Index Tier)

(b) he went to the shop to buy milk and cheese
H H* H-H% L H* L- L% (Tonal Tier)
1 0 1 0 4 0 1 1 1 4 (Break Index Tier)

```
(c)  he went to the shop        to buy milk and cheese
          H          H*H-L%        H        H*    L- L%     (Tonal Tier)
        1   0   1   0   4   0     1    1    1    4           (Break Index Tier)
(d)  he went to the shop        to buy milk and cheese
          H          H                  H         H*    L- H% (Tonal Tier)
       1   0   1   0    1   0    1    1    1    1   4        (Break Index Tier)
```

Example (a) consists of one intonation phrase that itself consists of two smaller intermediate phrases. The end of the initial intermediate phrase is signalled by the H- phrase accent. The H- phrase accent projects that the phrase is to be taken as signalling that it is to be interpreted as part of the larger intonation phrase. Examples (b) and (c) consist of two intonation phrases that differ only in the boundary tones found at the end of the initial intonation phrase. In (b) the presence of the H% tone signals a continuation rise (Pierrehumbert and Hirschberg 1990: 305) and indicates that the initial intonation phrase is to be interpreted in respect of the following unit. In (c) the two L% boundary tones do not signal any forward reference. The two intonation phrases are to be interpreted as independent units. Example (d) consists of a single intonation phrase with what traditional descriptions would describe as a fall-rise tone movement.

The ToBI system, commonly used to notate English, has in addition to the phrase and boundary tones, six starred tones. Two of the starred tones are simple: the H* that is perceived as relatively higher and the L* that is perceived as relatively lower. The remaining four starred tones are L+H* and H+L*, which in addition to the starred tone contain a leading tone movement up to the starred tone, and L*+H and H*+L which notate a trailing tone movement after the starred tone. The combination of starred tone plus H- or L- phrase tone and H% or L% boundary tone generate all the possible tone movements in English. Table 36 illustrates correspondences between ToBI notation and approaches that describe intonation in terms of tone movement.

Table 36 Correspondence between ToBI and tone movement

ToBI	Tone movement
H*H–L%	High level
H*L–L%	Fall
H*H–H%	High rise
H*L–H%	Fall-rise
L*H–L%	Low level
L*L–L%	Low fall
L*H–H%	Low rise
L*L–H%	Low rise
L+H*H–L%	High level (with low head)
L+H*L–L%	Rise-fall
L+H*H–H%	High rise
L+H*L–H%	High fall-rise
H+L*H–L%	Low level (with high head)

Table 36 (Continued)

ToBI	Tone movement
H+L*L–L%	Low fall (with high head)
H+L*H–H%	Low rise
H+L*L–H%	Low rise (high head)
L*+HH–L%	Low level tone or calling contour (Ladd 2008)
L*+HL–L%	Rise-fall
L*+HH–H%	Low rise
L*+HL–H%	Fall-rise
H*+LH–L%	Level tone or calling contour (Ladd 2008)
H*+LL–L%	Fall
H*+LH–H%	Fall-rise
H*+LL–H%	Fall-rise

Tone language

A tone language is one where word meanings can be distinguished by a lexical tone. In tone languages the lexical tone is a feature of the word. Words can be contrasted solely by differences in tone. The following monosyllabic examples from Cantonese (taken from Tench 1996: 3) illustrate:

_kha (low-level tone) *spice*
-kha (mid-level tone) *herb*
¯kha (high-level tone) *trade*
\kha (falling tone) *kill*
/ kha (rising tone) *leg*

In Cantonese, the string of segments *kha* can represent five different lexical items ranging in meaning from *spice* to *trade.* The pitch level or pitch contour attached to the lexical item is the sole means available of contrasting the lexical items. While English speakers may find the articulation of such minute phonetic detail exotic, it is worth remembering that an overwhelming majority of the languages of the world, perhaps up to 70 per cent, are tone languages. Furthermore, some of the most widely spoken languages such as Mandarin, Cantonese, Thai, Yoruba and Xhosa are tone languages. Tone languages are widespread in East Asia, Africa and in the indigenous languages of the Americas, especially in Central America.

Traditionally, linguists (such as Pike 1948) have distinguished *contour tone languages* found in East Asia and Central America from *register tone languages* found in Africa. Contour tone languages, as the name implies, are languages where the relevant feature of word identifying pitch is the trajectory of the pitch change across the word. In other words, does the pitch move upwards or downwards or remain relatively level within the word? Register tone languages are those languages where the relevant feature of word identifying pitch is the relative height of the syllabic pitches within an individual speaker's pitch span. In many register tone languages, the syllables may bear only static level pitches. What appear to be rises and falls in pitch are actually transitions between high level (h) and low level (l) pitch targets.

Three separate major traditions have traditionally described tone languages: first the description of African languages, second the description of Asian languages and third the description of Central American languages (for a comprehensive description see Yip 2002: ch. 2). African tone languages have been traditionally notated using an acute accent *á* for high tones, a grave accent *à* for low tones and a level accent for *ā* for mid tones. A combination of acute and grave accents has been used to signify contour tones, for example: *â* signals a fall from high to low. The Central American and Asian traditions have notated tone in a very different manner. Chinese tone has been notated using the system devised by Chao (1930) who proposed a series of 'tone letters', which somewhat confusingly are actually numbers! Chao divided the pitch range of the speaking voice into five levels, with 5 representing the highest pitch level and 1 the lowest. Each syllable was notated with usually two or three digits, with the first one representing the starting pitch and the last one representing the final pitch. In the Central American literature the notation is broadly similar, though 5 notates the lowest part of a speaker's pitch range while 1 notates the highest.

It is possible to transcribe all tone languages, as recent metrical transcriptions of African tone languages do, using 'h' and 'l' symbols that refer to high and low pitch targets. Mid-level tones can be notated as downstepped 'h' pitch targets. However, Yip (1995: 493) while acknowledging that 'the features required for Chinese must be those used by all tone languages, although of course, as with segmental features, no language will necessarily use all features distinctively', notes that downstepping is not found in Asian tone languages (ibid.: 492). Furthermore, East Asian tone languages have a far richer tonal inventory than African tone language. To resolve this apparent paradox, Yip (ibid.: 477) proposed two sets of features, one *register* divided into high and low and notated as H or L, and pitch targets notated as h or l. To illustrate, the earlier example is presented using both Chao's tone letters and Yip's autosegmental notation: see Table 37. Despite the exotic nature of tone languages to speakers of non-tone languages, the use of lexical tone as a contrastive feature of the word is very common and thus tone languages must somehow easily evolve. One explanation for tonogenesis (the birth of tone languages) lies in the attested phonetic fact that voiced obstruents lower the pitch of a following vowel, while voiceless obstruents raise the pitch of a following vowel (see Maddieson 1997 for phonetic details). If, over numerous generations of speakers, the consonants within a language become devoiced, one way of maintaining the lexical contrast previously signalled by voicing is to maintain the pitch difference on the vowel, and to pronounce the syllable that previously contained

Table 37 A comparison of different tone notations

		Chao (1930)	**Yip (1995)**
_kha (low-level tone)	*spice*	11	L, l
-kha (mid-level tone)	*herb*	33	H, l
¯kha (high-level tone)	*trade*	44	H, h
\kha (falling tone)	*kill*	41	H, hl
/ kha (rising tone)	*leg*	14	L, lh

the voiced obstruent with a low tone and the one originally containing a voiceless obstruent onset with high tone. However, Yip (2002: 37) notes that while the loss of a voicing contrast may explain tonogenesis in numerous languages, it is not sufficient to explain it in all languages. In some languages it appears that lexical tone may have arisen out of the effects of voiceless aspiration and glottalization on obstruents and not simply because of a voicing contrast. In any case, no matter what the ultimate cause of tonogenesis in a particular language is, lexical tone is an easily evolvable language feature, which is found in the majority of extant languages.

Transcription

A transcription is an orthographic and systematic record of speech. There are two main types of segmental transcriptions: broad transcriptions which record the **phonemic** contrasts, and narrow transcriptions which record the **phonetic** quality of an individual speaker. Broad transcriptions are enclosed by // brackets and contain only the letters necessary to describe the patterning of the phonemes of the language into meaningful lexical units. Narrow transcriptions are enclosed by [] brackets and contain all the letters used to represent the phonemes plus a series of diacritics that symbolize secondary articulations such as **aspiration, assimilation** and **nasalization**. To illustrate, the English sentence *the man's key is there on the mat* is transcribed in broad and narrow transcription:

/ðə mænz kiː ɪz ðɛə ən ðə mæt/ (broad)
[ðə mæ̃nz̥ k̟ʰiː z̥ ðɛəɹ ən̪ n̪ə mæ̃t̚] (narrow)

The additional diacritics in the narrow transcription notate details about how the sentence was uttered but do not alter the meaning of the sentence. In other words, they illustrate an individual speaker's accent. The speaker of the sentence produced *man's* with a nasalized vowel and a devoiced final consonant, *key* with a fronted and aspirated **velar stop**, *is* as a devoiced fricative. *On the* was pronounced with two **dentalized nasals** indicating the **coalescent assimilation** of the place of **articulation** of the nasal *in* to a dental place of **articulation** and the simultaneous assimilation of the manner of **articulation** of the **fricative** *the* to a nasal articulation. *Mat* was produced with a nasalized vowel and an unreleased final stop.

In addition to segmental transcriptions, linguists produce various types of **intonation** transcriptions. However, unlike segmental transcriptions there is no standard set of transcription conventions. Two recent attempts at producing a standardized broad intonation transcription system are **ToBI** (see Jun 2005) and the International Transcription System for Intonation (intsint) described in Hirst and Di Cristo (1998). While ToBI transcriptions can be considered broad, the intsint transcription was explicitly designed as a narrow transcription that could be utilized to describe the intonation patterns of languages whose inventory of tonal patterns have not yet been established. Both transcription systems argue against a transcription system based on tone movements. They argue instead that the most significant intonation primitives are pitch **targets**, which can be identified phonetically as turning points in the overall F_0 curve. At the time of writing, however, while the ToBI tradition has become widely accepted and used to produce broad transcriptions of many European languages, little if any work has been done beyond Hirst and Di Cristo (1998) in attempting to produce a narrow intonation transcription system.

Trill

A trill, which is also known as a roll, is a term used to refer to the classification of a **consonant** on the basis of its manner of **articulation**. Trills are produced by the rapid **tapping** of an **articulator** against the place of **articulation**. The IPA symbolizes trills made at the following places of **articulation**: **bilabial**, **alveolar** and **uvular**. English does not contain any **phonemic** trills. Trilled sounds are, however, recognizable. The Parisian <r> is realized as an uvular trill [ʀ]. The paralinguistic gesture, informally represented as *Brr,* which signals in English that the speaker is freezing, is a voiced bilabial trill [ʙ].

In traditional descriptions of English it was claimed that speakers of Scottish English trilled or rolled their <rs> (see Grant 1913: 83), though it is worth remembering that Abercrombie (1967: 49), writing more than 40 years ago, noted that an alveolar trilled <r> [r] is the articulation of a staged Scotsman. Recent evidence (see Stuart-Smith 2008: 64) notes that <r> in Scottish English is likely to be realized as a **post-alveolar approximant** [ɹ], **retroflex approximant** [ɻ] or **alveolar tap** [ɾ] snd not as a trill [r]. The trill [r] is, however, present in the spoken English of North and South Wales though not in areas that border England (Penhallurick 2008: 118).

Uvular

The term uvular refers to the classification of a **consonant** sound on the basis of the place of **articulation** of the sound. Uvular consonants are produced by contact or close proximity between the back of the tongue and the uvula, which is the fleshy appendage dangling behind the soft palate. Assuming a normal **pulmonic egressive airstream mechanism**, the following classes of consonants are classified by the IPA as uvular: **plosives** [q, ɢ], **nasals** [ɴ], **trills** [ʀ] and **fricatives** [χ, ʁ]. Uvular **phonemes** are not found in English but may be familiar to many readers from their experiences of hearing or learning French. French <r> may be realized as [ʁ] or as an uvular trill [ʀ], or even in some dialects as an apical trill [r] in the South of France (for further information see Harris 1988: 213, or Delattre 1965: 71ff.). Occitan, known informally as Provençal, which was widely spoken in Southern France, contains an uvular trill that may explain its presence in some French dialects.

As Table 38 indicates, uvular phonemes are not that common across languages but, of phonemes produced with an uvular articulation, fricatives are the most common. Ladefoged and Maddieson (1996: 167) report that uvular fricative phonemes are present in a range of Amerindian, African and Caucasian languages. They note (ibid.: 225) that uvular trills are rare outside of Western Europe, where they exist for some conservative speakers as **allophonic** realizations of uvular fricatives in French, German, some varieties of Italian and Russian and in Southern Swedish. Outside of Europe they exist in some varieties of Ashkenazi Hebrew – the Hebrew produced by the descendants of Jewish communities who lived along the Rhine. Their use of an uvular trill may be the result of extended contact with neighbouring German and French speakers.

Wells (1982b) reports the use of a voiced uvular trill as a substitute for <r> in a number of English dialects. It is a noted feature of the dialect of the historical country of Northumberland (excluding the urban centre of Newcastle upon Tyne) where it is known as the Northumbrian burr. Voiced uvular trills are also found in the traditional Welsh-speaking regions of Gwynedd and Dyfed, though Penhallurick (2008: 119) emphasizes both their rarity of occurrence and possible idiolectal nature. The sole other reference I have been able to locate in the literature concerning an uvular articulation of English concerns the pronunciation of some Afrikaans loan words in South African English, which contain /χ/, for example: *gogga* (an insect), which is pronounced /ˈχɒχə/ (Wells 1982b: 619).

Table 38 List of uvular phonemes found in 25 languages

Language	Plosive	Nasal	Fricatives
Amharic			
Arabic	q		
Bulgarian			
Cantonese			
Czech			
Dutch			χ
English			
French			ʁ
German			χ ʁ
Greek			
Hausa			
Hebrew			χ
Hindi			
Hungarian			
Igbo			
Italian			
Japanese		N	
Korean			
Mandarin			
Persian			
Portuguese			ʁ
Russian			
Spanish			
Swedish			
Thai			
Welsh			

Uvularization

Uvularization is a type of **secondary articulation** and occurs when a speaker produces a consonant while simultaneously moving the back of the tongue towards the **uvula**.

U

Velar

The term velar refers to the classification of a **consonant** sound on the basis of the place of **articulation** of the sound. Velar consonants are produced by contact or close proximity between the back of the tongue and the **soft palate** or velum. Assuming a normal **pulmonic egressive airstream mechanism** the following classes of consonants are classified by the IPA as velar: **plosives** [k, g], **nasals** [ŋ], **fricatives** [x, ɣ], **approximants** [ɰ] and **lateral appoximants** [ʟ]. As Table 39 indicates, velar **phonemes** especially plosives are extremely common across languages. Three velar phonemes /k, g, ŋ/ and the **labial-velar** approximant phoneme /w/ are found in standard British and American English.

The voiced velar fricative /x/ is a phoneme in Standard Scottish English, though not apparently a sound in the dialect of urban speakers, where it is replaced by /k/ (for further information see Jones 2002). Wells (1982b: 408) argues that in Standard Scottish English /x/ is restricted to proper names, such as *Balloch* pronounced as /ˈbæləx/, and to the pronunciation of words containing the letters <ch> of Greek and Hebrew origin. It will be noted that Greek but not Hebrew contains a /x/ phoneme. Some example words are *epoch* and *patriarch*, which are pronounced in Standard Scottish English as /ˈiːpɒx/ and /ˈpeɪtriɑːx/ and not /ˈiːpɒk/ and /ˈpeɪtriɑːk/. Words unique to Scottish English such as *dreich* and *loch* are pronounced as /dɹiːx/ and /lɒx/. A minimal pair found only in Scottish English where two lexical items differ only by the substitution of /k/ by /x/ is *keek* /kiːk/ and *keech* /kiːx/. The former word means a *peep* or a *glance*, the latter *excrement.* In other words, there is a considerable difference between taking a /kiːk/ and taking a /kiːx/.

In Irish English /x/ is not generally listed as a phoneme but it is found in some words of Irish origin such as *Taoiseach*, which is pronounced [ˈt̪iːʃəx], and *lough*, which is pronounced identically to the Scottish *loch.* /x/ while not phonemic in Welsh English is present in the sound system of Welsh and has a limited appearance in loan words from Welsh, especially in proper nouns, for example: *Amlwch* is pronounced as [ˈamlʊx]. However, Welsh English monolinguals tend to substitute /k/ for /x/ even in proper nouns (Wells 1982b: 389).

Finally, it is worth mentioning that in fast casual speech between vowels speakers may not fully close their stops, and the bilabial plosives /k/ and /g/ are in effect replaced by their fricative counterparts [x] and [ɣ]. This results in the following pronunciations: *faker* [ˈfeɪxə] *rugger* [ˈɹʌɣə] (Gimson 2008: 168).

Table 39 List of velar phonemes found in 25 languages

Language	Plosive	Nasal	Fricatives	Approximants
Amharic	k g			w
Arabic	k		x ɣ	w
Bulgarian	k g		x	
Cantonese	k kʰ	ŋ		
Czech	k g		x	
Dutch	k	ŋ		
English	k g	ŋ		w
French	k g			w
German	k g	ŋ		
Greek	k g	ŋ	x ɣ	
Hausa	k g			w
Hebrew	k g			
Hindi	k g kʰ gʱ			
Hungarian	k g			
Igbo	k g	ŋ	ɣ	w
Italian	k g	ŋ		w
Japanese	k g			w[1]
Korean	k kʰ g			
Mandarin	k kʰ	ŋ		w
Persian	k g		x ɣ	
Portuguese	k g			
Russian	k g		x	
Spanish	k g		x	
Swedish	k g	ŋ		
Thai	k kʰ	ŋ		w
Welsh	k g	ŋ	x	w

[1] The Japanese /w/ is unusual in that it is unrounded.

Velaric

The term velaric refers to an **airstream mechanism** that is initiated by the tongue. It is sometimes known as the oral airstream mechanism because all of the actions occur in the mouth. Laver (1994) suggests that it could reasonably be known as a lingual airstream mechanism because the initiator is the tongue. Like a **glottalic** airstream mechanism, a velaric airstream does not involve any respiratory activity. While it appears to be physiologically possible to produce a speech sound using either an **egressive** or **ingressive** velaric airstream, there do not appear to be any languages that employ an egressive velaric airstream mechanism to produce speech sounds. Sounds that are made on an ingressive velaric airstream are known as **clicks** and are found in some Southern African languages, especially those in the Khoisan language family.

Velarization

Velarization is a type of **secondary articulation**. It occurs when a speaker produces a consonant while simultaneously raising the back of the tongue towards the soft palate. The IPA symbol for velarization is [~] placed through the letter. This is the same as that for **pharyngealization** and no language is known to distinguish between these two secondary articulations. Velarized /l/ known as **dark** **<L>** is a regular allophonic variant in English and is discussed under dark <L>.

The number of languages reported to use a contrastive velarized/non-velarized consonant is extremely low. The sole unambiguous examples I have been able to locate in the literature are Marshallese (Ladefoged and Maddiesson 1996: 360) and a dialect of Gilbertese (Laver 1994: 326). It seems that this secondary articulation is not distinctive except in a few Austronesian languages.

Vocal folds

The vocal folds, previously known as the vocal bands or cords, are two flexible muscular folds that are contained within the larynx. Despite the older name, they are quite dissimilar to cords or strings. Instead they consist of two bands of muscle that are attached from a single point to the front of the thyroid cartilage and run backwards to the front ends of the arytenoid cartilages. The vibrations of the vocal folds result in the production of what we perceive as **voicing**. The rate of vibration of the vocal folds correlates with the **fundamental frequency** of a sound and is perceived by hearers as having a particular pitch. A significantly faster rate of vocal folds vibration is perceived as a higher pitch. The length and thickness of vocal folds varies between men and women, with adult males having vocal folds of between 17 mm and 25 mm in length, while adult females have vocal folds of between 12.5 mm and 17.5 mm. This results in male voices usually having a lower pitch than female ones. For reasons that are not totally clear, but may be related to the tension of the vocal folds, the pitch of the average male voice rises slightly in the later years of life, leading to some convergence in the pitch between elderly male and female voices.

Vocal organs

The term vocal organs is a collective term for all the anatomical features involved in the generation of speech and includes the organs that produce the **airstream mechanism** such as the lungs, as well as the passive and active **articulators**.

Vocal tract

The vocal tract is a phonetic term that is used to refer to the entire air passage above the larynx. It is divided into the oral tract, the mouth plus the pharynx, and the nasal tract, which is the air passage in the nose above the soft palate. If the soft palate is lowered, the airstream is able to flow through the nasal tract and the mouth simultaneously. Sounds produced with the soft palate lowered are referred to as **nasal** sounds. Sounds produced with the soft palate raised are **oral**.

Voice

Voiced sounds are produced when the **vocal folds** are held loosely together. The resulting blockage of the **glottis** impedes but does not stop the **airstream mechanism**. Assuming that the airstream is **egressive**, the blockage produced by the loosely held together vocal folds results in a build-up in air pressure beneath the glottis. Eventually, the aerodynamic force of the sub-glottal pressure results in the airstream mechanism pushing the vocal folds apart in order to equalize the air pressure above and below the glottis. This resulting drop in the sub-glottal air pressure, combined with the muscular tension used to hold the vocal folds loosely together, results in the vocal folds banging shut. This results in a build-up of higher air pressure below the glottis and the cycle starts once again. It is the sound made by the vibrating vocal folds that we perceive as voicing.

In English, all **vowels** are voiced while the **consonants** – with the exception of the voiced **nasals** /m, n, ŋ/, the voiced **semi-vowels** /j, w/, the voiced **liquids** /ɹ, l/, and the voiceless /h/ – contrast in terms of voiceless and voiced pairs. It is conventional when listing pairs of consonants produced with an identical manner and place of **articulation** to list the voiceless consonant on the left with the voiced one on the right. The remaining English voiced consonant phonemes are /b, d, g, v, ð, z, ʒ, dʒ/. In practice, however, voiced consonant phonemes tend to be only fully voiced when they are word intermediate and between two vowels. In other positions they tend to be (partially) devoiced – see **voice onset time**. Thus, in the following words, if spoken in isolation – *head, dean* and *header* – the /d/ is only fully voiced in *header*. In the other words, its partially devoiced status is indicated by the under ring:[hɛd̥] [d̥iːn] and [ˈhɛdə].

Word final devoicing is a common feature in German and Dutch, both of which are closely related to English. For instance, German and Dutch speakers pronounce the word *wind* as [vɪnt]. It is worth noting that, from a phonatory point of view, a fully devoiced voiced consonant phoneme is identical to its voiceless counterpart. See also **lenis**.

Voiceless

Voiceless sounds are produced when the **vocal folds** are held wide apart. Assuming that the **airstream mechanism** is **egressive** the air is able to freely flow through the **glottis**. The air flowing through the open glottis does not vibrate the vocal folds and consequently there is no perception of voice. In English, though not universally, only consonants are voiceless. The list of English voiceless consonants is as follows: /p, t, k, f, θ, s, ʃ, tʃ, h/. In standard accented English the voiceless **stops** /p, k, t/ are, when syllable initial, **aspirated**. See also **fortis**.

Voice Onset Time (VOT)

VOT is a **phonetic** term that refers to the point in time at which **vocal fold** vibration starts in relation to the release of a closure. In theory, voicing or vocal fold vibration could begin before the release of a closure, simultaneous to the release or after the release. If the vocal folds start to vibrate simultaneously with the release of the closure the VOT is zero. If the vocal folds start to vibrate prior to the release of the closure the VOT is negative, and if they start to vibrate after the release of the closure the VOT is positive. In English, in voiced plosives the vocal folds start to vibrate prior to the release of the closure and thus, they have a negative VOT, while in the case of voiceless plosives the vibration lags behind the release of the closure and, thus, the voiceless plosives have a positive VOT. As English voiced plosives are only fully voiced intervocalically they only have significantly negative VOT values when between vowels. Word initially they will have negative VOT values that approach zero.

Not all languages divide up what Catford (2001: 182) labels the VOT continuum in a similar manner. Unlike English, French voiced plosives are fully voiced in all positions. They have negative VOT values while French voiceless plosives are unaspirated and have a VOT of zero. Some languages (such as Korean) that contrast [pʰ] [p] and [b] contrast plosives with positive VOT values, zero and a negative VOT value approaching zero. See **aspiration**. Figure 11 summarizes:

	Negative VOT		Zero	Positive VOT	
French		[b]	[p]		
English	[b]			[pʰ]	
Korean		[b]	[p]		[pʰ]

Figure 11 The **VOT** continuum in three languages in word initial plosives

Voice quality

Voice quality is a phonetic term that refers to the long term articulatory and phonatory settings of an individual's vocal organs. The differences in settings between speakers allow us to identify the speaker. Gimson (2008: 293) notes that to date there has been little in the way of scientific study of the features that are unique to all individual speakers, though some accents appear to adopt perceptually different voice quality settings. American English is more nasalized than British English and RP is sometimes creaky voiced. It appears that, physiologically, voice quality between individuals varies as a result of the thickness and length of their **vocal folds** and the length and shape of their **vocal tract.**

Vowel

Vowels are speech sounds that are articulated without either a closure in the mouth or a narrowing of the mouth, which results in audible friction. In **phonological** terms, vowels can be defined as **sonorant** sounds that must occupy the **syllable** nucleus. Unlike **consonants** vowels cannot be described in terms of manner and place of **articulation**. Instead their position in the vowel space, the area where the tongue can be raised or lowered, fronted or backed to alter the resonance or echo of the mouth, determines the quality of the sound produced, which we perceive as a vowel. In addition, the degree of lip-rounding is used to identify vowels. Vowels differ from one another in terms of how high or low the tongue is, how front or back the tongue is in the mouth, and whether or not the lips are rounded. In addition, vowels can be long or short.

Phoneticians classify vowels into a number of discrete categories. *Front* vowels are those that are articulated with the highest point of the tongue towards the front of the mouth. An English example is /iː/, the vowel in FLEECE. Front vowels contrast with *back* vowels, which are articulated either at the back of the mouth or are articulated with the back of the tongue. In English this amounts to the same thing: an example is /uː/, the vowel in GOOSE. Any vowel that is neither front nor back is classified as central: an English example is /ɜː/, the vowel in NURSE. Vowels that are produced with the body of the tongue near the roof of the mouth are known as *close* or *high* vowels. The English vowels in FLEECE and GOOSE are both close. Close contrasts with *open* or *low* vowels, which are articulated with the tongue in the lowest possible position within the mouth. Two English examples are the vowels /æ/ in TRAP and /ɑː/ in PALM. Vowels immediately below close vowels are known as *close-mid* and vowels immediately above open vowels are known as *open-mid*. Front vowels tend to be unrounded, while back vowels (except open ones) tend to be rounded. As back vowels become closer they tend to become more rounded. The FLEECE vowel /iː/ chiefly differs from the vowel in KIT /ɪ/ in terms of length. The diacritic ː is used to notate a long vowel.

While the categories given above are sufficient for mapping out the vowel phonemes of any particular idiolect they are not particularly useful for mapping out differences between vowels in different languages or dialects. To do this we need to make use of the system of reference vowels known as **cardinal vowels**, devised by Daniel Jones to provide a means of reliably identifying vowels (see Jones 1956). Both Japanese and Spanish contain five vowels that can be transcribed with the IPA symbols a ɪ e o u[1] but this does not mean that vowels of both languages have the same phonetic qualities. Figure 12 charts both sets of vowels on vowel quadrilaterals to highlight the differences in how the individual vowels are articulated.

It is clear that with the exception of [a] the remaining four vowels differ phonetically. The Spanish [i] is closer to **cardinal vowel** (CV1) position while its Japanese equivalent is more slightly towards CV2 position. Both the Spanish and Japanese [e] are produced at the front of the mouth but the Spanish vowel is

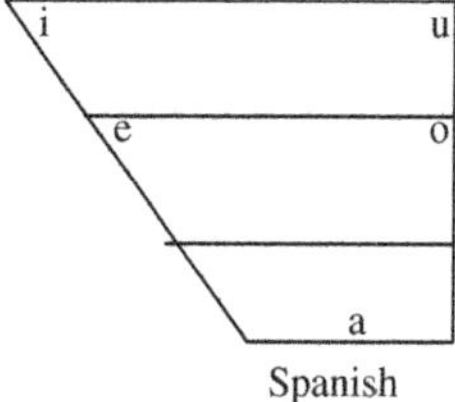

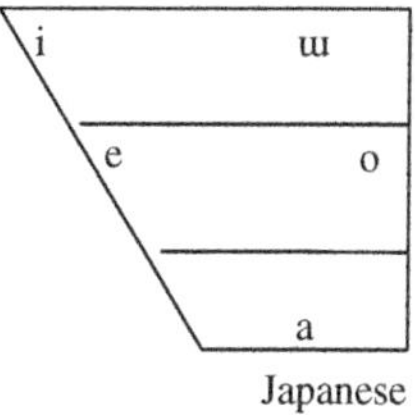

Figure 12 Comparison of Spanish and Japanese vowel systems

slightly closer than its Japanese equivalent. The Japanese [o] and [ɯ] vowels are slightly more open than their Spanish equivalents. They are also produced more towards the centre of the mouth. Without the cardinal vowel system it would not be possible to systematically and easily map out differences in the actual articulations of vowels between languages.

Studies of vowel inventories across languages have indicated a wide divergence in the number of vowels that a language contains. Ladefoged and Maddieson (1996: 286) and Maddieson (2008d) report the existence of four known languages that contain only two vowels either [i] and [a] or [ə] and [a]. They argue that the maximum vowel inventory is 14 vowels. It is important to note that this phonetic classification of vowels only takes account of tongue height, the tongue's position in the front versus back dimension, and the presence or absence of lip-rounding. Thus an individual language may contain considerably more than 14 vowel **phonemes**. For instance, **received pronunciation** contains 20 vowel phonemes.

Using the traditional three-way method of identifying vowels, Maddieson (2008d) surveyed the vowel systems of 564 languages and found that 93 languages had 4 or fewer vowels, 288 languages contained 5 or 6 vowels and the remaining 183 between 7 and 14 vowels. The minimal two-vowel systems, described above, differ only along the dimensions of vowel height, which appears to be the primary means by which vowels separate themselves off into the vowel space. Classical Arabic has the following three-vowel system, which takes triangular form:

i u
a

There is an opposition between a front close unrounded vowel, a back close rounded vowel and a central open unrounded vowel. The vowels are distinguished in terms of front versus back; open versus close and redundantly by unrounded versus rounded. More commonly, though, we find a vowel system with five vowels such as found in Latin, its modern descendant Spanish, Czech, some modern dialects of Arabic such as Egyptian and, as we saw above, Japanese. These vowel systems take the following phonological shape:

i u
e o
a

The addition of the two extra vowels results in a further distinction in terms of vowel height between close and close-mid, giving us a contrastive system of front versus back, and close versus close-mid versus open, and except in the case of Japanese a redundant contrast between rounded and unrounded vowels. Persian has a six-vowel system that has the following phonological shape:

i u
e o
a ɑ

It has the same set of oppositions as the five-vowel system. Italian has the following seven-vowel system:

i		u
e		p
ɛ		ɔ
	a	

There is an additional contrast in terms of height. There is a contrast between front versus back, close versus open-mid versus close-mid versus close. What appears to be occurring in these cases is that vowels space themselves along the extremities of the vowel space at the front or back of the mouth. It is only when further vowels are introduced into the vowel system that they tend to differentiate amongst themselves by being formed either in the centre of the mouth or by having non-redundant lip-rounding.[2] This can be illustrated by looking at the vowel systems of Portuguese and Danish:

i		u	i y		u
e		o	eø		o
ɛ	ə	ɔ	ɛœ		ɔ
	a			a	
Portuguese			Danish		

Portuguese uses a contrast of front versus centre versus back in open-mid position to distinguish the vowels. Danish uses only front versus back contrasts in close, close-mid and open-mid positions but distinguishes between front rounded and front unrounded vowels in these three positions. To conclude, we can say that vowel systems tend to be symmetrical. Ladefoged and Maddieson (1996: 296) state that vowels can differ from one another in terms of five degrees of height,[3] three degrees of backness and four types of lip-rounding, which could imply the presence of a theoretically possible language containing 60 vowels. But as we have seen using these three criteria, there is no known language that exploits more than around 23 per cent of the theoretical vowel contrasts and many language manage by only exploiting a mere 8 per cent of the available possibilities. Vowel phonemes within an individual language can additionally be distinguished by a number of other features: **nasalization**, which occurs in around 20 per cent of languages (including French and Portuguese) and by the articulatory gesture of **advanced tongue root**.

Now that we have seen that vowel systems tend to be symmetrical I would like to more closely examine the vowels of a single language, namely English. English is an interesting case in that it contains both a large number of vowels and is spoken with many different regional accents. Table 40 lists the vowel systems of ten commonly heard English accents in terms of the lexical sets devised by Wells (1982a: xvii–xix).

Table 40 illustrates not only the diversity of the vowel systems across English accents but also the systematicity of each individual accent. However, it somewhat downplays the differences in how typical speakers from different English speaking regions articulate vowels. As can be seen, the chief difference between the vowel systems of the different English accents is the effect of **rhoticity**. Rhotic accents neither contain centring **diphthongs** nor rhyme the palm and start vowels. Within rhotic accents the r-coloured vowel may be realized in different ways.

Table 40 The vowels of 10 English accents

Key word[1]	RP	Aust	NZ	Wales	West Mid	Tyne	GA	Irish	N Irish	Scots
KIT	ɪ	ɪ	ə	ɪ	ɪ	ɪ	ɪ	ɪ	e	ɪ
DRESS	ɛ	e	e	ɛ	ɛ	ɛ	ɛ	ɛ	ɛ	ɛ
TRAP	æ	æ	ɛ	a	a	a	æ	æ	a	a
LOT	ɒ	ɔ	ɒ	ɔ	ɒ	ɒ	ɑ	ɑ	ɒ	ɔ
STRUT	ʌ	ɐ	ɐ	ʌ	ʊ	ʊ	ʌ	ʌ	ʌ	ʌ
FOOT	ʊ	ʊ	ʊ	ʊ	ʊ	ʊ	ʊ	ʊ	ʉ	ʉ
BATH	ɑː	ɐː	ɐː	aː	a	a	æ	aː	ɑː	aː
CLOTH	ɒ	ɔ	ɒ	ɔ	ɒ	ɒ	ɑ	ɒ	ɒ	ɔ
NURSE	ɜː	ɜː	ɵː	œː	əː	øː	əː	ʌ(ɹ)	ʌ(ɻ)	ɜ(r)
FLEECE	iː	iː	iː	iː	iː	iː	iː	iː	iː	iː
FACE	eɪ	æɪ	æe	eː	ɛɪ	eː	eː	eː	eːə	eː
PALM	ɑː	ɐː	ɐː	aː	ɑː	ɒː	ɑ	aː	ɑ	a
THOUGHT	ɔː	oː	oː	ɔː	oː	ɔː	ɑ	ɒː	ɔː	ɔː
GOAT	əʊ	əʉ	ɐʉ	oː	oʊ	oː	oː	əʊ	ɔʊ	oː
GOOSE	uː	uː	uː	uː	uː	uː	uː	uː	ʉː	ʉː
PRICE	aɪ	ɑe	ɑe	aɪ	aɪ	aɪ	aɪ	aɪ	ɛɪ	ʌi
CHOICE	ɔɪ	oɪ	oe	ɔ	ɔɪ	oe	ɔɪ	ɒɪ	ɔɪ	ɔe
MOUTH	aʊ	æɔ	æo	aʊ	aʊ	æʊ	aʊ	aʊ	ɛu	ʌu
NEAR	ɪə	ɪə	ɪə	ɪə	ɪə	ɪɐ	iː(r)	iː(ɹ)	iː(ɻ)	i(r)
SQUARE	eə	eː	eə	ɛː	ɛ	ɛː	eː(r)	eː(ɹ)	əː(ɻ)	e(r)
START	ɑː	ɐː	ɐː	aː	ɑː	ɒː	ɑ(r)	ɑː(ɹ)	ɑː(ɻ)	ɛ(r)
NORTH	ɔː	oː	oː	ɔː	ɔː	o(r)	ɒː(ɹ)	ɒː(ɹ)	ɔː(ɻ)	o(r)
FORCE	ɔː	oː	oː	ɔː	ɔː	ɔː	o(r)	oː(ɹ)	oː(ɻ)	o(r)
CURE	ʊə	ʉə	ʉə	uwə	uːə	uɐ	u(r)	uː(ɹ)	ʉː(ɻ)	jʉː(r)
lettER	ə	ə	ɘ	ə - ʌ	ə	ə	ə	ə(ɹ)	ə(ɻ)	ʌ
commA	ə	ə	ɘ	ə - ʌ	ə	ə	ə	ə	ə	ʌ

[1]The data for RP is from Wells (2000), though to avoid confusion with cardinal vowel 2 I have replaced the Roman 'e' with the Greek 'ɛ'. The Australian data is from Cox and Palethorpe (2007). The New Zealand data is from Bauer, Warren, Bardsley, Kennedy and Major (2007). The Welsh English data is from Penhallurick (2008). The data from the West Midlands is from the Birmingham variety and is from Clark (2008). The Tyneside data is from Watt and Allen (2003). The General American data is from Ladefoged (1999). Both the Irish and the Northern Irish data is based on Hickey (2008) with the Irish data representing what Hickey labels 'supraregional southern' while the Northern Irish data is rural and representative of traditional Ulster Scots. While I have indicated length marks for some Northern Irish and Scottish vowels it is true to say that Northern Irish and Scottish vowels tend not to be distinguished for length and tend to be realized as half-long. The Scottish English data is a slightly simplified form of Stuart-Smith (2008) and represents Scottish Standard English. The symbol [r] has been used as a neutral representation of the post-vocalic Scottish <r>. Some speakers will pronounce post vocalic <r> as a tap [ɾ], others as an approximant [ɹ] and yet others as a retroflex [ɻ].

One of the unique features of the vowel system in Scottish English and in some forms of Northern Irish English is that vowel phonemes are not intrinsically long or short. Instead, their phonetic realization as long or short depends on the surrounding phonetic context. Vowels become long before the /r v ð z ʒ/ and at the end of a word (see Table 41).

Readers interested in exploring the historical background to the Scottish Vowel Length Rule should consult (McMahon 2000a: 160–9). In other varieties of English, vowel phonemes are phonemically long or short though long vowels before **lenis** consonants are phonetically longer than long vowels before **fortis** ones. For instance, the vowel in *heed* is longer than the vowel in *heat*.

The following paragraphs briefly describe how the English vowels using RP as a standard are articulated by plotting them on a cardinal vowel chart (see Figure 13). They also set out some of the major realizational differences between the different English accents found within Britain and Ireland. Readers interested in exploring more deeply should see Gimson (2008: 105–33).

The FLEECE vowel is a high front unrounded vowel. To make the vowel (which is long) the front of the tongue – the part lying across from the hard palate when at rest – is raised to a height slightly below and behind CV1 position. The lips

Table 41 Scottish vowel length

	Long		Short	
	Before /r v ð z ʒ/ and word final		All other contexts	
/o/	[foː] *foe*	[foːr] *four*	[got] *goat*	
/i/	[miː] *me*	[biːz] bees	[bip] *beep*	
/a/	[maː] *ma*	[faːrm] *farm*	[palm] *palm*	
/ʉ/[1]	[mʉː] *moo*	[mʉːz] *moos*	[mʉd] *mood*	
/ɔ/	[lɔː] *law*		[θɔt] *thought*	

[1]The diacritic indicates that the Scottish GOOSE vowel is more fronted than other English pronunciations of the vowel.

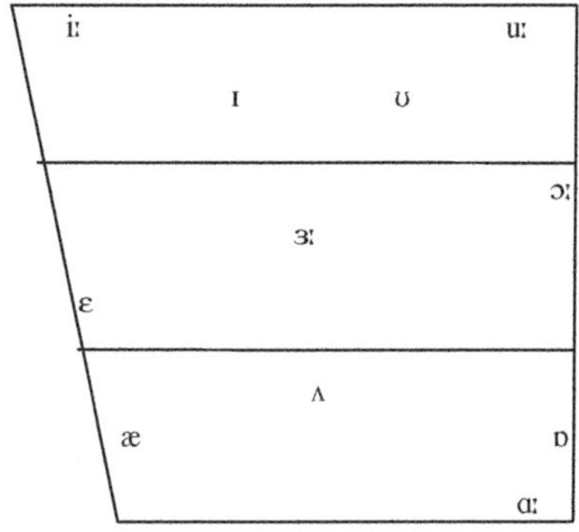

Figure 13 The RP vowels

are spread. The tongue is tense with the side rims making a firm contact with the upper molars. The FLEECE vowel does not normally occur in a syllable that is closed by /ŋ/. Many speakers realize this vowel as a diphthong with the starting point being around the position of the KIT vowel. In other accents, such as that of the West Midlands, the glide starts more centrally. **RP** speakers produce a shortened variant of the FLEECE vowel at the end of words such as *happy* and *city*.

The KIT vowel is a short vowel that is made by raising the part of the tongue that is nearer to the centre than it is to the front to a position just above the mid-close position. The tongue is lax or less tense than it is for /iː/. In West Midlands speech the KIT vowel is much closer to CV1 position and is articulated with the front of the tongue. The DRESS vowel is made by raising the front of the tongue between close-mid and open-mid, though it approaches more closely to open-mid. The lips are loosely spread and slightly wider apart than they are when producing the FLEECE vowel. Within Britain there are numerous variants in how the DRESS vowel is pronounced. In Yorkshire it is pronounced slightly below CV3, while in Northern Ireland the pronunciation is much more open and the sound approaches CV4.

The TRAP vowel is a more open vowel than the DRESS vowel. The front of the tongue is raised to a position just above open, with the side rims making a very slight contact with the upper back molars. The lips are open. The TRAP vowel has in recent times become more open by moving closer to CV4; it was previously situated nearer CV3. In Northern varieties of English, such as Yorkshire, it is realized in a much more open manner near CV4 than it is in RP. This is not surprising, as the Northern realization of the DRESS vowel was slightly below CV3. So the TRAP vowel has moved to maintain its distinctiveness. Similarly the Northern Irish realization of the TRAP vowel is backed and approaches CV5. The fact that vowels spread across the vowel space to maintain their distinctiveness has significant consequences for diachronic sound change.

The STRUT vowel is a relatively recent addition to the sound inventory of English and is absent in Northern varieties of English. Words that in RP contain the STRUT vowel are articulated with the FOOT vowel. The vowel is short and articulated with a considerable separation of the jaws, with the lips in neutral position. The centre of the tongue is raised just above the fully open position and no contact is made between the tongue and the upper molars. In many Irish accents the strut vowel approaches CV5, while in South Wales it is realized as considerably raised and centralized and articulated near CV14. In unstressed syllables it does not contrast with schwa.

The PALM vowel is a long vowel that is articulated with a considerable separation of the jaws, with the lips neutrally open. A part of the tongue between the centre and the back is in fully open position. No contact is made between the rims of the tongue and the upper molars. In non-rhotic accents alone, the PALM vowel is homophonous with the START vowel. In many forms of English the PALM vowel is considerably fronted. which leads to a neutralization between the PALM and TRAP vowels. The CLOTH vowel is a short vowel that is articulated with wide open jaws and slight lip-rounding. The back of the tongue is in fully open position. There is no contact between the tongue and the upper molars. The RP vowel approaches CV5.

The THOUGHT vowel is a long vowel that is articulated with medium lip-rounding. The back of the tongue is raised between open-mid and close-mid. There is no contact between the tongue and the upper molars. In recent times there has been some evolution of this sound, which has resulted in the loss for **RP** speakers between *saw* /sɔː/ and *sore* /sɔə/. For most people, both words are now pronounced as /sɔː/. A number of other words – such as *sure, poor, your* – which historically were pronounced with the /ʊə/ CURE vowel have changed pronunciation and are now realized by the THOUGHT vowel. In non-rhotic accents the THOUGHT, NORTH and FORCE vowels are homophonous. In Scottish English, the thought vowel is realized in open-mid position near CV6 and, except where it is long, it is homophonous with the CLOTH vowel. Thus, the words *caught* and *cot* are not distinguishable.

The FOOT vowel is a short vowel that is pronounced with the part of the tongue nearer to the centre than to the back, raised slightly above close-mid position. As a result it exists in a symmetrical relationship with the KIT vowel. There is no firm contact between the tongue and the upper molars. Historically it was a rounded vowel but there appears to be an increased tendency, according to Gimson, for this vowel to be unrounded. The GOOSE vowel is a long close back vowel that exists in a symmetrical relationship with the FLEECE vowel. It is realized in a slightly less close position and a slightly more central position than CV8. Like the FLEECE vowel, many speakers tend to realize the vowel as a short diphthong commencing from around the position of the GOOSE vowel. In Scottish English, as previously noted, this vowel is considerably fronted.

The NURSE vowel is a long vowel that is only found in non-rhotic accents. It is articulated with the centre of the tongue raised between close-mid and open-mid. There is no firm contact made between the tongue and the upper molars. The lips are neutrally spread. This vowel is highly unusual in the languages of the world and, as a result, it is not particularly useful to try to plot this vowel on a CV quadrilateral. In GA the nurse vowel is **retroflexed** due to the fusion of the vowel and a following /r/. On Tyneside the vowel is considerably fronted and is articulated near CV10. The most common vowel in English speech is the commA vowel /ə/ which is known as *schwa*. This is basically a shortened variant of the NURSE vowel. In English, with the sole exception of the New Zealand accent, the *schwa* cannot appear in **stressed** syllables. Table 42, adapted from Fry (1947), shows the text frequencies of vowels and diphthongs in RP. Despite the data being more than 70 years old, there seems little reason to suppose that *schwa* is not still the most frequent vowel in English. However, see **diphthong** for a discussion of the current trends in the use of the SQUARE and CURE diphthongs.

Phonologically the English steady state vowels can be classified as free and checked vowels. Diphthongs are free vowels (see Kreidler 2004; Collins and Meese 2008: 53–65). Kreidler (ibid.: 103) states that free vowels alone can occur in:

- open syllables
- before a limited number of consonant clusters such as *nt* – as in *paint, pint; nd* as in *friend, wound, pound; ld* as in *field, wild, bold*; and *nch* as in *change, lounge*; and less commonly before the following clusters */ps/* as in *traipse*; */ks/* as in coax; and */lt/* as in *bolt.*

Table 42 Text frequencies of vowels in RP

Rank	Vowel	Vowel keyword	%
1	ə	commA, lettER	27.4
2	ɪ	Kit	21.2
3	ɛ	Dress	7.6
4	aɪ	Price	4.7
5	ʌ	Strut	4.5
6	eɪ	Face	4.4
7	iː	Fleece	4.2
8	əʊ	Goat	3.9
9	æ	Trap	3.7
10	ɒ	Cloth	3.5
11	ɔː	thought, north, force	3.2
12	uː	Goose	2.9
13	ʊ	Foot	2.2
14	ɑː	palm, start	2
15	aʊ	Mouth	1.6
16	ɜː	Nurse	1.3
17	eə	Square	0.9
18	ɪə	Near	0.5
19	ɔɪ	Choice	0.4
20	ʊə	Cure	0.2

Checked vowels, on the other hand, can only occur in closed syllables. The steady state free vowels of what Collins and Meese label **nrp** are as following: /iː ɑː ɔː uː ɜː/ as in the vowels of FLEECE, PALM, THOUGHT, GOOSE and NURSE.[4] See **stress**.

V

Weak forms

In **connected speech** non-lexical items such as prepositions and pronouns have two possible pronunciations. If the word is **unaccented** it is articulated with a reduced vowel such as *schwa* or even in extremely fast unconnected speech with the vowel elided. Weak forms are found only in non-syllable timed languages such as English. The term 'weak form' contrasts with **strong form**. Table 43 sets out some typical examples of weak and strong forms in English.

The grammatical item *that* may function either as a conjunction or as a demonstrative adjective or pronoun. In these cases the word is always articulated as a strong form. The difference can be seen in the following example:

[ðæts] the man [ðət] did it.

When functioning as a demonstrative *that* is often **accented**. The lexical item *some* can also function as a pronoun, in which case it is articulated as a strong form. The difference can be seen in the following pair:

I've got [səm] money.
Has anyone got any money? I've got [sʌm].

The verb *have* functions both as an auxiliary and as a main verb and, when functioning as a main verb, it is articulated as a strong form. The following examples illustrate that the substitution of a strong for a weak form can result in a change of meaning:

The things he [həz] or [əz] left (= the things remaining to him) are precious.
The things he [hæz] left (= the things he left behind) are precious.

Table 43 Weak and strong forms in English

Auxiliary and modal verbs					
	Strong	**Weak**		**Strong**	**Weak**
BE	biː	bi	AM	æm	əm, m
ARE	ɑː(r)[1]	ə(r), r[2]	IS	ɪz	ɪz, z, s
BEEN	biːn	bɪn	WAS	wɒz	wəz
WERE	wɜː(r)	wə(r)	HAVE	hæv	həv, əv, v
HAS	hæz	həz, əz, z, s	HAD	hæd	həd, əd, d
DO	duː	də, du, d	DOES	dʌz	dəz, dz
CAN	kæn	kən	COULD	kʊd	kəd
MUST	mʌst	məst	SHALL	ʃæl	ʃəl, ʃl
SHOULD	ʃʊd	ʃəd	WILL	wɪl	wəl, əl, l
WOULD	wʊd	ʍəd, əd[3]			
Determiners					
A	eɪ	ə	AN	æn	ən, n
SOME	sʌm	səm	ANY	ɛni	ɛni, əni
MANY	mɛni	mɛni, məni[4]			
THE	ðiː	ðɪplus vowel, ðə plus consonant[5]			
Prepositions					
AT	æt	ət	FROM	frɒm	frəm
FOR	fɔː(r)	fə(r)	OF	ɒv	əv, ə, v
TO	tuː	tə plus consonant, tʊ or tu plus vowel.[6]			
Pronouns					
YOU	juː	ju, jʊ	HE	hiː	hi, i,
SHE	ʃiː	ʃi, ʃɪ	WE	wiː	wi
THEY	ðeɪ	ðeɪ	WHO	huː	hu, u
ME	miː	mi	HIM	hɪm	ɪm
HER	hɜː(r)	hɜː(r), hə(r), ə(r)			
US	ʌs	əs, s[7]	THEM	ðɛm	ðəm, əm, m
HIS	hɪz	ɪz	OUR	aʊə(r)	ɑː(r)[8]
THERE	ðeə, ðɜː(r)	ðə plus consonant, ðər plus vowel.[9]			

Conjunctions					
and	ænd	ənd, ən, n	but	bʌt	bət
or	ɔː(r)	ə(r)[10]	nor	nɔːr	nə(r)
as	æz	əz	than	ðæn	ðən
that	ðæt	ðət			
because	bɪˈkɒz	bɪkəz, bəkəz			

[1]The /r/ is present only in rhotic accents.

[2]The reduced form /r/ is only found in rhotic accents.

[3]*Would* and *should* can be further reduced to [d] if preceded in casual speech by a vowel, for example: *he would/should* can be articulated as [hɪd].

[4]The weak forms [əni] and [məni] are classed as being occasional (see Wells 2000). Otherwise, even though the vowel retains the same quality in the weak form as it had in the strong form in connected speech it is produced and perceived as being much reduced. See Brazil (1994: 26–9) for a fuller description of what he labels 'protected vowels' or in other words vowels in weak form which retain their vowel quality.

[5]Wells (2000: 774) notes that native speakers often ignore the distinction between [ðɪ] and [ðə] and use [ðə] in all environments. Windsor Lewis (2007) in Gimson (2008: 268) notes that this occurs only when the vowel is glottally re-enforced by the addition of [ʔ] before the vowel.

[6]Wells (2000: 783) notes that American speakers tend to use [tə] in all environments. British speakers in formal speech may employ [tu] even before a consonant and otherwise may use [tə] even before a vowel as long as it has been glottally reinforced.

[7]To my ears US, both in strong and weak form is being increasingly pronounced in the UK with a voiced fricative as [ʊz] or [əz].

[8]Some speakers use [ɑː(r)] as a weak form but for others the vowel sequence [aʊə] has undergone compression to [ɑː] and thus, for these speakers the vowel has no weak form (Wells 2000: 542).

[9]This applies even for non-rhotic accents.

[10]The weak forms of OR and NOR in British English are rare and usually occur only in fixed expressions, for example: *twenty* [ə] *more*. In GA there are usual weak forms [^{ə}r] and [n^{ə}r].

Notes

Aa

1. Wells (2000: 499) reports that in a 1998 poll panel of British English speakers 89 per cent pronounced the word even in careful speech with /z/ and not /s/, which indicates that the voicing assimilation may have led to a sound change.

Bb

1. Maddieson admits that in the case of one of the five languages that was spoken in Alaska, Eyak (a language from the Na-Dene language family) contained bilabial nasal sounds. These, however, have been interpreted as allophones and not phonemes. In any case the last known speaker of Eyak is reported to have died in January 2008.

Cc

1. Because lip-rounding lowers the first formant it is not possible to plot rounded vowels accurately on a two-dimensional vowel chart.

Dd

1. In the past few years, the overwhelming majority of my undergraduate students have produced the SQUARE vowel as a monophthong. The decline in the use of the diphthong appears to be an ongoing but not yet complete sound change.
2. In a discussion I had with an undergraduate class consisting of English and Welsh students there was severe resistance to accepting the following pronunciations /dʊə/, /lʊə/ and /mʊə/. Instead, the students argued forcefully that dour, lure and moor should be pronounced as /dɔː/, /lɔː/ and /mɔː/.
3. In the full analysis 12 binary features were proposed. Two of these [± Checked] and [±Sharp] are not relevant for the analysis of the English phonemic system and consequently they are not discussed here.
4. On page 329 they sketch a fifth type of feature, namely Prosodic features, which presumably includes features such as [± stress], [± duration] and [± pitch/tone].
5. The classification of /h/ as [+Sonorant] is in line with their definition, though at odds with most of the literature that would, in my opinion, correctly classify the segment as [−Sonorant].
6. In Halle's later work (1995) he restricts the feature [± Distributed] to [+Coronal] sounds.
7. On page 318 Chomsky and Halle detail their difficulty in classifying /l/ in terms of [±Continuant] by noting that 'if the defining characteristic of a stop is taken as total blockage of airflow then [l] must be viewed as a continuant... If, on the other hand, the defining characteristic of stops is taken to be blockage of air past the primary stricture then [l] must be included among the stops.'
8. There are individual feature theories that recognize this and employ a set of features used to define vowel heights that depend on the number of vowel heights available within an

individual language, for instance, Clements and Hume (1995). Thus, CV2 would be classified as [+High 2] while CV1 would be classified as [+High 3].

9. The diacritic # refers to the end of a word.

Ee

1. In the shortened form *oft* the /t/ has been preserved. The presence of the orthographic <t> has resulted in free variation between pronunciations with the <t> and those without the <t>.
2. Spellings of surnames such as *Thompson*, *Simpson* and *Sampson* indicate the historical nature of the process in English. I thank Paul Tench for this observation.

Ff

1. The superscripts in the example below signify the following: ^{h} indicates that the vowel is high, ^{l} indicates that the vowel is low and ^{r} indicates that the vowel is rounded.
2. In fact, when plotting vowels on a formant chart, phoneticians calculate the degree of backness by subtracting the F1 value from the F2 value. They do this primarily to make the formant charts fit more closely to the traditional vowel charts produced by phoneticians, who were ostensibly describing articulatory factors such as tongue height, etc., and because there is a better correlation between the degree of backness and the distance between F2 and F1 (see Ladefoged 2001 for further details).

Gg

1. K is an ad hoc symbol for a velar consonant and X for a palatalized consonant.
2. For pedagogical purposes I have ignored the operation of earlier rules which tense and diphthongize the underlying vowel /ɪ/ in the discussion of the underlying form of the words *expedite, ignite, delight* and *right*. Thus, /ɪgnɪt/ is proposed as the underlying form of *ignite*.

Hh

1. In this section all information on Niger-Congo languages is taken from *Ethnologue*.
2. Laver employs the symbol 'h' as a phonological indicator that the consonant is a member of the lax set of consonants (1994: 388).

Nn

1. There is a discrepancy between the chart in chapter 18, which lists ten languages with no nasals, one language with no bilabials or nasals and one language with no nasals or fricatives, and the subsequent text that states, 'A total of 13 languages in the sample are listed as having no nasals in their consonant inventories.' Regardless, it is clear that nasal phonemes are a near universal feature.
2. Of course, a real speaker might elide the [h] and substitute [ʊ] for [ʌ].

Oo

1. The following marginal exceptions of words borrowed from Welsh – Gwen, Gwent and Gwynedd, etc. – violate the ocp. /kw/ clusters are not uncommon in English, for example, *queer, queen, question, queasy*, etc.
2. This constraint is identical to the view expressed in Halliday (1967) that in the unmarked case a tone unit is coterminous with a clause – see **intonation**.

Pp

1. This could be pronounced as /ʃriːˈlæŋkə/.
2. As a verb *schlep* means to carry something in a clumsy manner or with difficulty. As a noun it has two quite distinct meanings and can refer to an arduous journey or a clumsy or stupid person.
3. This word, which is apparently of Scots origin, means to strike the ground with a golf club prior to hitting the ball.
4. The former word refers to a financial penalty and the latter to the residue of metal left after calcification.

Ss

1. The initial consonant in *drei* has undergone fortition in German; the old high German initial consonant was θ.
2. The intial [h] is a product of lenition from [x] → [h].
3. Some scholars, though not all, transcribe the occurrence of secondary stress after the primary stressed syllable in lexical items such as *anecdote* /ˈænɪkdəʊt/, where the initial syllable is the most prominent and receives the primary stress but the final syllable is more prominent than the middle one!
4. The differences in vowel quality between *record* (noun) and *record* (verb) and *below* and *billow* arise chiefly from the differences in stress patterning.
5. The following paragraphs are largely based upon the work of Kreidler (2004: 179–95).
6. It is clear that even if the vowel is checked it retains the quality of a short /əʊ/ and cannot be reduced to a schwa.
7. The noun *a downgrade* would have the opposite stress pattern and be articulated as /ˈdaʊngɹeɪd/.
8. In all three languages there are marginal exceptions to the generalization that the three languages contain only open syllables. For instance, the Japanese word for *book* is *hon,* the Italian word for *part* is *par+te*, the Mandarin word place name *Nan+jing* contain codas containing nasals and liquids. But in all three languages it is the case that, except in the case of gemination, codas are never closed by obstruents, for example: the Japanese word for ticket *kip+pu.*
9. Syllables and moras are notated by the Greek letters Sigma σ and Mi μ, respectively. The letters O, R, N and Cd refer to onset, rhyme, nucleus and coda, respectively.

Vv

1. The Japanese u vowel is unusual in that it is unrounded and accordingly it is notated as [ɯ].
2. This is only a tendency and it is possible to find languages such as Turkish which have the following vowel system:

   i y ɯ u
   e ø o
   a

   Even though a fourth degree of height is theoretically available, Turkish chooses to differentiate three sets of vowels in terms of lip-rounding rather than height.
3. There are non-European languages such as Tswana or Sitswana a Bantu language spoken in Botswana which apparently have five degrees of height.
4. Collins and Mees (2008) additionally include /ɛː/ but see the discussion of the SQUARE vowels in **diphthongs**. In any case, regardless whether the vowel is described as a monophthong or a diphthong, it is free.

References

Abercrombie, D. 1967. *Elements of General Phonetics*. Edinburgh: Edinburgh University Press.

Aceto, M. 2008. 'Eastern Caribbean English-derived language varieties: phonology', in B. Kortmann and C. Upton (eds.), *Varieties of English*. Berlin: Mouton de Gruyter, 290–311.

Altendorf, U. n.d. 'Estuary English: Is English going Cockney?', http://www.phon.ucl.ac.uk/home/estuary/altendf.pdf. Last accessed on 17 May 2010.

Altendorf, U. and D. Watt. 2008. 'The dialects in the South of England: phonology', in B. Kortmann and C. Upton (eds.), *Varieties of English*. Berlin: Mouton de Gruyter, 194–222.

Archangeli, D. and D. T. Langendoen. 1997. *Optimality Theory: An Overview*. Oxford: Blackwell.

Ball, M. J. and J. Rahilly. 1999. *Phonetics: The Science of Speech*. London: Edward Arnold.

Bauer, L. and P. Warren. 2004. 'New Zealand English: phonology', in B. Kortmann, E. W. Schneider, K. Burridge, R. Mesthrie and C. Upton (eds.), *A Handbook of Varieties of English*. Berlin: Mouton de Gruyter, 580–602.

Bauer, L., P. Warren, D. Bardsley, M. Kennedy and G. Major. 2007. 'New Zealand English', *Journal of the International Phonetic Association*, 37, 97–102.

Beal, J. 2008. 'English dialects in the North of England: phonology', in B. Kortmann and C. Upton (eds.), *Varieties of English*. Berlin: Mouton de Gruyter, 122–44.

Beckman, M. E. 1992. 'Evidence for speech rhythm across language', in Y. Tohkura, E. Vatikiotis-Bateson and Y. Sagisaka (eds.), *Speech Perception, Production and Linguistic Structure*. Tokyo: IOS Press, 457–63.

Berko Gleason, J. and N. Bernstein Ratner. 1998. 'Language acquisition', in J. Berko Gleason and N. Bernstein Ratner (eds.), *Psycholinguistics*. 2nd edition. Belmont, CA: Wadsworth, 347–88.

Blom, J. P. and J. J. Gumperz. 2000. 'Social meaning in linguistic structure: code switching in Norway', in L. Wei (ed.), *The Bilingualism Reader*. London: Routledge, 111–36.

Bok Lee, H. (1999). 'Korean', in *Handbook of the International Phonetic Association*. Cambridge: Cambridge University Press, 120–23.

Bolinger, D. 1962. 'Contrastive accent and contrastive stress', *Language*, 37, 83–96.

Bolinger, D. 1981. *Two Kinds of Vowels, Two Kinds of Rhythm*. Bloomington, IN: Indiana University Linguistics Club.

Brazil, D. 1994. *Pronunciation for Advanced Learners of English: Teacher's book*. Cambridge: Cambridge University Press.

Brazil, D. 1997. *The Communicative Value of Intonation in English*. Cambridge: Cambridge University Press.

Cassidy, F. G. 1982. 'Geographical variation of English in the United States', in R. W. Bailey and M. Görlach (eds.), *English as a World Language*. Cambridge: Cambridge University Press, 177–209.

Catford, J. C. 1977. *Fundamental Problems in Phonetics*. Edinburgh: Edinburgh University Press.

Catford, J. C. 2001. *A Practical Introduction to Phonetics*. 2nd edition. Oxford: Oxford University Press.

Chambers, J. K. and P. Trudgill. 1998. *Dialectology*. 2nd edition. Cambridge: Cambridge University Press.

Chao, Y. R. 1930. 'A System of tone letters', *Le Maître Phonetéique*, 45, 24–7.

Chinn, C. and S. Thorne. 2001. *Proper Brummie: A Dictionary of Birmingham Words and Phrases*. Studley, Warks: Brewin Books.

Cho, T., S. A. Jun and P. Ladefoged. 2002. 'Acoustic and aerodynamic correlates of Korean stops and fricatives', *Journal of Phonetics*, 30, 193–228.

Chomsky, N. 1990. *On Language*. New York: The New Press.

Chomsky, N. and M. Halle. 1968. *The Sound Pattern of English*. New York: Harper and Row.

Clark, J., C. Yallop and J. Fletcher. 2007. *An Introduction to Phonetics and Phonology*. 3rd edition. Oxford: Blackwell.

Clark, U. 2008. 'The English West Midlands: phonology', in B. Kortmann and C. Upton (eds.), *Varieties of English*. Berlin: Mouton de Gruyter, 145–77.

Clements, G. G. and E. V. Hume. 1995. 'Internal organization of speech sounds', in J. A. Goldsmith (ed.), *The Handbook of Phonological Theory*. Oxford: Blackwell, 245–306.

Collins, B. and I. Mees. 2008. *Practical Phonetics and Phonology*. 2nd edition. London: Routledge.

Cox, F. and S. Palethorpe. 2007. 'Australian English', *Journal of the International Phonetic Association*, 37, 341–50.

Cruttenden, A. 1997. *Intonation*. 2nd edition. Cambridge: Cambridge University Press.

Crystal, D. 1969. *Prosodic Systems and Intonation in English*. Cambridge: Cambridge University Press.

Crystal, D. 1997. *The Cambridge Encyclopaedia of Language*. 2nd edition. Cambridge: Cambridge University Press.

Crystal, D. 2003. *A Dictionary of Linguistics and Phonetics*. 5th edition. Oxford: Blackwell.

Crystal, D. and D. Davy. 1975. *Advanced Conversational English*. London: Longman.

Davenport, M. and S. J. Hannahs. 2010. *Introducing Phonetics and Phonology*. 3rd edition. London: Hodder Education.

Delattre, P. 1965. *Comparing the Phonetic Features of English, French, German and Spanish*. Heidleberg: Jules Groos Verlag.

Deutscher, G. 2005. *The Unfolding of Language*. London: William Heinemann.

Devonish, H. and O. G. Harry. 2008. 'Jamaican Creole and Jamaican English: phonology', in B. Kortmann and C. Upton (eds.), *Varieties of English*. Berlin: Mouton de Gruyter, 256–89.

Edwards, W. F. 2008. 'African American Vernacular: phonology', in E. W. Schneider (ed.), *Varieties of English: The Americas and the Caribbean*. Berlin: Mouton de Gruyter, 181–91.

Engstrand, O. 1999. 'Swedish', in *Handbook of the International Phonetic Association*. Cambridge: Cambridge University Press, 140–2.

Esling, J. H. 1998. 'Everyone has an accent except me', in L. Bauer and P. Trudgill (eds.), *Language Myths*. London: Penguin, 169–82.

Firth, J. R. 1957. 'Sounds and prosodies', in J. R. Firth (ed.), *Papers in Linguistics 1934–1951*. Oxford: Oxford University Press, 121–38.

Fougeron, C. and C. L. Smith. 1999. 'French', in *Handbook of the International Phonetic Association*. Cambridge: Cambridge University Press, 78–81.

Fromkin, V. 1973. *Speech Errors as Linguistic Evidence*. The Hague: Mouton.

Fry, D. B. 1947. 'The frequency of occurrence of speech sounds in southern English', *Archives Néerlandaises de Phonétique Expérimental*, 20.

Gimson, A. 2008. *Gimson's Pronunciation of English*, revised by Alan Cruttenden. 7th edition. London: Hodder Education.

Goldsmith, J. A. 1990. *Autosegmental and Metrical Phonology*. Oxford: Blackwell.

Goldsmith, J. A. 1999. 'An overview of autosegmental phonology', in J. Goldsmith (ed.), *Phonological Theory: The Essential Readings*. Oxford: Blackwell, 137–61.

Grant, W. 1913. *The Pronunciation of English in Scotland*. Cambridge: Cambridge University Press.

Gussenhoven, C. 2004. *The Phonology of Tone and Intonation*. Cambridge: Cambridge University Press.

Gussenhoven, C. and H. Jacobs. 2005. *Understanding Phonology*. London: Hodder Arnold.

Halle, M. 1995. 'Feature geometry and feature spreading', *Linguistic Inquiry*, 26, 1–46.

Halliday, M. A. K. 1967. *Intonation and Grammar in British English*. The Hague: Mouton.

Halliday, M. A. K. 1970. *A Course in Spoken English*. Oxford: Oxford University Press.

Halliday, M. A. K. 1994. *An Introduction to Functional Grammar*. 2nd edition. London: Edward Arnold.

Halliday, M. A. K. and W. S. Greaves. 2008. *Intonation in the Grammar of English*. London: Equinox.

(1999). *Handbook of the International Phonetic Association*. Cambridge: Cambridge University Press.

Harrington, J. 2010. *Phonetic Analysis of Speech Corpora*. London: Wiley-Blackwell.

Harris, M. 1988. 'French', in M. Harris and N. Vincent (eds.), *The Romance Languages*. London: Routledge, 209–45.

Hayes, B. 2009. *Introductory Phonology*. London: Wiley-Blackwell.

Hayward, K. and R. J. Hayward. 1999. 'Amharic', in *Handbook of the International Phonetic Association*. Cambridge: Cambridge University Press, 45–50.

Hickey, R. 2008. 'Irish English: Phonology', in B. Kortmann and C. Upton (eds.), *Varieties of English*. Berlin: Mouton de Gruyter, 71–105.

Hirst, D. and A. Di Cristo. 1998. *Intonation Systems: A Survey of Twenty Languages*. Cambridge: Cambridge University Press.

Hoberman, R. D. 1995. 'Current issues in semitic phonology', in J. A. Goldsmith (ed.), *The Handbook of Phonological Theory*. London: Blackwell, 839–47.

Hughes, A., P. Trudgill and D. Watt. 2005. *English Accents and Dialects*. 4th edition. London: Hodder Arnold.

Jakobson, R. 1990. *On Language*. L. Waugh and M. Monville-Burston (eds). Cambridge MA: Harvard University Press.

Jakobson, R. and M. Halle. 1956. *Fundamentals of Language*. The Hague: Mouton.

Jakobson, R. and L. Waugh. 1987. *The Sound Structure of Language*. Bloomington, IN: Indiana University Press.

Jenkins, J. J., W. Strange and T. R. Edman. 1983. 'Identification of vowels in vowelless syllables', *Perception and Psychophysics*, 34(5), 44–50.

Jones, C. 2002. *The English Language in Scotland: An Introduction to Scots*. East Linton: Tuckwell.

Jones, D. 1956. *An Outline of English Phonetics*. 8th edition. Cambridge: Heffer.

Jones, D. 1967. *The Phoneme: Its Nature and Use*. 3rd edition. Cambridge: Cambridge University Press.

Johnson, P. 1997. 'Regional variation', in C. Jones (eds.), *The Edinburgh History of the Scots Language*. Edinburgh: Edinburgh University Press.

Jun, S. -A. 2005. *Prosodic Typology: The Phonology of Intonation and Phrasing*. Oxford: Oxford University Press.

Kerswill, P. 2003. 'Dialect levelling and geographical diffusion in British English', in D. Britain and J. Cheshire (eds.), *Social Dialectology: In honour of Peter Trudgill*. Amsterdam: John Benjamins, 223–43.

Kretzschmar, W. A. 2008. 'Standard American English pronunciation phonology', in E. Schneider (ed.), *Varieties of English: The Americas and the Caribbean*. Berlin: Mouton de Gruyter, 37–51.

Kreidler, C. W. 2004. *The Pronunciation of English*. 2nd edition. Oxford: Blackwell.

Kurath, H. 1949. *A Word Geography of the Eastern United States*. Ann Arbor, MI: University of Michigan Press.

Labov, W. 1966. *The Social Stratification of English in New York City*. Washington, D.C.: Center for Applied Linguistics.

Labov, W., S. Ash and C. Boberg. 2006. *The Atlas of North American English: Phonetics Phonology and Sound Change*. Berlin: Mouton de Gruyter.

Ladd, D. R. 1996. *Intonational Phonology*. Cambridge: Cambridge University Press.

Ladd, D. R. 2008. *Intonational Phonology*. 2nd edition. Cambridge: Cambridge University Press.

Ladefoged, P. 1999. 'American English', in *Handbook of the International Phonetic Alphabet*. Cambridge: Cambridge University Press, 41–4.

Ladefoged, P. 2001. *A Course in Phonetics*. 4th edition. Boston, MA: Heinle and Heinle.

Ladefoged, P. 2005. *Vowels and Consonants*. 2nd edition. Oxford: Blackwell.

Ladefoged, P. and I. Maddieson. 1996. *The Sounds of the World's Languages*. Oxford: Blackwell.

Lass, R. 1976. *English Phonology and Phonological Theory*. Cambridge: Cambridge University Press.

Lass, R. 1984. *Phonology: An Introduction to Basic Concepts*. Cambridge: Cambridge University Press.

Lass, R. 1987. *The Shape of English: Structure and History*. London: Dent.

Laufer, A. 1999. 'Hebrew', in *Handbook of the International Phonetic Alphabet*. Cambridge: Cambridge University Press, 96–9.

Laver, J. 1994. *Principles of Phonetics*. Cambridge: Cambridge University Press.

Liberman, A. 1996. *Speech: A Special Code*. Cambridge, MA: M.I.T. Press.

Liberman, M. 1985. *The Intonational System of English*. New York: Garland.

Lindau, M., K. Norlin and J. O. Svantesson. 1985. 'Cross-linguistic differences in diphthong'. *UCLA Working Papers in Phonetics*, 61, 40–4. Available online at http://escholarship.org/uc/item/6z50c4zv#page-3. Last accessed on 7 September 2010.

Ling, L. E., E. Grabe and F. Nolan. 2000. 'Quantitative characterizations of speech rhythm: syllable-timing in Singapore English', *Language and Speech*, 43(4), 377–401.

Local, J. 1996. 'Conversational phonetics', in E. Couper-Kuhlen and M. Selting (eds.), *Prosody in Conversation*. Cambridge: Cambridge University Press, 177–230.

Lodge, K. 2009. *A Critical Introduction to Phonetics*. London: Continuum.

Lyons, J. 1991. *Chomsky*. 3rd edition. London: Fontana.

Macafee, C. 2003. *Glasgow*. Amsterdam: John Benjamins.

McCarthy, J. J. 2004. *Optimality Theory in Phonology: A Reader*. Oxford: Blackwell.

McCarthy, J. J. 2008. *Doing Optimality Theory: Applying Theory to Data*. Oxford: Blackwell.

McMahon, A. 2000a. *Lexical Phonology and the History of English*. Cambridge: Cambridge University Press.

McMahon, A. 2000b. *Change, Chance and Optimality*. Cambridge: Cambridge University Press.

McMahon, A. 2006. 'Restructuring renaissance English', in L. Mugglestone (ed.), *The Oxford History of English*. Oxford: Oxford University Press, 147–77.

MacNeilage, P. 2008. *The Origin for Speech*. Oxford: Oxford University Press.

Maddieson, I. 1984. *Patterns of Sounds*. Cambridge: Cambridge University Press.

Maddieson, I. 1997. 'Phonetic universals', in W. J. Hardcastle and J. Laver (eds.), *Handbook of Phonetic Sciences*. Oxford: Blackwell, 619–39.

Maddieson, I. 2008a. 'Absence of common consonants', in M. Haspelmath, M. S. Dryer, D. Gil and B. Comrie, Bernard (eds.), *The World Atlas of Language Structures Online*. Munich: Max Planck Digital Library, chapter 18. Available online at http://wals.info/feature/18. Last accessed on 16 July 2012.

Maddieson, I. 2008b. 'Presence of uncommon consonants', in M. Haspelmath, M. S. Dryer, D. Gil and B. Comrie, Bernard (eds.), *The World Atlas of Language Structures Online*. Munich: Max Planck Digital Library, chapter 19. Available online at http://wals.info/feature/19. Last accessed on 16 July 2012.

Maddieson, I. 2008c. 'Lateral consonants', in M. Haspelmath, M. S. Dryer, D. Gil and B. Comrie, Bernard (eds.), *The World Atlas of Language Structures Online*. Munich: Max Planck Digital Library, chapter 8. Available online at http://wals.info/feature/19. Last accessed on 16 July 2012.

Maddieson, I. 2008d. 'Vowel quality inventories', in M. Haspelmath, M. S. Dryer, D. Gil and B. Comrie, Bernard (eds.), *The World Atlas of Language Structures Online*. Munich: Max Planck Digital Library, chapter 2. Available online at http://wals.info/feature/19. Last accessed 16 July 2012.

Mathisen, A. G. 1999. 'Sandwell, West Midlands: ambiguous perspectives on gender patterns and models of change', in P. Foulkes and G. Docherty (eds.), *Urban Voices: Accent Studies in the British Isles*. London: Edward Arnold, 107–23.

Melchers, G. 2008. 'English spoken in Orkney and Shetland: phonology', in B. Kortmann and C. Upton (eds.), *Varieties of English*. Berlin: Mouton de Gruyter, 37–47.

Mieke, J. 2008. *The Emergence of Distinctive Features*. Oxford: Oxford University Press.

Milroy, J. 1981. *Regional Accents of English: Belfast*. Belfast: Blackstaff.

Mitchell, A. G. and A. Delbridge. 1965. *The Speech of Australian Adolescents a Survey*. Sydney: Angus and Robertson.

Mitchell, T. F. 1969. 'Review of Abercrombie 1967', *Journal of Linguistics*, 5, 153–64.

Mugglestone, L. 2003. *Talking Proper: The Rise of Accent as Social Symbol*. Oxford: Oxford University Press.

Nagy, N. and J. Roberts. 2008. 'New England: phonology', in E. Schneider (ed.), *Varieties of English: The Americas and the Caribbean*. Berlin: Mouton de Gruyter, 52–66.

Nathan, G. S. 2008. *Phonology: A Cognitive Grammar Introduction*. Amsterdam: John Benjamins.

Ní Chasaide, N. 1999. 'Irish', in *Handbook of the International Phonetic Association*. Cambridge: Cambridge University Press, 111–15.

O'Connor, J. D. 1973. *Phonetics*. Harmondsworth: Penguin.

O'Grady, G. 2010. *A Grammar of Spoken English Discourse: The Intonation of Increments*. London: Continuum.

Ohala, M. 1999. 'Hindi', in *Handbook of the International Phonetic Association*. Cambridge: Cambridge University Press, 100–3.

Painter, C. 1963. 'Black country speech', *Maître Phonétique*, 120, 30–3.

Penhallurick, R. 2008. 'Welsh English: phonology', in B. Kortmann and C. Upton (eds.), *Varieties of English*. Berlin: Mouton de Gruyter, 105–21.

Pierrehumbert, J. 1980. 'The phonology and phonetics of English intonation'. Unpublished PhD dissertation. *M.I.T.* Available online at http://faculty.wcas.northwestern.edu/~jbp/publications/Pierrehumbert_PhD.pdf. Last accessed on 14 December 2010.

Pierrehumbert, J. 2003. 'Probabilistic phonology: discrimination and robustness', in R. Bod. J. Hay and S. Jannedy. (eds.), *Probabilistic Linguistics*. Cambridge, MA: M.I.T. Press, 177–228.

Pierrehumbert, J. and J. Hirschberg. 1990. 'The meaning of intonational contours in the interpretation of discourse', in P. Cohen, J. Morgan and M. Pollack (eds.), *Intentions in Communication*. Cambridge, MA: M.I.T. press, 271–311.

Pike, K. 1943. *Phonetics*. Ann Arbor, MI: University of Michigan Press.

Pike, K. 1948. *Tone Languages*. Ann Arbor, MI: University of Michigan Press.

Prince, A. and P. Smolensky. 2004. *Optimality Theory: Constraint Interaction in Generative Grammar*. Oxford: Blackwell.

Przedlacka, J. 2002. *Estuary English?* Frankfurt: Peter Lang.

Roach, P. 1982. 'On the distinction between 'stress-timed' and 'syllable-timed languages', in F. R. Palmer and D. Crystal (eds.), *Linguistic Controversies*. London: Edward Arnold, 73–9.

Roach, P. 1991. *English Phonetics and Phonology*. 2nd edition. Cambridge: Cambridge University Press.

Roach, P. 2009. *English Phonetics and Phonology*. 4th edition. Cambridge: Cambridge University Press.

Roca, I. and W. Johnson. 1999. *A Course in Phonology*. Oxford: Blackwell.

Rogerson-Revell., P. 2011. *English Phonology and Pronunciation Teaching*. London: Continuum.

Rosewarne, D. 1984. '"Estuary English": David Rosewarne describes a newly observed variety of English', *Times Higher Education Supplement*, October 19.

Searle, J. 1998. *Mind, Language and Society*. New York: Basic Books.

Shattuck-Hufnagel, S. 1979. 'Speech errors as evidence for a serial ordering mechanism in speech production', in W. E. Cooper and E. C. T. Walker (eds.), *Sentence Processing: Psycholinguistic Studies Presented to Merrill Garret*. Hillsdale, NJ: Erlbaum, 295–342.

Silverman, D. 2006. *A Critical Introduction to Phonology*. London: Continuum.

Stampe, D. 1979. *A Dissertation on Natural Phonology*. New York: Garland.

Stenson, N. 1991. 'Code-switching vs. borrowing in modern Irish', in P. Sture Ureland and G. Broderick (eds.), *Language Contact in the British Isle. Proceedings of the Eight International Symposium on Language Contact in Europe*. Tübingen: Niemeyer, 559–79.

Stevens, K. N. and M. Halle. 1967. 'Remarks on analysis by synthesis and distinctive features', in W. Wathen-Dunn (ed.), *Models for the Perception of Speech and Visual Form*. Cambridge, MA: M.I.T. Press, 88–102.

Stockwell, R. P. and D. Minkova. 1988. 'The English vowel shift: problems of coherence and explanation', in D. Kastovsky and G. Bauer (eds.), *Luick Revisted*. Tübingen: Gunter Narr Verlag, 355–94.

Stuart-Smith, J. 2008. 'Scottish English: phonology', in B. Kortmann and C. Upton (eds.), *Varieties of English*. Berlin: Mouton de Gruyter, 48–70.

Tench, P. 1990. *The Roles of Intonation in English Discourse*. Frankfurt am Main: Peter Lang.

Tench, P. 1996. *The Intonation Systems of English*. London: Cassell.

Thelwall, R. and M. Akram Sa'adeddin. 1999. 'Arabic', in *Handbook of the International Phonetic Alphabet*. Cambridge: Cambridge University Press, 51–4.

Thomas, C. K. 1958. *Phonetics of American English*. New York: Ronald.

Thomas, E. R. 2008. 'Rural Southern white accents', in E. W. Schneider (ed.), *Varieties of English: The Americas and the Caribbean*. Berlin: Mouton de Gruyter, 87–114.

Tillery, J. and G. Bailey. 2008. 'The urban South: phonology', in E. W. Schneider (ed.), *Varieties of English: The Americas and the Caribbean*. Berlin: Mouton de Gruyter, 115–28.

Trudgill, P. 1974. *The Social Differentiation of English in Norwich*. Cambridge: Cambridge University Press.

Trudgill, P. 2000. *The Dialects of English*. 2nd edition. Oxford: Blackwell.

Trudgill, P. 2008. 'The Dialect of East Anglia', in B. Kortmann and C. Upton (eds.), *Varieties of English*. Berlin: Mouton de Gruyter, 178–93.

Upton, C. 2006. 'Modern regional English in the British Isles', in L. Mugglestone (ed.), *The Oxford History of English*. Oxford: Oxford University Press, 305–33.

Upton, C. 2008a. 'Received Pronunciation', in B. Kortmann and C. Upton (eds.), *Varieties of English*. Berlin: Mouton de Gruyter, 237–52.

Upton, C. 2008b. 'Synopsis: phonological variation in the British Isles', in B. Kortmann and C. Upton (eds.), *Varieties of English*. Berlin: Mouton de Gruyter, 269–82.

Walters, J. R. 2003. 'On the intonation of a South Wales 'Valleys accent' of English', *Journal of the International Phonetic Association*, 33(2), 211–38.

Watt, D. and W. Allen. 2003. 'Tyneside English', *Journal of the International Phonetic Association*, 33, 261–71.

Waugh, L. and M. Monville-Burston. 1990. 'Editor's note', in L. Waugh and M. Monville-Burston (eds.), *Roman Jakobson on Language*. Cambridge, MA: Harvard University Press, 259–60.

Wells, B. and S. Peppé. 1996. 'Ending up in Ulster', in E. Couper-Kuhlen and M. Selting (eds.), *Prosody in Conversation*. Cambridge: Cambridge University Press, 101–30.

Wells, J. C. 1982a. *Accents of English 1: An Introduction*. Cambridge: Cambridge University Press.

Wells, J. C. 1982b. *Accents of English 2: The British Isles*. Cambridge: Cambridge University Press.

Wells, J. C. 1982c. *Accents of English 3: Beyond the British Isles*. Cambridge: Cambridge University Press.

Wells, J. C. 1994. 'The cockneyfication of RP', in G. Melchers and N. L. Johannesson (eds.), *Nonstandard Varieties of Language. Papers from Stockholm Symposium: Stockholm Studies in English LXXXIV*. Stockholm: Almqvist and Wiksell International, 198–205.

Wells, J. C. 2000. *Longman Pronouncing Dictionary*. 2nd edition. Harlow: Longman.

Wichmann, A. 2000. *Intonation in Text and Discourse*. Harlow: Longman.

Williams, A. and P. Kerswill. 1999. 'Dialect levelling: change and continuity in Milton Keynes, Reading and Hull', in P. Foulkes and G. Docherty (eds.), *Urban Voices: Accent studies in the British Isles*. London: Edward Arnold, 141–62.

Wright, M. 2011. 'On clicks in English talk in interaction', *Journal of the International Phonetic Association*, 41(2), 201–30.

Yavas, M. 2006. *Applied English Phonology*. Oxford: Blackwell.

Yeni-Komshian, G. H. 1998. 'Speech perception', in J. Berko Gleason and N. Bernstein Ratner (eds.), *Psycholinguistics*. 2nd edition. Belmont, CA: Wadsworth, 107–56.

Yip, M. 1995. 'Tone in East Asian languages', in J. A. Goldsmith (ed.), *The Handbook of Phonological Theory*. Oxford: Blackwell, 476–94.

Yip, M. 2002. *Tone*. Cambridge: Cambridge University Press.

Yuasa, I. P. 2008. *Culture and Gender of Voice Pitch*. London: Equinox.

Index

CPI Antony Rowe
Eastbourne, UK
December 21, 2018